Trends, Discovery, and
People in the Digital Age

CHANDOS DIGITAL INFORMATION REVIEW SERIES

Series Editors: Professor David Baker and Wendy Evans
(emails: d.baker152@btinternet.com and wevans@marjon.ac.uk)

The Chandos Digital Information Review Series aims to be a summary and a summation of the key themes, advances and trends in all aspects of digital information and explores the impact on the information world. The emphasis is on both the key current topics and future developments; an international perspective is taken throughout. Each publication in the series has a dynamic set of contents that respond to and, more importantly, anticipate digital information futures. The relevant chapters are written by experts in the field, drawing widely from Europe, North America, Australasia and South East Asia. If you would like a full listing of current and forthcoming titles, please visit our website, www.chandospublishing.com, email wp@woodheadpublishing.com or telephone +44 (0) 1223 499140.

New authors: we are always pleased to receive ideas for new titles; if you would like to write a book for Chandos, please contact Dr Glyn Jones on gjones@chandospublishing.com or telephone +44 (0) 1993 848726.

Bulk orders: some organisations buy a number of copies of our books. If you are interested in doing this, we would be pleased to discuss a discount. Please email wp@woodheadpublishing.com or telephone +44 (0) 1223 499140.

Trends, Discovery, and People in the Digital Age

EDITED BY

DAVID BAKER AND WENDY EVANS

CP

CHANDOS
PUBLISHING

Oxford Cambridge New Delhi

Chandos Publishing
Hexagon House
Avenue 4
Station Lane
Witney
Oxford OX28 4BN
UK
Tel: +44 (0) 1993 848726
Email: info@chandospublishing.com
www.chandospublishing.com
www.chandospublishingonline.com

Chandos Publishing is an imprint of Woodhead Publishing Limited

Woodhead Publishing Limited
80 High Street
Sawston
Cambridge CB22 3HJ
UK
Tel: +44 (0) 1223 499140
Fax: +44 (0) 1223 832819
www.woodheadpublishing.com

First published in 2013

ISBN: 978-1-84334-723-1 (print)
ISBN: 978-1-78063-389-3 (online)

Chandos Digital Information Review ISSN: 2050-6651 (print) and ISSN: 2050-666X (online)

Typeset by Domex e-Data Pvt. Ltd., India
Printed in the UK and USA.

Printed in the UK by 4edge Ltd, Hockley, Essex.

Contents

List of figures and tables

Figures

Tables

Foreword: the paradox of a commonplace revolution

Martin Hall

An overarching paradox of our contemporary world is this. The transition in the use, and abuse, of digital information is so comprehensive and profound that it is largely taken as commonplace. We take for granted that we can carry a terabyte or two of data in our pockets and find out where we are, almost anywhere in the world, from a cheap phone. We seem largely unconcerned that we may be photographed by hidden cameras a dozen times a day and that we can be tracked by digital face recognition. We expect to be able to find anything we want, from anywhere in the world, on the Internet, and we become impatient if access takes more than a minute. And yet for any adult alive today, these transitions have taken place within their lifetime. A person who was aged ten in 1990 was growing into a world with nothing like the digital resources we take for granted today. None of us would accept a return to the standards of digital information that we found path-breaking just ten years ago.

The chapters in this book force a momentary pause in this whirlwind of change. By looking critically at significant aspects of this digital juggernaut, they tease apart some of the fault-lines that, inevitably, are features of such a profound transition. And in doing so, they cast light on the paradox that such profound and recent changes are taken as routine. A suitable anchor for these fault-lines is the current predicament of the library, as both a place where information professionals work and as an institution. As David Baker and Wendy Evans put it in their Introduction, 'the very future of that thing we call "the library" is in question: even if there are to be collections, services, users – and librarians to support them – it will be something new and radically different from what has gone before.' The roles and operations of libraries – and the expenditure that this necessitates – are being widely questioned (Steve O'Connor, Chapter 17). But however significant these issues are for professionals and policy-makers closely concerned with information services, they are mostly hidden from the wider world. As Lorraine Estelle notes, the library as an institution becomes invisible in the face of fast and effective online searches from home or the office. For academic users, automated authorisation of access to licensed e-journals makes them appear to be free at the point of use, disguising the essential role of information professionals. In this sense, the library has become a sort of back office to the Internet, where its lack of visibility is an index of its efficiency and effectiveness. Information professionals are responding to these changes in a range of ways, as contributions here show. In Caroline Williams' eloquent turn of phrase, 'as a flock of birds moves as one in response to stimuli then we should assume the behaviour of complex adaptive systems to ensure long-term survival through agility and flexibility as individuals, teams and services.'

This situation can be understood, in part, as a disconnection between those who provide information, and those who use it – a second fault-line that is highlighted in this book. Baker and Evans see the loss of the librarian as an intermediary as matched by an increasing shortfall in the sophistication of online users. A number of contributors refer to the myths about 'digital natives' and show that, contrary to popular assumption that people born after 1980 are hard-wired into the digital world, there are prevalent and increasing deficits in information literacy. This, again, calls for new adaptive systems, such as the User-Centred Design approaches that Anthony Chow reviews in detail. Chow shows that, while the need for engaging and efficient user interfaces is all too apparent, designing and implementing such interfaces is demanding and still imperfectly understood. Closing the growing divide between information professionals and their clients is a pressing priority.

Of course, interfaces can only be effective if users are provided with the content that they require. Given how rapidly the nature and scope of digital information is evolving, there is constant pressure on information professionals to advance their capabilities and to provide appropriate opportunities for keeping pace with advances in technology. For example, Estelle shows how researchers increasingly want seamless access to both online publications and their associated data sets and analytical programmes. Processes of disintermediation are blurring distinctions between data sets, analysis and publication.

In turn again, this is sparking interest in new approaches to data curation (Aldalin Lyngdoh, Chapter 10). And data curation is inseparable from the immense challenges of metadata design and management:

Without tags, terms or descriptors describing the 'aboutness' of something, it is extremely challenging for even the best search engines to correctly retrieve results or makes it difficult or impossible for curators to find and showcase content on a particular topic. Reviewing knowledge resources that are of strategic importance is an extremely valuable service for digital curators to perform, one that is closely related to traditional work of librarians and information professionals. (Abby Clobridge, Chapter 11)

The future potential of these convergences is exemplified in Everall and Fernando's Mirrorworld platform, which integrates and visualises massive and scattered datasets drawn from local, regional and national government sources. This, in turn, opens up the possibilities of new ways of working for a wide range of professional fields and facilitates new forms of governance and decision-making based on intelligent, evidence-based policy models.

A fourth fault-line, following from the disconnections between providers and users of digital information and between analysis and data centres on issues of access. Traditionally, librarians, archivists and publishers managed access to formalised knowledge, and there was a clear distinction between such formalised knowledge and the sources of information on which it was based. But with new technologies, the massive expansion of readily available and cheap memory, and ubiquitous broadband and location-aware devices, these old distinctions are increasingly irrelevant. As Baker and Evans note in their Introduction, the efficacy of the future digital library will be largely determined by the extent to which the principles of open access are applied. Indeed, the advances in interoperability noted by several contributors to this volume will mean that, from the perspective of the future digital client, the world of digital information may function as a massive and, for practical purposes, infinite single resource.

Whether, and how, this potential is realised will be influenced by commercial considerations. Whittemore, Allen and Dobson point out that the Internet contributed 7.2 per cent of Britain's GDP in 2009 – a proportion that will undoubtedly continue to grow. And Richard Otlet draws attention to the growing significance of 'walled garden' applications that are accessible only to subscribers, creating restricted information platforms. There is clear and growing tension between the growth of the 'semantic web', across which there is sufficient metadata to allow software to identify and analyse significance, allowing information users to roam freely wherever they need to go, and the pay-walls that limit access in return for rent. This loops back to the future of the library as a public interest organisation.

For Susan Myburgh libraries, galleries, museums and archives are institutions that are both socially constructed and also serve to shape the customs and behaviours of the communities that they serve. This is as much so now as when public libraries were places of note. And there is strong innovation here, as information professionals respond, like Williams' birds responding to new stimuli, Vivien Sieber's study of Open Education Resources, and Joanne John and John Dolan's analysis of *Enquire* and the key role it has played as an open-to-all web service for libraries and their publics.

Myburgh's point is that, in a networked world, the selection of sources and the paths followed through the Web of online resources is both a proxy for key aspects of our social condition and a structure that shapes future behaviour that 'aggregates the results of all the perceptive and cognitive functions undertaken by individuals.' Google knows this, and has grown very rich. If the commercial functions of the Internet are not balanced through the work of strong, public-interest organisations, the consequences will be the privatisation of both choice and that which is available to choose. LiLi Li surely writes for many: in the digital age a library should be 'a centre for information access and distribution, learning and teaching activities, presentations and exhibitions, and social network connections.'

What of the future? Given the rapidity of changes in digital information and its uses over the past few decades, who really knows? What seems certain is that the digital world that today's ten-year-old will know as an adult will be very different. Not surprisingly, those contributors to this volume who dare to look to this future come to very different conclusions. For Anthony Chow, our children will evolve into informavores hunting for information scents. For David Vogt, the humans of the future will have 'augmented individuality' as the biological brain merges seamlessly into the digital cloud of information and as people 'aggregate, amplify, cross-fertilise and promote, in advantageous ways (exactly as their brain does) all of the separate and collective digital elements of their existence.' But for Chérifa Boukacem-Zeghmouri and Joachim Schöpfel much of this will pass:

> We do not deny latent age effects and some Google generation-like phenomena. Nevertheless, we think that this effect may be transitional and a kind of collateral effect of emerging ICT in research work. When all Internet users are digital natives, variation

related to the hypothetical generation gap will decrease and disappear, and disciplinary differences will (again) become a central factor, reflecting the richness and diversity of fields of science.

Take your choice.

These fault-lines, carefully identified and teased apart by the contributors to this volume, resolve the paradox of the 'commonplace revolution' in digital information and its uses. Because an overall direction in the development of both technology and practice has been towards increasing seamlessness of ever richer, and exponentially larger, sources of digital information, intermediation has become automated, extremely rapid and largely invisible. Like the oxygen we breathe and depend on for life, vast and unseen quantities of digital information, intelligently ordered and analysed, is expected to flow into our homes and offices without any evident agency getting in the way. In providing the professional expertise to make key aspects of this service possible, the lack of visibility that is a signal of their success may be mistaken for irrelevance. This book contributes to the avoidance of such an error.

Preface

The book aims to be a summary and a summation of the key themes, advances and trends in all aspects of digital information at the present time. It explores the impact of developing technologies on the information world. The emphasis is on the key current topics as well as future developments, and an international perspective is taken throughout. The publication is based on a dynamic set of contents that respond to and anticipate what is happening and may well happen in the field of digital information.

The book will be of interest and value to all involved in digital information provision, library developments and digital collections and services (whether or not library based), including managers, subject specialists, project directors, technical staff, content creators and editors. It will also be of interest to researchers, lecturers and students of library and information science and students, researchers and lecturers of the Internet and of digital provision.

All web links were correct at the time of checking (November 2012).

David Baker and Wendy Evans
January 2013

Acknowledgements

The editors are especially grateful to all who made this book possible: to the authors of the various chapters for their contributions and their willingness to be involved in the project; to Glyn Jones for his support throughout the development of the proposal and the actual production of the book; to Nina Hughes, research assistant for the project, and Sharon Holley for her help and support during the final stages; and also to University College Plymouth St Mark & St John for their support.

List of abbreviations

ACT-IF	Adaptive Control of Thought in Information Foraging
ADA	Americans with Disabilities Act
ADDIE	Analyse, Design, Develop, Implement and Evaluate
AI	Adobe Illustrator
AI	Artificial Intelligence
API	Application Programming Interface
ASK	Anomalous State of Knowledge
ASP	Active Server Pages
AURIL	Association for University Research and Industry Links
BBC	British Broadcasting Corporation
BCE	Business and Community Engagement
BL	British Library
BLLD	British Library Lending Division
BMA	British Medical Association
CAUL	Council of Australian University Librarians
CC	Creative Commons
CERN	European Organisation for Nuclear Research
CIBER	Centre for Information Behaviour and the Evaluation of Research
CILIP	Chartered Institute of Library and Information Professionals
CNN	Cable News Network
CNRS	Centre National de la Recherche Scientifique
COPAC	National, Academic and Specialist Library Catalogue

CPD	Continuing Professional Development
CRM	Customer Relationship Management
CSS	Cascading Style Sheets
CURL	Consortium of University Research Libraries
DAM	Digital Asset Management
DDE	Design, Develop and Evaluate
DNA	Deoxyribonucleic Acid
DNER	Distributed National Electronic Resource
DTD	Document Type Definition
EAD	Encoded Archival Description
EARL	Electronic Access to Resources in Libraries Consortium
EES	Effectiveness, Efficiency and Satisfaction
EIT	Electronic and Information Technology
EPSRC	Engineering and Physical Sciences Research Council
EPUB	Electronic Publication
ESP	Extra-Sensory Perception
FE	Further Education
FOAF	Friend of a Friend
GDP	Gross Domestic Product
HAL	Hyper Article en Ligne
HCD	Human-Centred Design
HCI	Human–Computer Interaction
HE	Higher Education
HEA	Higher Education Academy
HEFCE	Higher Education Funding Council for England
HR	Human Resources
HSS	Humanities and Social Science
HTML	HyperText Markup Language
Hz	Hertz

ICT	Information and Communications Technology
IE	Information Environment
IFLA	International Federation of Library Associations
ILL	Interlibrary Loan
IM	Instant Messaging
IP	Intellectual Property
IPR	Intellectual Property Rights
IRs	Institutional Repositories
ISO	International Organization for Standardization
IT	Information Technology
ITT	Invitation to Tender
JISC	Joint Information Systems Committee
JPEG	Joint Photographic Experts Group
JSP	Java Server Pages
JURA	Joint Universities Research Archive
LASER	London and South Eastern Library Region
LF&G	Lead, Follow and Get Out of the Way
LIBRIS	Library Information System
LIDAR	Light Detection and Ranging
LIS	Library and Information Science
MARC	Machine Readable Cataloguing
MBTI	Myers-Briggs Type Indicator
MEDEV	Medicine, Dentistry and Veterinary Medicine
MIT	Massachusetts Institute of Technology
MLA	Museums, Libraries and Archives Council
MSP	Managing Successful Programmes
MT	Machine Translation
NCCPE	National Coordinating Centre for Public Engagement
NHS	National Health Service

NLL	National Lending Library for Science and Technology
OAI-PMH	Open Archives Initiative Protocol for Metadata Harvesting
OAPEN	Open Access Publishing in European Networks
OCLC	Online Computer Library Center
OCW	OpenCourseWare
OER	Open Educational Resources
OGC	Office of Government Commerce
OOER	Organising Open Educational Resources
OS	Ordnance Survey
OWL	Web Ontology Language
PC	Personal Computer
PCT	Primary Care Trusts
PDA	Patron Driven Acquisitions
PDF	Portable Document Format
PHP	Hypertext Preprocessor
PLoS	Public Library of Science
POS	Parts-of-Speech
PRINCE	Projects in Controlled Environments
RDF	Resource Description Framework
RDF	Researcher Development Framework
RDFS	Resource Description Framework Schema
RFID	Radio Frequency Identification
RIN	Research Information Network
RLO	Reusable Learning Object
RLUK	Research Libraries United Kingdom
ROI	Return on Investment
RSS	Really Simple Syndication
SAF	Self-Analysis Framework
SCL	Society of Chief Librarians

SCOAP3	Sponsoring Consortium for Open Access Publishing in Particle Physics
SCONUL	Society of College, National and University Libraries
SCORM	Sharable Content Object Reference Model
SME	Small to Medium Enterprises
SPIRIT	Strategic Priority Investments in Research and Innovation Translation
STM	Science, Technology and Medicine
SUNCAT	Serials Union Catalogue
TCR	The Combined Regions
TIFF	Tagged Image File Format
UCD	User-Centered Design
UCT	University of Cape Town
UI	User Interface
UKNUC	United Kingdom National Union Catalogue
UKOLN	United Kingdom Office for Library and Information Networking
URI	Uniform Resource Identifiers
URL	Universal Resource Locator
UX	User Experience
VDT	Visual Display Terminals
VLE	Virtual Learning Environment
VR	Virtual Reality
W3C	World Wide Web Consortium
WCAG	Web Content Accessibility Guidelines
XML	Extensible Markup Language
ZETOC	Z39.50-compliant access to the British Library's Electronic Table of Contents

About the contributors

Robert Allen has over 15 years experience in education, training, development and research, primarily in the fields of innovation and change programmes, and particularly the use of new technology within organisations. He is a qualified organisational psychologist and experienced business manager with a PhD and MBA among other qualifications. He has worked with many organisations including numerous universities and colleges, public libraries and local authorities, small and large businesses and business support bodies. Internationally he has been involved in projects such as with the British Council in Sri Lanka and the European Trade Union Association in Florence and Stockholm.

Previously deputy director at JISC Netskills, part of JISC Advance, he took over management of the Business and Community Engagement (BCE) activity across JISC Advance in 2008. Now working part-time in his BCE role, he is also managing director of training and consultancy Hapsis Innovation Ltd working with organisations on team and leadership development including innovation and entrepreneurship.

David Baker was Principal of University College Plymouth St Mark and St John (UCP Marjon) 2003–9 and is Emeritus Professor of Strategic Information Management. He has published widely in the field of Library and Information Studies, with 14 monographs and some 100 articles to his credit. He has spoken at numerous conferences, led workshops and seminars and has undertaken consultancy work in most countries in the European Union, along with work in Ethiopia, Kuwait, Nigeria and the Sudan. He was Deputy Chair of the Joint Information Systems Committee (JISC) 2008–12, having also led a number of large technology-based projects, both in relation to digital and hybrid library development and content creation for teaching and learning. He has published the following books with Chandos: *Strategic Information Management*, *Strategic Change Management in Public Sector Organisations*; co-produced (with Wendy Evans) *Digital Library Economics: An Academic Perspective* and *Libraries and Society: Role, Responsibility and Future in an Age of Change*; and (with Bernadette Casey) *Eve on Top: Women's Experience of Success in the Public Sector.*

Chérifa Boukacem-Zeghmouri is Lecturer in Information and Communication Science at the Université de Lyon (Lyon 1 University – Sciences). She is a research member of the ELICO Research Laboratory. Her PhD was devoted to an economic analysis of the transition of the academic library services in an electronic context (defended in 2004). From 2006 to 2010, she chaired a national project on the usage of electronic resources in the French academic context, using a socio-economic research approach. She is now coordinating a national study on the return on investment (ROI) of electronic resources in the French academic network.

Since October 2011, she has been Head of the Regional Scientific and Technical Information Training Unit (URFIST Lyon) dedicated to scholars, PhD students, librarians and information professionals.

Rachel Bruce is Innovation Director for Digital Infrastructure for JISC, a body that works on behalf of UK universities and colleges to provide world-class ICT infrastructure. She has many years of experience in the development of socio-technical infrastructure for the provision of quality information for education and research. In 1999 she scoped and established the UK Archives Hub through JISC, and has since overseen strategies and multi-million pound programmes for digital repositories, open access, digital preservation, research tools and resource discovery. She holds an MSc in Information Science from City University, and sits on a number of committees, including the UK Data Forum, the UKPMC Funders Forum, the SCONUL Shared Services Committee, the JISC-RLUK Resource Discovery Taskforce, the Mimas Management Board and the DCMI Oversight Committee. Currently she also chairs the JISC e-Journal Archiving Implementation Group and Repository and Curation Service Oversight Group. As well the above, she oversees the development of JISC resource discovery infrastructure for UK universities and is active in the development of policy and infrastructure for sustainable and open solutions to research data management and use. The overriding aim of her work is to exploit technologies, including the Web, for more effective and innovative research and learning.

Anthony Chow teaches library management, technology, and web design and usability as an assistant professor in the Department of Library and

Information Studies at the University of North Carolina at Greensboro (UNCG). He has been teaching at the graduate university level for over 12 years and is the author of over 70 academic presentations, articles and books. He has a doctorate in instructional systems (systems design) and a Master's degree in Educational Psychology (learning and cognition) from Florida State University. Currently he also serves as the Director of Online Learning for UNCG's School of Education. Anthony also serves as an educational consultant specialising in online information and evaluation systems and has overseen the IT for a large academic unit, served as a usability lab director, managed training and quality assurance for an Internet company and oversaw computer-based instruction training for a government agency. His dissertation was published as a book entitled *Systems Thinking and 21st Century Education*. Anthony Chow's professional and academic experience has allowed him views of the complex interactions between users and technology from a diverse set of perspectives and settings.

Abby Clobridge is the managing director and lead consultant at Clobridge Consulting, a firm designed to support organisations with information management, knowledge management and library-related challenges such as digital curation, taxonomy development and user tags, open access, scholarly communication, digital repositories, and strategic planning for information, knowledge-sharing and library initiatives. She has worked with a wide range of organisations, including United Nations agencies, non-governmental and non-profit organisations, universities, the news media and private sector companies. Her experience spans the United States, Europe and Africa.

Previously, Abby was the Associate Director of Research & Knowledge Services at Harvard University, Kennedy School of Government, and she worked at Bucknell University where she developed the university's digital repository programme. She was the co-recipient of the 2009 Association of College and Research Libraries Instruction Sector Innovation Award for a project developed while at Bucknell. Earlier in her career, Abby worked as a news librarian and investigative researcher for CNN. Her recent book, *Building a Digital Repository Program with Limited Resources*, was published by Chandos in 2010.

Abby holds a BA with honours from Tufts University and an MS in Library and Information Science from Florida State University.

Marc Dobson is the Programme Liaison Manager within the JISC Advance Business and Community Engagement (BCE) Team, based at

Newcastle University. Marc has been involved in supporting and managing projects across JISC Advance Services and those funded by the JISC BCE programme across further and higher education institutions since 2008.

With experience in the education sector since 1999, Marc has been involved in collaborative research projects in Internet technologies with partners from across the European Union and in EU-funded regional business support projects in the area of web enablement for small to medium enterprises. He has also worked with the Association for University Research and Industry Links (AURIL) in providing accredited programmes and CPD resources for BCE practitioners.

Marc has also worked in project management roles on development projects in a regional development agency and local authority.

John Dolan's formative career was in Manchester. He worked in business information then community librarianship. In St Helens in a new leisure directorate he led a modernisation programme for library, archive and museum services.

In Birmingham he was strategic manager for Libraries and Archives, Early Years and Family Learning, the Youth Service and Adult Education. He led on the first concept design for the Library of Birmingham. He was also project leader for the strategic development of the People's Network. At the Museums, Libraries and Archives Council (MLA) he worked on policy and partnership programmes for public libraries. He has contributed to national strategies for public libraries in Bulgaria and India.

Recent work includes a shared services study with a group of West Midlands library authorities, a study programme for German library directors working towards a national policy on library services for new communities and the drafting of guidelines on public libraries for the Chartered Institute of Library and Information Professionals (CILIP).

He is Head of Community Regeneration at Eye (*http://www.thisiseye. com*). With Eye he has worked as a library specialist on a feasibility study for a joint public/academic library in Southend and on three regeneration projects in Nottingham focusing on community need and consultation.

John Dolan was awarded an OBE for services to libraries and information provision. He is an Honorary Fellow at the Department of Information Studies at Aberystwyth University. In January 2011 he was elected as a trustee of CILIP.

Lorraine Estelle is Chief Executive of JISC Collections, the organisation that manages the national procurement and licensing of a broad array of intellectual property for UK academic libraries. JISC Collections collaborates with its library members and the publishing community to undertake research that drives the development of licensing and business models in line with user needs, innovative technology and the future of digital content. Recent projects in this area include the OAPEN-UK exploring open access scholarly monograph publishing in the humanities and social sciences and the e-books for FE project. She is a member of the Knowledge Exchange Licensing Group, which looks at the issues of digital licensing and procurement at the multinational level, she is an active participant in the International Coalition of Library Consortia conferences, and she is a member of the EDINA Management Board. Lorraine is also co-editor of *Insights: The UKSG Journal*, which aims to facilitate communication between the many stakeholders in the global knowledge community. Prior to joining JISC Collections she worked in the publishing industry, firstly in trade book publishing and then in the area of children's educational books and multimedia.

Wendy Evans is Head of Library at University College Plymouth St Mark & St John (UCP Marjon). She has a keen interest in the Internet and electronic resources and in particular access to journals and databases. She also has an expertise in data protection and freedom of information. Wendy has published, lectured and researched in the field of electronic journal and database usage and also access versus ownership of journals. She has co-authored and edited *Digital Library Economics: An Academic Perspective* and *Libraries and Society: Role, Responsibility and Future in an Age of Change* and is currently working on *A Handbook of Digital Library Economics*, also to be published by Chandos. Wendy has recently been awarded an Associate Teaching Fellowship at UCP Marjon.

Ian Everall has over 25 years' experience in the public sector. He works as a consultant advising local authorities and local strategic partnerships on the use of digital technologies to support urban regeneration and public sector transformation programmes. He has an established track record working in demanding partnership environments developing strategies and programmes to help public sector stakeholders improve access to local services, tackle issues of social and digital inclusion, promote skills development and progression, worklessness, business enterprise and economic growth. Over the last five years Ian has also worked as a Senior Research Fellow at the THINKlab as an industry expert researching and promoting the use of emerging visualisation and simulation technologies to support public sector regeneration and transformation programmes.

Ian recently set up a new company, Mirrorworld Technologies Ltd, to help promote wider adoption and use of the technology by government and local government in the UK and internationally.

Terrence Fernando is the Director of the THINKlab at the University of Salford (*http://www.thinklab.salford.ac.uk*). He has a track record in developing technology platforms for a range of sectors such as local government, police, health, aerospace, automotive, building construction and media. His main recent research focus has been on developing collaborative workspaces for multi-functional teams. Within this context, he has been conducting research to develop flexible collaboration platforms and multi-user interface frameworks for remote teams in engineering and media, urban regeneration and public sector transformation programmes. He has worked on many interdisciplinary research projects such as the North West Research Centre for Advanced Virtual Prototyping (EPSRC), Vivacity (EPSRC), FIRM(EPSRC), Future Workspaces (EU) and CoSpaces (EU) involving large numbers of research teams and private and public organisations.

Martin Hall is Vice Chancellor of the University of Salford. He is also Professor Emeritus, University of Cape Town (UCT), where he is affiliated with the Graduate School of Business. Previously Professor of Historical Archaeology, he was inaugural Dean of Higher Education Development and then Deputy Vice Chancellor at UCT (from 1999 to 2008). He is a past-President of the World Archaeological Congress and is a Fellow of the Royal Society of South Africa and of the University of Cape Town. He is an accredited mediator with the Africa Centre for Dispute Settlement. He has written extensively on pre-colonial history in Southern Africa, on the historical archaeology of colonialism, on contemporary public culture and on issues in higher education and social mobility.

Joanne John has a background spanning finance and accountancy for a major brewing company and local government to information and reference within a regional cooperative: Co-East, the link being a high-quality customer service ethic. As part of the management team that set up *People's Network Enquire*, Joanne is a service administrator, trainer and practitioner and has been in this role first with Co-East and now the OCLC for eight years; prior to this Joanne worked on *Ask-A-Librarian* and other digital strategies as part of Co-East. This provides a unique position from which to advocate for digital reference as well as to understand the local needs of participating in a national service. Joanne's experience and commitment to raising the profile of access to information through digital reference as well as visibility through collaboration is well known throughout current and past *Enquire* participants.

LiLi Li is Associate Professor/E-Information Services Librarian at the Georgia Southern University Library, which is located in Statesboro, Georgia in the United States. Before serving the university, Professor Li worked for several American IT business companies as IT consultant, software developer, and software engineer separately. Since 2005, Professor Li has started publishing and lecturing on information technologies applicable to academic libraries at state, national and international conferences. In 2009, Chandos Publishing in Oxford in the UK published his first book titled *Emerging Technologies for Academic Libraries in the Digital Age*. According to the statistics collected by the OCLC WorldCat Basic Search, 180 libraries from 25 countries and regions in the world, including the British Library, Cambridge University, Cornell University, Duke University, Hong Kong University, Princeton University, Purdue University, Rice University, Stanford University, University of California at Los Angeles, etc., have purchased his work.

Aldalin Lyngdoh is an Assistant Librarian at the British Medical Association (BMA) in London. She has a Master's degree in Information Science from University College London and an undergraduate degree in Biotechnology from North Eastern Hill University (India) where she completed her dissertation in autoimmune diseases.

Having worked in a variety of roles at the BMA, she developed an interest in information and data storage and retrieval in the sciences. Attending the 4th Bloomsbury Conference at University College London on Data Curation furthered her enthusiasm for the subject. Libraries are required to play a role in data curation more than ever before. This is a result of what Tony and Jessie Hey term the 'e-science revolution', data being generated at an exponential rate which changes the very nature of information. The format, speed of dissemination, user needs and expectations all together are transforming the very nature of scholarly communication. As information and data providers it becomes our responsibility to keep up with this digital revolution.

She is also a member of CILIP and is in the process of gaining chartered status.

Andy McGregor works in JISC's Innovation Group as a Programme Manager. Andy is currently responsible for three programmes of work:

- an exploration of the use of activity data in higher education: *http://www.activitydata.org/*;
- fostering a community of software developers working in further and higher education: *http://devcsi.ukoln.ac.uk/*;
- the Discovery Programme – an initiative to improve access to library, museum and archive collections: *http://discovery.ac.uk/*.

Before working for JISC Andy worked as a librarian for Middlesex University and the Institute of Cancer Research. He may be contacted via Twitter: *@andymcg*.

Susan Myburgh has been an information professional for several decades, mostly as an academic, at the University of Cape Town, University of South Australia and, most recently, as Professor at the University of Parma, where she teaches and engages in research with regard to digital cultural institutions. She has investigated and worked in many areas of library and information science, including cataloguing and metadata, recordkeeping and archives, information retrieval and strategic information management, and knowledge management and community informatics. She is widely published, including two volumes by Chandos (*The New Information Professional*, 2005, and *Educating Digital Librarians*, 2012). She has also won several awards and honours, including the Britt Literary Award and a Fulbright Scholarship. Her main areas of research remain how social information problems can be solved and how information is used.

Steve O'Connor is a Director of Information Exponentials, a company specialising in future-proofing libraries. He has extensive experience in managing organisations large and small, income-based as well as expenditure-based. Most recently he has been the University Librarian at the Hong Kong Polytechnic University. He has held similar posts as a CEO and University Librarian in Australia.

He has researched, published, presented, consulted and taught very extensively in the areas of change, organisational management, leadership, scenario planning and authorship as well as on the future of the wider library and information environment. He has assisted libraries and consortia to explore new thinking and service delivery through scenario planning methodologies.

His current focus is on the creation of sustainable new business models for our future libraries. He has been the editor of the international peer reviewed journal *Library Management* for over ten years as well as the editor of a new journal *Library Management China* published completely in simplified Chinese.

He has recently published a book *Imagine Your Library's Future* (Chandos, 2011) which will be translated into Chinese in 2012. He has published over 50 journal articles and numerous conference presentations.

Richard Otlet is a graduate of the University of Wales College Newport and the University of Bristol, his career spanning both the commercial business sector in marketing intelligence and the public sector, initially as a lecturer in education and latterly in communications and marketing. Richard's experience includes working for a multinational corporation, the Imperial Group, in central marketing intelligence and the IMI Group.

Moving into the public sector in the 1990s, Richard lectured in education at a further education college and holds a Master of Education degree from the University of Bristol, specialising in information management and policy in education. Richard joined the Joint Information Systems Committee (JISC) in 2000 and moved to the newly formed JISC communications and marketing team in 2003 where he heads up the outputs team responsible for corporate communications outputs across events, press, public relations, publications, branding and multimedia. Richard is passionate about improving the user information experience and building innovative information architectures to support a total user experience that is both on and offline. Richard has continued his research specialising in information behaviours and improving the student experience as part of his doctoral research, again at the University of Bristol. Richard can trace his lineage back to Paul Otlet, one of several people who have been considered the father of information science, a field he called 'documentation'.

Joachim Schöpfel is head of the LIS department at the University of Lille 3, director of the French digitisation centre for PhD theses and a member of the GERiiCO research laboratory. He was manager of the INIST (CNRS) scientific library from 1999 to 2008. He teaches in library marketing, auditing, intellectual property and information science. His research interests are scientific information and communication, especially open access and grey literature.

Vivien Sieber is currently Head of Learning and Research Support and Development at the University of Surrey where she is responsible for

Academic Liaison Librarians, Learning Developers, the Researcher Development Team and Additional Learning Support. Her interest in using technology to support learning developed before the Web, and she has learnt alongside the technological evolution. Vivien is committed to using technology in her own teaching and to encouraging others to use technology.

Vivien's initial training was as a bioscientist, her PhD being in ecological genetics, and she conducted a range of research projects before moving into teaching. A sideways move to education development and technology-enhanced learning led to interests in virtual learning environments and online learning. Recognising that creating quality online resources is time-consuming and costly, coupled with the possibilities offered by the Web for sharing and reuse, led to an interest in Open Educational Resources (OER). Vivien has been involved in a number of subject-based OER projects exploring what is involved in sharing materials while the 'Skills Portal' is an example of reusing resources.

David Vogt is a scientist, entrepreneur and innovation leader in Vancouver, Canada. He currently leads two start-up companies, advises others and runs the Mobile Muse Network, which undertakes collaborative innovation in mobile media technologies for public engagement. David Vogt is also Director of Innovation Strategy at the Media and Graphics Interdisciplinary Centre (MAGIC) Lab of the University of British Columbia.

Caroline Williams has a BA in English Language and Literature, an MA in Library and Information Studies and an MBA. While studying for her MBA Caroline worked at both the Open University and Manchester Metropolitan University, where she became increasingly interested in information technology, management and leadership practice. These interests developed and in 2004 Caroline became Executive Director of Intute (formerly the RDN) at the national data centre Mimas based at the University of Manchester; in 2008 she was appointed to the role of Mimas Deputy Director. It was in these positions that Caroline gained experience of leading organisational transition and change. She became an MSP Advanced Practitioner in 2006, and in 2007 was the winner of the Jason Farradane Award in recognition of outstanding work in the field of information science.

Caroline joined the University of Nottingham in 2011 as Director of Research and Learning Resources within Information Services. Her portfolio of work spans libraries, learning technology, manuscripts and special collections, and research data management. She is co-Director of the Centre for Research Communications and Director of the Centre for International e-Portfolio Development.

Simon Whittemore has a background in the public and private sectors, in a range of policy development, business change and improvement roles, working at national and international levels.

He leads the Business and Community Engagement (BCE) programme and strategy at the Joint Infrastructure Systems Committee (JISC): *http:// www.jisc.ac.uk/supportingyourinstitution/cribsheets/engagingbusiness. aspx*. The BCE programme helps institutions develop their capabilities for managing and optimising their strategic partnerships and collaboration with external organisations, and the associated services, through the innovative use of ICT.

Simon was previously Deputy Head of the Business and Community team at HEFCE from 2003 to 2007, developing the strategic and conceptual coherence of knowledge transfer and exchange (KT), the national innovation funding policy and related good practices. Prior to that, he led multinational teams developing, authoring and deploying online group-wide methods and quality standards at Cap Gemini headquarters in France, in areas such as Programme Management, Documentation Development and the establishment of global Application Management Service Centres. He has also taught in further education and held various IT change, service and account management roles. An advocate of cross-cultural engagement and a linguist, he is fluent in Italian and French.

The future of digital information provision

David Baker and Wendy Evans

Abstract. In this first chapter, the authors aim to summarise the main themes and issues, successes and opportunities, challenges and threats that the developing information environment – in its broadest sense – encompasses, as evinced and explored in the rest of this book. The topics covered are wide-ranging indeed, but this is a sign of the times, the all-embracing nature of the Internet and the very many challenges that are evident for us all, whether creators, providers or users of information.

Keywords: access, digital, future, information

Introduction

In this first chapter, we aim to summarise the main themes and issues, successes and opportunities, challenges and threats that the developing information environment – in its broadest sense – encompasses, as evinced and explored in the rest of this book. The topics covered are wide-ranging indeed, but this is a sign of the times, the all-embracing nature of the Internet and the very many challenges that are evident for us all, whether creators, providers or users of information.

The future of the library and the library of the future

It is clear from even a cursory study of the essays contained within this volume and the relevant literature more broadly, that the information world – and indeed the world more generally – is experiencing a significant period of discontinuous change (Lynch, 2005; Dempsey, 2006; JISC, 2010; Curtis et al., 2011). As Richard Otlet (Chapter 5) points out, information has always been inherently unstable, and no more so than now. The library has typically been a stabilising influence, albeit along with other groups, such as publishers. But the traditional information environment is breaking down, as discussed here and throughout the rest of the book. As a result, the very future of that thing we call 'the library' is in question: even if there are to be collections, services, users – and librarians to support them – it will be something new and radically different from what has gone before. We have not even used the word 'library' in either the title or the subtitle of this book, though a number of authors do explore what it will mean to run or use such an entity in the coming years and many give much cause for optimism in terms of a vibrant future for the profession of librarianship.

But the world is much bigger that just physical space or volumes on shelves, and even specific digital collections and services. We really do live in an era of global access to (almost) endless resources (Curtis et al., 2011) which has the potential to pose a threat to the library as a place (Watson, 2010). The information environment is very complex, and the chapters in this volume aim, as Otlet stresses, to map the landscape as a means of understanding what the future might hold, both generally and particularly in terms of library and information services and the skills that will be necessary to navigate through that landscape. Librarians must recognise their changing role and that their activities will take place outside of the four walls of the physical library (Plutchak, 2012): the idea of bringing the library and the librarian to the user wherever they may be (Kesselman and Watstein, 2009) and in the academic context 'to work with researchers on their own turf'.[1] This is where library and information professionals come in, as discussed later in the book, and especially Chapters 14 and 15.

While there are clear threats, then, to the continued existence of libraries – especially traditional ones – there are also a number of pointers to what a library might in the future look like and consist of, even though it will be radically different from what we are used to. For example, the descriptions of the *Enquire* service (Chapter 3), the Skills Portal (Chapter 13) and the Salford THINKlab (Chapter 8) could all be said to take over some of the functions of the traditional library. Their success is seemingly based on the fact that they have identified a need and the potential of technology – in some cases more advanced than others – and married the two to provide novel applications that are of real benefit, both now and in the future.

Discovery

The ability to discover relevant information, content and resources quickly, easily and (cost) effectively is more crucial than ever in the digital age (see, for example, Canadian Heritage Information Network, 2009). The developments of the last decade or so have certainly enabled seemingly instant access to infinite amounts of material, and the ways in which people research, the changing nature of user ability and expectations (Law, 2009) and the nature of the results and outcomes which they achieve – at all levels and in all subjects – are being transformed. Yet there remain issues and challenges – which should be and are being taken up by librarians, information officers and others. There are particular questions relating to quality of provision and seamlessness of access, underpinned by openness of materials and sustainable business models – or the lack of them – which still need clear answers. Free at the point of use does not guarantee quality of resource, but subscription-based services to highly rated quality content will suffer if they are not easy to use, cost-effective to maintain and seen as good value for money by those who pay for them. At the same time, approaches that assume users think in the same way as librarians are generally agreed as being doomed to failure. Similarly, designers of digital information spaces must connect with the user in order to be successful (Chow, Chapter 2). Librarians need to understand who their users are, what they want and need, how user expectations are changing and how we respond to this (Neal, 2009). The advent of Google – and the development of the Internet (as, for example, with regard to social networking) more broadly – has seen to that. A number of projects are looking at how discovery can be improved in this new information environment, where the user rather than the provider is ostensibly in control. The Joint Information Systems Committee's Discovery programme[2] is discussed by Andrew McGregor and Rachel Bruce in Chapter 7. It is already clear that in order to achieve the vision of high-quality, flexible, any-time access to resources for a wide variety of purposes and to satisfy almost endless needs, and on a global scale, a number of issues must be resolved, of which the widespread engagement of all the key stakeholders – including publishers and authors – is but one critical success factor. There is also an increasing emphasis on shared services, at regional, national and international level, though the ability to have localised – and indeed personalised – flexibility seems to be crucial to the success of such collaborative projects. The benefits are considerable, both in terms of cost-efficiency and enhanced services to users. As evinced by the *Enquire* project (Chapter 3), for example, national leadership, collaborative management, local buy-in and an emphasis on quality access are also required for such projects.

Open access, intellectual property rights, interoperability

The efficacy of the future digital library, then, will be largely determined by the extent to which the principles of open access are embraced by all the key stakeholders[3] (Krishnamurthy, 2008). The debates continue, with the creators and the curators yet to reach significant and widespread agreement with publishers, though, as a number of authors in this book imply, there does now seem to be significant movement, even though robust business models remain largely elusive (Creaser, 2011). The latest area where agreements must be concluded soon if research in particular is not to be impeded is the area of data mining in relation to intellectual property rights, as McDonald and Kelly (2012) point out. Managing the issue of intellectual property rights in a positive way that benefits all parties in the communication chain continues to be of paramount importance (see, for example, Korn and Oppenheim, 2006; Zhang, 2007). There has been a change in the role of the stakeholders/ researchers/libraries/publishers involved in publishing research resulting in a not so linear process, overlap and confusion in roles (Hunter et al., 2009). While publishers – like librarians – could and should have a significant role to play in the future information environment, it is not yet entirely clear what this might be, though in academic publishing the quality assurance frameworks traditionally provided by publishers remain important in the digital world. Partnership and collaboration at a technical level will be essential in the future if that crucial prerequisite of interoperability – supported by universally agreed and implemented standards, frameworks and models – is to be achieved as recommended in the Finch Group Report.[4] At the time of writing new legislative measures are being announced to modernise and strengthen the UK copyright licensing system with a view to boosting its contribution to the economy and society.[5]

Sustainability

So, while old models of provision and access are breaking/have broken down, there is yet to be a clear set of new business models that fit with the emergent environment. This includes not just electronic publication, but any and every area relating to digital content (Hamilton, 2004; Houghton et al., 2009; JISC, 2009; Maron et al., 2009; Maron and

Loy, 2011). Given the very diverse nature of that environment, it may be some considerable time before such models emerge, as for example in the case of e-books, though even here a number of authors report progress and interesting experiments are already taking place (see also, for example, Franklin, 2012). At the present time, as noted by Lorraine Estelle in Chapter 6, both librarians and publishers are struggling with how to sustain provision in a world where ever increasing amounts of material seem to be available to the end user free of charge. As she goes on to argue, however, there have been successes, of which arguably the most obvious to date is in the field of (scholarly) journal publishing. At the extreme end of the spectrum, with changing communication patterns, could this be the death of the journal as we know it (Hunter et al., 2009)? Even the long-heralded e-book is now proving popular as both academic tool and general reading device,[6] though this is one of a number of areas where intermediaries such as libraries and booksellers are being bypassed.

A key attraction of digital content is the anytime, anywhere availability of materials. Without this feature as a given, users will not even contemplate accessing content. As several authors, such as Chérifa Boukacem-Zeghmouri and Joachim Schöpfel (Chapter 9) point out, Google is very much the dominant design at the present time, even though there may be discipline-specific variations in use on the Internet. Library responses to this situation have been to work with rather than against Google (see, for example, Manuel and Oppenheim, 2007; Cahill, 2008). This has been echoed by discovery services fully integrating library content and making it accessible through a Google-type search engine. There seems little alternative, given that power has very much shifted from provider to user, though ensuring that users are information literate (see later in this chapter and also Chapters 5 and 13) – as Richard Otlet argues (Chapter 5) – should mean that we are not overwhelmed by the sheer amount of material that is available without any quality control mechanism in place. There continues to be an exponential growth in digital content and an ever greater divergence in its provenance: content creation is no longer the preserve of professionals or organisations. The application of digital curation principles in order to add meaning and content – as discussed by Aldalin Lyngdoh in Chapter 10 and Abby Clobridge in Chapter 11 – and thus aid effective discovery is vital (Walton, 2011), not least in the Humanities (see, for example, Reisz, 2011).

Users, resources, intermediation

All of the trends described here have two things in common – the predominance of the user and the infiniteness of resources. Paradoxically, there is an increasing disconnect between those who provide information (typically, still, libraries) and those who use it. A number of authors comment on the fact that most, if not all, users are now blind to the origin of the information and data that they locate and access through the Internet. It could be argued this could be attributed to today's users being 'digital natives' (those born after the Internet was invented in 1993) as opposed to 'digital immigrants'.[7] As Lorraine Estelle (Chapter 6) in particular points out, the 'very ease of access' means that the significant costs of provision and access are largely hidden from public view, even though, in the case of research endeavour, there is a strong correlation between quality and depth of provision and the excellence of outcomes.

Personalisation has been a major outcome of the development of the Internet and user-centred design is now becoming rightly popular, not least as a way of ensuring that the user remains in control through continuously improving usability (Chapter 2; see also: Chowdhury et al., 2006; Kani-Zabihi et al., 2006). But, as David Vogt (Chapter 4) points out, who is in charge of this personalisation, the individual user or the conglomerates that increasingly dominate the Web and have the potential to control what can and cannot be seen and used? There are certainly dangers in a personalisation process that denies the individual access to all material, relevant or otherwise. Richard Otlet (Chapter 5) discusses how the ease with which digital content can be accessed has resulted in the decentralisation of information and disintermediation (Nicholas, 2012), or the obviating of the need for an intermediary – typically the librarian (Curtis et al., 2011). Similarly, the marginalisation of physical collections – as housed in library buildings – has dislocated content from obvious common or public ownership on the one hand and raised the possibility of significant sets of resources being *less* easily available – without a fee payment – because they are privately owned. This is as true of much born-digital material (thanks to the current business models in publishing, as already noted) as it is of retrospectively digitised content. In addition, the explosion in information creation, provision and access has meant that its currency is declining. The half-life of its usefulness may be shorter, but the tail of decay is longer.

Information literacy

There is evidence – as discussed later in this book – to suggest that the comprehensiveness of the Internet is not matched by the sophistication of its users. Information literacy – the need for it and the need to develop ways of engendering and inculcating it – is a burgeoning topic, at least among those who aim to provide quality resources if not those who may or may not use them.[8] Skills Portal (Chapter 13) is one example of the ways in which users can be helped to help themselves using, in this case, open education resources. It is interesting that the project report notes the importance of ensuring the engagement of users with the resources as being crucial to the success of an information literacy programme and the extent to which resources are being imported from Google. Just as important, though, is the way in which the value of subject specialists is being recognised as a key element in the selection of appropriate material for the programmes.

Information literacy is also an important aspect in the engagement of communities – public and private, commercial and not-for-profit. Without a sufficiently deep understanding of technology and the knowledge of how to use it to best effect, knowledge transfer between, for example, universities and industries will be significantly hampered. Simon Whittemore and colleagues (Chapter 12) report on a major initiative designed to improve such synergies in the United Kingdom by the development of 'economic competencies' in order to make a substantial contribution to the country's international competitiveness.

Whither librarianship?

A number of the contributions to this volume consider the future of librarianship and information science. In recent years, as already noted, there has been a significant move away from the librarian as intermediary between content and user. If librarians are to have a future, then they must renew their profession in the context of a very different environment, as already described in this chapter and throughout the rest of this book. Librarians are moving more towards having a role as content aggregators, access managers and educators in digital literacy (Norman, 2012). Susan Myburgh (Chapter 14) argues that in particular there needs to be not only a new theoretical basis for librarianship but also a broadening out of the roles that librarians need to play – especially in the education of users and the provision of easy access to quality content. Put another way, as Richard Otlet stresses (Chapter 5), librarians need to re-intermediate between content and user, not least in the area of information literacy.

But librarianship will still be one profession among many that collectively lead, manage and provide library-type services. A recurring theme – already noted – is the importance of leadership and the continued fostering and development of leaders willing to take risks as they innovate through the harnessing of new technologies to create vital services in the new information environment. However, as Steve O'Connor (Chapter 17) points out, there is a significant mismatch between the organisational structures currently in place in most library and information services and the types of requirement that are becoming more central as the digital age unfolds.[9] Caroline Williams (Chapter 15) focuses on the maintenance and development of skilled, motivated, agile and flexible teams organised into project and matrix-based groupings as a way of providing libraries with the necessary differentiating factor to ensure their meaningful future at a time – as discussed earlier – when the need for such services is widely questioned.

What next?

After a long period of seeming stability, the world of information management has been turned upside down in little more than a decade. Yet David Vogt (Chapter 4) reminds us that the Internet is in its infancy and describes the significant untapped potential that it still holds for us. The 'elaboration' of current social web developments offers the ultimate personalisation (already a major trend) of digital information through emulation of the software architecture of the brain itself. Certainly the process of human thought and our phenomenal ability to process data (and to 'overlook' or 'ignore' most of it in highly individual ways unless or until required) offers the most impressive possible model for future developments. At the same time, the Web provides the potential for supporting the brain's information management processes as new applications are developed. The underlying question implicit in this challenge relates to the identity of the agency or agencies that could possibly deliver such applications, especially when it comes to the 'common good'. Perhaps this is where the reinvention and renewal of the librarian offers an opportunity to redress the balance through a process of re-intermediation between users and resources, as referred to earlier.

End note

This, then, is the likely future environment in which we will live, work and play. It is one where electronic publication is the norm and, indeed, almost certainly in the longer term, the sole means of dissemination of information; where global and local combine in a myriad ways; where everyone is – or believes themselves to be – an expert, or at least a contributor and certainly a user; it is a world where we will all soon be digital natives; and it will be one where there is no single landscape to be viewed and no prime roadmap to be navigated in order to find a way forward. Will there be a future for the traditional players in the information chain? Ease of access to quality resources will be the core goal of librarians and information managers. As Lyngdoh discusses in Chapter 10, metadata will continue to play an important part in helping them to achieve this goal by the addition of real value and meaning in a complex world (as, for example, McDonald and Kelly, 2012).

Whether or not librarians and information managers will be able to achieve this aim remains to be seen, for it is not yet clear which business models will succeed and whether or not free-at-point-of-use will remain the norm. And what of publishers? Traditional models of communication are breaking down. But there is a danger that many (commercial) organisations would have the world's knowledge available only on their terms when there is so much more to be gained by making it (freely) available to all, for whatever reasonable purpose and perhaps especially for the pursuit of knowledge through academic research, learning and teaching.[10] Collaboration rather than competition would seem to be the way forward. Perhaps in future, then, librarians and information managers will be 'fixers': the people who bring it all together through collaborative arrangements that are in everybody's interests and which, in consequence, are likely to have the best chance of success (see, for example, Deegan and Tanner, 2002; Watson, 2010; Gannon-Leary and Bent, 2011; Bevan, 2012). If this challenge of the availability, accessibility, reusage and repurposing of quality information can be met, then the future holds much promise in terms of improving the human condition for all.

Notes

1. *http://www.insidehighered.com/news/2010/06/09/hopkins*
2. The Discovery project publishes a newsletter at: *http://discovery.ac.uk/files/ newsletter/Discovery_Newsletter.pdf.* To keep up with the latest news you can visit *http://discovery.ac.uk/news/* and *http://blog.discovery.ac.uk* at any time or keep an eye on the *#ukdiscovery* hashtag on Twitter. See also J. Esposito, 'The problem of discovery for patron-driven acquisitions (PDA)', at: *http://scholarlykitchen.sspnet.org/2012/06/12/the-problem-of-discovery-for-patron-driven-acquisitions-pda/?utm_source=feedburner&utm_ medium=twitter&utm_campaign=Feed%3A+ScholarlyKitchen+%28The+Sc holarly+Kitchen%29.*
3. See, for example, *http://www.guardian.co.uk/science/2012/jun/19/open-access-academic-publishing-finch-report* (accessed 19 June 2012).
4. *Expanding Access to Research Publications*, Report of the Working Group on Expanding Access to Published Research Findings – the Finch Group. The Finch Report is at: *http://www.researchinfonet.org/publish/finch/.* See also, for example, P. Jump, 'Push for gold will cost millions, open access report says', at: *http://www.timeshighereducation.co.uk/story.asp?sectioncod e=26&storycode=420307&c=1; http://www.dw.de/dw/episode/0,,15836242, 00.html* and *http://www.timeshighereducation.co.uk/story.asp?sectioncode= 26&storycode=420326&c=1.*
5. *http://www.bis.gov.uk/news/topstories/2012/Jul/modernising-copyright-to-strengthen-growth*
6. See also M. Reisz (2012) 'Farewell, obscure object of desire', *Times Higher Education*, 2033, 11 June.
7. *http://www.marcprensky.com/writing/prensky%20-%20digital%20natives, %20digital%20immigrants%20-%20part1.pdf*
8. See, for example: 'Digital literacy: trial and error?', at: *http://blog.lboro. ac.uk/elearning/?p=1244&utm_source=rss&utm_medium=rss&utm_ campaign=jisc-news-release-developing-digital-literacy-trial-and-error.*
9. See also L. Dempsey (2012) 'Regional Council meeting', *CILIP Update*, January, 41–3.
10. See, for example, 'The $99 question: could this be the future of open-access publishing?', *Times Higher Education*, 2054, 14–20 June 2012, pp. 6–7; E. Hyams (2012) 'Are academic journals fit for purpose?', *CILIP Update*, June, pp. 35–7.

References

Bevan, N. (2012) 'Preliminary to reading', *Times Higher Education*, 28 February. Online at: *http://www.timeshighereducation.co.uk/story.asp?storycode=419086.*

Cahill, K. (2008) 'An opportunity, not a crisis: how Google is changing the individual and the information profession', *Journal of Library Administration*, 47(1/2): 67–75.

Canadian Heritage Information Network (2009) *The Impact of Search Engine Optimisation on Organisations' Websites*. Bristol: JISC.

Chowdhury, S., Landoni, M. and Gibb, F. (2006) 'Usability and impact of digital libraries: a review', *Online Information Review*, 30(6): 656–80.

Creaser, C. (2011) 'Open access to research outputs – institutional policies and researchers' views: results from two complementary surveys', *New Review of Academic Librarianship*, 16(1): 4–25.

Curtis, G., Davies, C., Hammond, M., Hawtin, R. and Ringland, G. (2011) *Academic Libraries of the Future: Scenarios Beyond 2020*. British Library, JISC and others. Online at: *http://www.futurelibraries.info/content/system/ files/Scenarios_beyond_2020_ReportWV.pdf*; see also: *http://www. futurelibraries.info*.

Deegan, M. and Tanner, S. (2002) *Digital Futures: Strategies for the Information Age*. New York: Neal Schuman.

Dempsey, L. (2006) 'The (digital) library environment: ten years after', *Ariadne*, 46. Online at: *http://www.ariadne.ac.uk/issue46/dempsey/*.

Franklin, A. (2012) 'Printing pressed', *Times Higher Education*, 29 March. Online at: *http://www.timeshighereducation.co.uk/story.asp?storycode=419464*.

Gannon-Leary, P. and Bent, M. (2011) 'Writing for publication and the role of the library', *New Review of Academic Librarianship*, 16(1): 26–44.

Hamilton, V. (2004) 'Sustainability for digital libraries', *Library Review*, 53(8): 393–5.

Houghton, J., Rasmussen, B., Sheehan, P., Oppenheim, C., Morris, A., Creaser, C., Greenwood, H., Summers, M. and Gourlay, A. (2009) *Economic Implications of Alternative Scholarly Publishing Models: Exploring the Costs and Benefits*. Bristol: JISC.

Hunter, K., Waters, D., Wilson, L. and Heath, F. (2009) 'Panel 3: Into the Glass Darkly: future directions in the 21st century', *Journal of Library Administration*, 49(3) 281–301.

Joint Information Systems Committee (JISC) (2009) *Sustainable ICT in Further and Higher Education*. Bristol: JISC; see also: *http://www.susteit.org.uk*.

Joint Information Systems Committee (JISC) (2010) *Transformation Through Technology: Illustrating JISC's Impact Across Two Decades*. Bristol: HEFCE.

Kani-Zabihi, E., Ghinea, G. and Chen, S.Y. (2006) 'Digital libraries: what do users want?', *Online Information Review*, 30(6): 395–412.

Kesselman, M. and Watstein, S. (2009) 'Creating opportunities: embedded librarians', *Journal of Library Administration*, 49(4): 383–400.

Korn, N. and Oppenheim, C. (2006) 'Creative commons licences in higher and further education: do we care?', *Ariadne*, 49. Online at: *http://www.ariadne. ac.uk/issue49/korn-oppenheim/*.

Krishnamurthy, M. (2008) 'Open access, open source and digital libraries', *Program*, 42(1): 48–55.

Law, D. (2009) 'Academic digital libraries of the future: an environment scan', *New Review of Academic Librarianship*, 15(1): 53–67.

Lynch, C. (2005) 'Where do we go from here ? The next decade for digital libraries', *D-Lib Magazine*, 11(7/8). Online at: *http://www.dlib.org/dlib/ july05/lynch/07lynch.html*.

McDonald, D. and Kelly, U. (2012) *The Value and Benefits of Text Mining to UK Further and Higher Education.* Bristol: JISC. Online at: *http://www.jisc.ac.uk/media/documents/publications/reports/2012/value-text-mining.pdf.*

Manuel, S. and Oppenheim, C. (2007) 'Googlepository and the University Library', *Ariadne,* 53. Online at http://www.ariadne.ac.uk/issue53/manuel-oppenheim/.

Maron, N. and Loy, M. (2011) *Revenue, Recession, Reliance: Revisiting the SCA/Ithaka S+R case studies in sustainability.* London: JISC, SCA, Ithaka S+R. Online at: *http://sca.jiscinvolve.org/wp/files/2011/10/iDF158-SCA_Ithaka_ReportPlus_Sep11_v1-final1.pdf.*

Maron, N., Kirby Smith, K. and Loy, M. (2009) *Sustaining Digital Resources: An On-the-Ground View of Projects Today.* London: JISC, SCA, Ithaka S+R. Online at: *http://www.jisc.ac.uk/media/documents/publications/general/2009/scaithakaprojectstoday.pdf.*

Neal, J. (2009) 'What do users want? What do users need? W(h)ither the academic research library?', *Journal of Library Administration,* 49(5): 463–8.

Nicholas, D. (2012) 'Disintermediated, decoupled and down', *CILIP Update,* April, pp. 29–31.

Norman, M. (2012) 'Frail, fatal, fundamental: the future of public libraries', *Aplis,* 25(2): 94–100.

Plutchak, T. (2012) 'Breaking the barriers of time and space: the dawning of the great age of librarians', *Journal of the Medical Library Association,* 100(1): 10–19.

Reisz, M. (2011) 'Surfdom', *Times Higher Education,* 8 December. Online at: *http://www.timeshighereducation.co.uk/story.asp?storycode=418343.*

Walton, G. (2011) 'Data curation and the academic library', *New Review of Academic Librarianship,* 16(1): 1–3.

Watson, L. (2010) 'The future of the library as a place of learning: a personal perspective', *New Review of Academic Librarianship,* 16(1): 45–56.

Zhang, W. (2007) 'Digital library intellectual property right evaluation and method', *Electronic Library,* 25(3): 267–73.

2

The usability of digital information environments: planning, design and assessment

Anthony Chow

Abstract. The proliferation of Internet-based digital resources has increased the need for well designed digital information environments. Competition is fierce as users rapidly 'surf the web' in search of information, entertainment and social connection. Twenty-first-century information-seekers have little patience for confusing interfaces, poor use of media, or sites that are difficult to navigate and understand. This chapter explores and defines the concept of usability and establishes its place and value in designing digital environments for use with the technology devices used to access them. It examines the body of research on information and information-seeking behaviour followed by a set of guidelines for designing digital information spaces for both adults and youth. Lastly, assessment and evaluation are discussed as essential aspects of the design and continuous improvement foundation for any highly usable system. Readers will be provided with a set of applicable guidelines in which to design, implement and evaluate highly usable digital environments within the context of a sound theoretical framework.

Keywords: information-seeking behaviour, navigation, usability, user-centred design

Introduction

The proliferation of Internet-based digital resources has increased the need for well designed digital information environments: competition is fierce as users rapidly 'surf the web' in search of information, entertainment and social connection. Twenty-first-century information-seekers have little patience for confusing interfaces, poor use of media or sites that are difficult to navigate and understand. On average, users will spend only 25–30 seconds on a web page to determine whether it will meet their information needs (Nielsen and Loranger, 2006). This finding is consistent with Poole's (1985) *principle of least effort* that posits humans will take the path of least effort to fill an information need; make the information-seeking task too difficult and information-seekers will quickly go elsewhere.

User-centred design: usability and digital environments

The chapter will first explore and define the concept of usability and establish its place and value in designing digital environments for use with the technology devices used to access them, especially in Web 2.0 and the emerging tablet, mobile and projected Web 3.0 environments.

User-centred design

User-centred design (UCD) is 'the practice of creating engaging, efficient user experiences' (Garrett, 2011). The terms *engaging*, *efficient* and *experiences* are all, however, uniquely subjective to both designers of digital environments and the people that use them. Another definition of UCD as defined by the United States government is:

> User-centered design (UCD) is an approach for employing usability. It is a structured product development methodology that involves users throughout all stages of Web site development, in order to create a Web site that meets users' needs. This approach considers an organization's business objectives and the user's needs, limitations, and preferences.[1]

Rubin (1984), cited in www.w3.org,[2] describes UCD as an interrelated set of concentric circles involving eight factors, where '... users are in the center of a double circle' comprised of an inner ring that represents 'Context, Objectives, Environment and Goals' and an outer ring that represents 'Task Detail, Task Content, Task Organization and Task Flow' (see Figure 2.1).

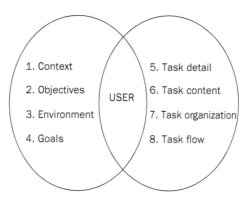

1. Context
2. Objectives
3. Environment
4. Goals

USER

5. Task detail
6. Task content
7. Task organization
8. Task flow

Figure 2.1   User-centred design factors

According to the World Wide Web Consortium (W3C), UCD can also be considered *human-centred design* (HCD).[3] The International Organization for Standardization (ISO) defines HCD in its standard ISO 13407 (1999) as '... an approach to interactive system development that focuses specifically on making systems usable. It is a multi-disciplinary activity.'[4] According to this standard, HCD is comprised of four core principles: 'active involvement of users, appropriate allocation of function to system and to user, iteration of design solutions, [and] multi-disciplinary design' involving four major activities: understand and specify the context of use, specify user and organisational requirements, produce more than one candidate design solution, and evaluate designs against requirements (see Table 2.1).[5]

While easy to understand, the successful implementation of the UCD process is much more difficult. One of the central problems is that designers frequently develop digital information spaces utilising their own paradigms – what they deem to be important, organised in a fashion that makes the most sense to them – *in absentia* of the people that will actually be using it. This disconnect creates a gap between designer and user.

Chow et al. (2012) coined the term *concept actualisation* in their research with 53 middle- and high-school-aged youth in the United States. The research focused on how to deliver marketing and career-oriented information about computing and information technology in an age-appropriate fashion that youth found the most usable. The study

Table 2.1	User-centred design principles and activities

Core principles	UCD core activities
▪ Active involvement of users ▪ Appropriate allocation of function to system and to user ▪ Iteration of design solutions ▪ Multi-disciplinary design	1. Understand and specify the context of use 2. Specify user and organisational requirements 3. Produce more than one candidate design solution 4. Evaluate designs against requirements

found that it was difficult for adult web designers to develop digital information spaces for youth because their adult paradigm differed so greatly from that of youth. For example, what was considered clean, uncluttered design shaped by and for the adult-centric priority for seeking and accessing information as quickly and efficiently as possible was not appropriate for youths' need for bright colours, use of animation and preference for exploration and social interaction. They found that only by practising collaborative design or working with youth as design partners (Druin et al., 1999) did *concept actualisation* take place where the UCD concepts of *engaging*, *efficient* and (satisfying) *experience* could be implemented effectively for youth.

While UCD is the process for people-centred design, usability represents the overall utility and ease-of-use[6] a person experiences in a digital environment while attempting to accomplish their information-seeking goals. The ISO formally defines usability as the 'extent to which the product can be used by specified users to achieve specified goals with effectiveness, efficiency and satisfaction in a specified context of use.'[7] *Effectiveness* is the 'percentage of goals achieved, percentage of users successfully completing tasks and average accuracy of completed tasks', *efficiency* is the 'time to complete a task, tasks completed per unit time and monetary cost of performing the task' and *satisfaction* is a 'rating scale for satisfaction, frequency of discretionary use and frequency of complaints' (Chow et al., 2012). According to Nielsen (2008), 'Usability allows us to make everyday life more satisfying by empowering people to control their destiny and their technology rather than be subjugated by computers.'[8] In fact, John Gould and Clayton Lewis (1983) held that there were three primary principles of usability that designers and developers of any product or service must adhere to: (1) establish an early focus on users; (2) run field studies before starting any design work; and (3) conduct empirical usability studies throughout development.[9]

While usability as a concept can be extremely complex to understand and consider in terms of application and implementation, it is actually quite elegantly simple to apply three basic processes:

1. Identify and engage representative users as design partners from the very start of the project.
2. Iteratively test at all design and development stages, including paper copies detailing only the information architecture and mock-up of a projected digital environment.
3. Continuously improve, refine and collect representative user feedback. (Garrett, 2011)

Information-seeking behaviour: need, information, access

Developers of digital spaces often mistake aesthetic design as the primary outcome, forgetting that most often visitors to digital environments are usually there for an explicit purpose centred around an information need; that is, visitors are on the hunt for information that makes the usability concepts of effectiveness (finding what one is looking for), efficiency (minimising the time and effort it takes to find what you are looking for) and satisfaction (a combination of effectiveness, efficiency and design aesthetics) extremely relevant and essential. Nielsen and Loranger's (2006) research suggests that users give a web page on average only 25–35 seconds to convince them that they are likely to be able to find what they are looking for. Google's web statistics analytics program calls this a *bounce rate* or the percentage of visitors that leave the page without visiting another page on the site (which suggests they may have not found what they are looking for).[10]

What is information-seeking behaviour?

Taylor (1968) defines information-seeking behaviour as information someone is searching for that helps 'fill out his picture of the world'. Belkin et al. (1982) define information need as an anomalous state of knowledge (ASK) and Derwin (1992) defines it as a process of 'sense-making'. Morris (1994) describes the information-seeking process in general as '[u]sers seek information to meet an information need and this process is highly unique, contextualized and constructivist in nature' (Chow and Bucknall, 2011).

Taylor (1968) defined four linear levels of information need:

1. A conscious or unconscious need for information where it '... may be only a vague sort of dissatisfaction. It is probably inexpressible in linguistic terms.'
2. A conscious mental description of an ill-defined area of indecision usually articulated or conceptualised as '... an ambiguous and rambling statement'.
3. A qualified and rational statement of the question. The indecision becomes better defined as an '... area of doubt in concrete terms and he (she) may or may not be thinking within the context or constraints of the system from which he wants information.'
4. The question is articulated within the context of the environment with the anticipation of success. The information-seeker must 'think in terms of the organization of particular files and of the discrete packages that are available – such as books, reports, papers, drawings, or tables (etc.).'

Taylor describes this as the question-negotiation process where information-seekers approach an information system or organisation with an information need in various stages of concreteness and articulation and 'negotiates' this need within the context of the information-seeking environment.

Pirolli and Card (1999) use a behavioural-based hunting metaphor, *information foraging*, to describe the information need and information-seeking relationship within technology environments. Their adaptive control of thought in information foraging (ACT-IF) theory suggests that humans are *informavores* hunting for *information scents* and that they will '... modify their strategies, or modify the structure of the interface if it is malleable, in order to maximize their rate of gaining valuable information.' At the same time, the information provider will also tend to evolve – when '... feasible, natural information systems evolve toward stable states that maximize gains of valuable information per unit cost.' This theory is especially useful in helping designers develop information architectures that make information scents especially strong so that users can find what they are looking for quickly and with little effort (Morville and Rosenfield, 2008).

Information-seeking and information-provision match

> *Jacob's Law of the Web User Experience states that* 'users spend most of their time on *other* websites.'[11]

If you want highly usable digital environments, then design information spaces for those who will use them and the information they usually seek. It is really that simple. The science of doing this, however, is more complex and represents an integration of the organisation and the user's goals. Websites, for example, have gone through several major changes in terms of information and user interaction. In the early 1990s, the primary focus for first-generation websites was making sure that they worked; second-generation websites began allowing users to customise their experience as browsers became capable of displaying more than just text through the use of colour, icons and images. Third-generation websites utilised expanded design and multimedia options to 'give visitors a complete experience, from entry to exit' (Siegal, 1997).

One of the most popular models for developing any kind of high-performance product or service is the ADDIE model, which stands for Analyse, Design, Develop, Implement and Evaluate (Pirolli and Card, 1999). This model serves as the foundation of systems thinking and '… performance technology because it details an easy to understand, systematic way of achieving goals in an efficient and effective manner', which closely aligns with both UCD principles and its recommended four activities – *understand the context of use, specify user and organisational requirements, produce multiple iterations* and *evaluate design based on requirements* (Garrett, 2011) (see Figure 2.2).

The concept of *pervasive usability* is 'a principle of design that advocates the application of usability methods in every stage of the design process.'[12] Applying the ADDIE model with usability methods included at each stage led Chow et al. (2012) to create an integrated web design and usability model called the Design, Develop and Evaluation (DDE) model (see Figure 2.3).

The *design* phase of these digital environments involves establishing both user and organisational requirements regarding decisions around who, what and how technology will be used to provide information to a discrete set of users. A few representative users should be brought in as design partners to help provide authentic perspectives and contexts for deciding preliminary needs and the system requirements necessary to

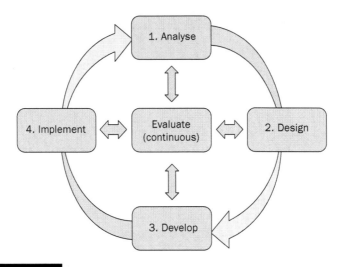

Figure 2.2 ADDIE model

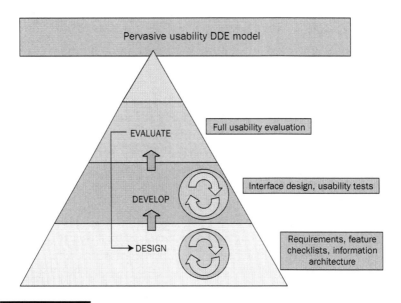

Figure 2.3 DDE model

meet these needs. It is also especially critical to attempt to ensure *concept actualisation* (Chow et al., 2012) with representative users, as what is considered good design, in terms of colour, use of animation, graphics and so on, may be operationalised in drastically different ways given the likely divergent paradigms of designers, developers and users of the site.

Once requirements have been established, priority feature checklists identifying 5–7 of the most important ways a user group will be using the site should be created. This can be done as a simple table listing each unique user group and their respective information needs. For example, for a university website, typical users can be broken down into prospective students, current students, faculty and staff, alumni and other potential non-affiliated visitors. Table 2.2 illustrates a potential set of features each respective group may require.

The final step in the *design* phase is to create an information architecture based on the preliminary analysis of user needs, informed by the project user design partners and identified feature checklists. For websites, this means organising content around major navigational links. Users want to find what they are looking for quickly and easily, and pushing the high priority items to the front of the home page, based on what users want, is an excellent way to make this happen. Continuing with this example, a preliminary information architecture map may look something like Figure 2.4.

An initial usability test can be conducted with only a paper or electronic version of a preliminary information architecture by asking users what pathways they would take if they were searching for the high-priority information identified in the feature checklists. This will test how well organised and how well the navigation has been labelled using

Table 2.2   Feature checklist

Priority	Prospective student	Current student	Alumni	Faculty and staff	Other
1	Degree information	Course offerings	News and events	Contact information	Contact information
2	Tuition	Faculty	Faculty	News and events	Job opportunities
3	Faculty	News and events	Contact information	Policies and procedures	Faculty
4	Overview of programme	Academic calendar			Directions and map
5	Contact information	Policies and procedures			
6	Application information	Graduation information			
7	Course offerings	Contact information			
8	Directions and map				

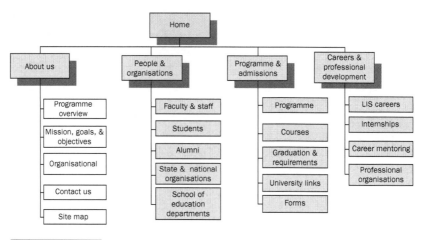

Figure 2.4 Information architecture map

language and words representative users understand. Early problems can be identified and multiple iterations of the site's information architecture may be required. Similar to building a house, once the structure and foundation are well designed, the house will be solid and well made.

The *develop* phase entails establishing a preliminary interface design, which can be defined as all of '[t]he ways in which a user comes into contact with any system or technology product' (Moran, 1981). Garrett (2011) defines the 'user experience development process' as 'taking into account every possibility of every action the user is likely to take and understanding the user's expectations at every step of the way through that process'. He suggests websites are comprised of five discrete 'planes' – the *surface* plane (what a user sees – text, photos, colour and so on), the *skeleton* plane (the architecture and organisation of the site and the infrastructure that resides underneath the surface plane), the *structure* plane (specific content and functionality and what a user will find and can do), the *scope* plane (the totality of what a user will be able to accomplish on the site) and the *strategy* plane (the shared goals of both the organisation and its users).

Similar to the design phase, the develop phase will involve multiple iterations informed by the project's design partners. Formal usability testing also begins at this stage where representative users will be asked to actually seek information and perform high-priority tasks on the design iterations. This is where the three factors of usability become more clearly apparent, where users can accomplish their intended goals with high levels of effectiveness, efficiency and satisfaction. The third and final phase will be a full usability evaluation after the site has been made available to the public.

Let us now discuss some general design guidelines based on information-seeking behaviour and tendencies.

Heuristics and design guidelines

Molich and Nielsen (1990) generated a list of ten design standards or heuristics that have since been revised in 2005.[13] These ten design standards are as follows:

1. *Consistency* – designing a product so that similar tasks are done in similar ways.

2. *Compatibility* – designing a product so that its method of operation is compatible with users' expectations based on their knowledge of other types of products and the 'outside world'.

3. *Consideration of user resources* – designing a product so that its method of operation takes into account the demands placed on the users' resources during interaction.

4. *User control* – designing a product so that the extent to which the user has control over the actions taken by the product and the state that the product is in is maximised.

5. *Visual clarity* – designing a product so that information displayed can be read quickly and easily without causing confusion.

6. *Prioritization of functionality and information* – designing a product so that the most important functionality and information are easily accessible to the user.

7. *Explicitness* – designing a product so that cues are given as to its functionality and method of operation.

8. *Match between system and real world* – the system should speak the users' language, with words, phrases and concepts familiar to the user, rather than system-oriented terms. Follow real-world conventions, making information appear in a natural and logical order.

9. *Recognition rather than recall* – make objects, actions and options visible. The user should not have to remember information from one part of the dialogue to another. Instructions for use of the system should be visible or easily retrievable whenever appropriate.

10. *Aesthetic and minimalist design* – dialogues should not contain information which is irrelevant or rarely needed. Every extra unit of information in a dialogue competes with the relevant units of information and diminishes their relative visibility.

Kamper (2002), in his work with IBM, developed a theory of human–computer interaction (HCI) referred to as Lead, Follow and Get Out of the Way (LF&G), which theorises that the optimal HCI experience is analogous to a facilitative learning relation:

> Like a good teacher, mentor, or coach, the usable user interface leads the user to successful completion of tasks and goals; follows the user's progress and provides appropriate feedback and information when needed; and gets out of the way of the user to allow efficient and effective completion of tasks as the user attains mastery of the system, its concepts, and operations. A set of 18 heuristics grouped under the 3 general principles of the title are provided for use across the tasks of design guidance, development refinement, and end-user evaluation of computer systems.

Information-seeking trends

Adult information-seeking

Research into adult information retrieval began with the notion that adult information-searching represented a 'berry-picking' style – search strategies usually focused on gathering information in pieces (Bates, 1989). Contemporary studies suggest that adult information-seekers typically are mainly concerned with the information search and retrieval process, often ignoring features such as navigation bars, animation and sound effects and rarely paying attention to logos, mission statements or advertising within a website in their quest for obtaining information with relevant content.[14] They prefer quick downloads, predictable responses, text-based links and broad, shallow tree structures for a site's information architecture (Lazar et al., 2003). Also, unlike children, adults are not averse to finding information through scrolling and reading text if necessary.[15]

Adult information-seekers become easily frustrated with seeking information on the Web when navigation and search time becomes too long and/or requires too much mental effort due to poor design, unpredictable interference, dropped connections and pop-up advertisements.[16] They often have little patience and do not take the time to learn about the site they are on, instead moving on to another site to find the information they are looking for (Lazar et al., 2003). Problems also occur because adults may not really understand where they are within a website's information architecture.[17] Recent literature supports the theory that relevant education and training as well as effective website design would improve general information retrieval and usability for adults.[18] Studies suggest that research on information-seeking could be incorporated into interface design[19] and has found marked improvements in software interface design since incorporating user feedback (Large et al., 2002).

Age-appropriate web design for children and adolescents

The general misconception adults have about younger information-seekers is that they are 'techno-wizards' who, because of their frequent use of iPods, smart phones, gaming systems and social media, are similarly adept at understanding how to navigate websites for information-seeking purposes (Large et al., 2002). Considine et al. (2009) found that while the 'Google generation' could access materials, their ability to process those texts was somewhat limited. Their search strategies could be characterised as 'skimming and squirrelling behaviour', they did not have a strong understanding of their own information needs, they had difficulty utilising effective information-seeking strategies and they spent little time processing whether the information found was either accurate, relevant or from a trusted source.

There is a growing body of knowledge about designing youth-oriented websites, and some design models, such as Druin et al.'s (1999) *cooperative inquiry*, Read et al.'s (2002) *participatory design* and Large et al.'s (2006) *bonded design* place youth at the centre of any design efforts. Cooper (2005) suggests that youth-oriented websites emphasise '... user control, [are] open-ended (encouraging exploration), active (as opposed to passive), involve multiple senses, offer quick feedback, balance novelty with familiarity, allow for and [are] responsive to child input, allow for progressive levels of expertise facilitating competence while offering new challenges, and support social interaction'.

Websites for children should be 'colorful, relevant, and easy-to-use' (Dubroy, 2010) and animation and interactivity must not be used in a 'gratuitous' fashion as 'bells and whistles are useless if the content is irrelevant' (Blowers and Bryan, 2004). The design should be simple and easy to navigate, which ironically is often not the case for youth-oriented websites: in 2002, Nielsen[20] conducted a study with 55 children and actually found that they tended to have an easier time navigating websites for adults rather than those for children because children's sites are often 'convoluted' (Nielsen, 2002, cited in Dubroy, 2010). Using metaphors and having help features available are also important website elements for youth as they can help reduce cognitive load for children by scaffolding new information being presented to pre-existing mental structures and images (Large and Beheshti, 2005). Help features also have been found to be extremely important to children so there is somewhere to turn to if they get lost or confused (Large et al., 2002; Bilal and Kirby, 2002).

Nielsen (2005) created a matrix that summarises and compares some of the major differences between younger groups and adult information-seekers (see Figure 2.5).[21]

Druin's (2002) youth design model (Figure 2.6) suggests a conceptual framework for a child's role as part of the design team, which starts at the very beginning, serving multiple roles through the design and development cycle as it evolves.

As websites are typically developed by adults, including youth from the very beginning of a site's conceptual and interface design is essential to developing user-friendly, age-appropriate digital environments for youth.

Nielsen's web design table across users

	Animation and sound effects	Mine sweeping for links	Advertising	Scrolling	Reading
Kids	☺	☺	☺	☹	☹
Teens	☺	☹	☺	☺	☹
Adults	☹	☹	☹	☺	☺

Key:

☺ Enjoyable, interesting and appealing, or users can easily adjust to it.

☺ Users might appreciate it to some extent but overuse can be problematic.

☹ Users dislike it, don't do it or find it difficult to operate.

Figure 2.5 **Nielsen's kids, teens and adult preferences**

Source: Nielsen (2005).

The child as...

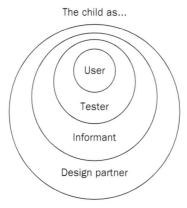

User

Tester

Informant

Design partner

| **Figure 2.6** | Including children in the web design process in multiple ways |

Source: Druin (2002).

Accessibility

In 1990, the US Department of Justice passed landmark legislation in addressing and establishing design guidelines for accessibility called the Americans with Disabilities Act (ADA).[22, 23] This Act '… prohibits discrimination on the basis of disability in employment, State and local government, public accommodations, commercial facilities, transportation, and telecommunications' (Bates, 1989). In 1998, the US Congress amended the Rehabilitation Act of 1973 to address ADA requirements regarding federal electronic and information technology (EIT), by creating Section 508 (29 U.S.C. '794 d) ensuring that 'agencies must give disabled employees and members of the public access to information that is comparable to access available to others'.[24] Section 508 addresses accessibility in electronic environments and defines accessible technology as 'one that can be operated in a variety of ways and does not rely on a single sense or ability of the user. For example, a system that provides output only in visual format may not be accessible to people with visual impairments and a system that provides output only in audio format may not be accessible to people who are deaf or hard of hearing' (Bates, 1989). Section 508 is comprised of four subparts, Standards A–D, addressing Technical Standards, Functional Performance Criteria, and Information, Documentation and Support. Subpart B, standard 1194.22: Web-based intranet and Internet information and applications, specifically addresses Web guidelines and is comprised of 16 rules[25] (see Table 2.3).

Table 2.3	ADA compliance rules for web-based intranet and Internet information and applications

The 16 Rules of Section 508, §1194.21 'Web-based intranet and internet information and applications'
(a) **A text equivalent for every non-text element** shall be provided (e.g., via "alt", "longdesc", or in element content).
(b) **Equivalent alternatives for any multimedia presentation** shall be synchronized with the presentation.
(c) Web pages shall be designed so that **all information conveyed with color is also available without color**, for example from context or markup.
(d) Documents shall be organized so they are readable without requiring an associated style sheet.
(e) **Redundant text links shall be provided** for each active region of a server-side image map.
(f) **Client-side image maps shall be provided instead of server-side image maps** except where the regions cannot be defined with an available geometric shape.
(g) **Row and column headers** shall be identified for data tables.
(h) **Markup shall be used to associate data cells and header cells for data tables** that have two or more logical levels of row or column headers.
(i) **Frames shall be titled with text** that facilitates frame identification and navigation.
(j) Pages shall be designed to avoid causing the screen to flicker with a frequency greater than 2 Hz and lower than 55 Hz.
(k) When pages utilize scripting languages to display content, or to create interface elements, **the information provided by the script shall be identified with functional text that can be read by assistive technology.**
(l) When a web page requires that an applet, plug-in or other application be present on the client system to interpret page content, **the page must provide a link to a plug-in or applet that complies with §1194.21**(a) through (l).
(m) When electronic forms are designed to be completed online, the form shall allow people using assistive technology to access the information, field elements, and functionality required for completion and submission of the form, including all directions and cues.
(n) A method shall be provided that permits users to skip repetitive navigation links.
(o) When a timed response is required, the user shall be alerted and given sufficient time to indicate more time is required.

The rules were derived from the Web Content Accessibility Guidelines 1.0 (WCAG 1.0) (May 5, 1999) published by the Web Accessibility Initiative of the World Wide Web Consortium (Jordan, 1998), which were created with:

> The primary goal ... to promote accessibility. However, following them will also make Web content more available to *all* users, whatever user agent they are using (as for example desktop browser, voice browser, mobile phone, automobile-based personal computer, and so on) or constraints they may be operating under (as for example noisy surroundings, under- or over-illuminated rooms, in a hands-free environment, and so on). Following these guidelines will also help people find information on the Web more quickly.[26]

These guidelines are defined by two primary themes of accessible design – *ensuring graceful transformation* and *making content understandable and navigable* – which inform 14 recommended guidelines (Lazar et al., 2003). These guidelines are identified by priority order at three levels: Priority 1 (**must** satisfy), Priority 2 (**should** satisfy) and Priority 3 (**may** satisfy). Each of the priorities has checkpoint items that can be used as checklist items to ensure appropriate accessibility criteria are met. Table 2.4 includes a list of all 14 guidelines and their respective priority 1 checkpoints.

Table 2.4   Priority 1 web accessibility guidelines

14 Web Accessibility Guidelines
1. Provide equivalent alternatives to auditory and visual content.
1.1 Provide a text equivalent for every non-text element.
1.2 Provide redundant text links for each active region of a server-side image map.
1.3 Provide an auditory description of the important information of the visual track of a multimedia presentation.
1.4 For any time-based multimedia presentation (e.g. a movie or animation), synchronize equivalent alternatives (e.g. captions or auditory descriptions of the visual track) with the presentation.
2. Don't rely on color alone.
2.1 Ensure that all information conveyed with color is also available without color, for example from context or markup.

| **Table 2.4** | Priority 1 web accessibility guidelines (*cont'd*) |

3.	Use markup and style sheets and do so properly.
4.	Clarify natural language usage.
	4.1 Clearly identify changes in the natural language of a document's text and any text equivalents (e.g. captions).
5.	Create tables that transform gracefully.
	5.1 For data tables, identify row and column headers.
	5.2 For data tables that have two or more logical levels of row or column headers, use markup to associate data cells and header cells.
6.	Ensure that pages featuring new technologies transform gracefully.
	6.1 Organize documents so they may be read without style sheets.
	6.2 Ensure that equivalents for dynamic content are updated when the dynamic content changes.
	6.3 Ensure that pages are usable when scripts, applets or other programmatic objects are turned off or not supported.
7.	Ensure user control of time-sensitive content changes.
	7.1 Until user agents allow users to control flickering, avoid causing the screen to flicker.
8.	Ensure direct accessibility of embedded user interfaces.
	8.1 Make programmatic elements such as scripts and applets directly accessible or compatible with assistive technologies.
9.	Design for device-independence.
	9.1 Provide client-side image maps instead of server-side image maps except where the regions cannot be defined with an available geometric shape.
10.	Use interim solutions.
11.	Use W3C technologies and guidelines.
	11.1 If, after best efforts, you cannot create an *accessible* page, provide a link to an alternative page that uses W3C technologies, is accessible, has *equivalent* information (or functionality) and is updated as often as the inaccessible (original) page.
12.	Provide context and orientation information.
	12.1 Title each frame to facilitate frame identification and navigation.
13.	Provide clear navigation mechanisms.
14.	Ensure that documents are clear and simple.
	14.1 Use the clearest and simplest language appropriate for a site's content.

Source: W3C.org.

Usability evaluation: building sites high in utility and ease of use

Jordan (1998) more precisely defined the usability factors of effectiveness, efficiency and satisfaction and Chow (2011) adapted it into a usability scale consisting of eight factors. *Effectiveness*, the extent to which a goal or task is reached, is comprised of two criteria: (1) task completion; and (2) quality of output. *Efficiency*, the amount of effort required to accomplish goals, is comprised of four criteria: (3) deviations from the critical path; (4) error rate; (5) time on task; and (6) mental workload. *Satisfaction*, the level of comfort a user feels in being able to accomplish goals, is comprised of both a (7) quantitative rating and (8) qualitative rating. These eight factors allows for explicit testing of the three core usability factors in terms of both quantitative and qualitative ratings, which allows for comparing ratings across iterations and helps provide the specificity required to continuously improve and refine a website (see Table 2.5).

There are two types of usability evaluations – empirical (with users) and non-empirical (without users) (Chow, 2011). Empirical usability methods include surveys, focus groups, natural observation, task analysis (try to complete high-priority tasks) and think-aloud protocols (verbalise thought processes during task analysis). Non-empirical (without users) methods include cognitive walkthroughs (mentally attempt to seek and find information as effectively and efficiently as possible), heuristic evaluation (rate the site based on established design standards) and log analysis (view site statistics for trends and user needs) (Chow, 2011). In the end, designing, developing and maintaining usable digital environments requires clear communication between users and information provider.

It is not possible to design an information space that everyone will experience the same way due to a wide variety of physical, mental and technological factors. How do you know if your digital environment is usable? Let us look at a combination of empirical (with users) and non-empirical ways to answer this question:

1. Create a feature checklist with the top five to seven primary information-seeking needs your users want from your digital environment. You do this by:

   (a) interviewing a few representative users (once a year);

   (b) conducting a focus group of representative users (once a year);

   (c) forming and talking to an advisory group of representative users (several times a year);

   (d) sending out an electronic survey to representative users (once a year).

Table 2.5   EES usability rating scale

Criteria	Rating	Comments
Effectiveness: extent to which a goal or task is reached		
1. **Task completion** Could you complete your tasks?		
2. **Quality of output** What was the quality of your output?		
Efficiency: amount of effort required		
3. **Deviations from critical path** (note: a low number of deviations means that user should have a high satisfaction score) Did you deviate from the critical path?		
4. **Error rate** (note: a low error rate means that a user should have a high satisfaction score) How many errors did you make?		
5. **Time on task** (note: low time on task means a user should have a high satisfaction score) How long did it take (okay, too long?)		
6. **Mental workload** (note: low mental workload means a user should have a high satisfaction score) How much mental effort did it take you?		
Satisfaction: level of comfort user feels in being able to attain goals.		
7. **Quantitative** Rate it on scale of 1–10		
Average your ratings		
8. **Qualitative** Why did you rate it as you did?		

2. Design your site's information architecture and interface design around the primary information needs of users as well as standard web design conventions. You do this by:

   (a) redesigning or creating a navigation scheme around the main information needs you have identified (validated empirically with representative users);

   (b) creating a quick links area on your home page with most used and accessed information;

   (c) designing your home page for maximum access to high-priority information as well as quick, at-a-glance information about what your digital environment contains;

(d) ensuring your page follows these standard conventions: logo is top left or centre of your page, navigation is on the top or left of your page, search feature is top right of your page and your footer contains your organisation's contact information (address, phone, email address);

(e) designing kids' pages accordingly;

(f) collecting and reviewing site statistics which will tell you overall site visits, which pages are being visited and what information is being accessed and/or downloaded;

(g) conducting a cognitive walkthrough ensuring the path to high-priority information is as efficient and effective as possible;

(h) conducting a heuristic evaluation ensuring your digital environment takes into account primary design conventions;

(i) having representative users review your interface design and navigation;

(j) having representative users test your design by attempting to locate high priority information.

3. Develop and/or add tested changes to a test digital environment (alpha or beta versions) and conduct quick usability testing:

(a) Nielsen's five user rule suggests that testing with only five representative users can find 85 per cent of a site's usability problems. Have your advisory group or a random sample of five representative users try and accomplish your identified high-priority information needs and then complete the EES usability scale.

(b) These tests can be conducted in person or by emailing your users the tasks you want them to complete and then asking them to complete an EES scale.

(c) Make recommended changes and then seek follow-up input to ensure the changes are satisfactory.

4. Read and react – have a permanent online feedback form for users to provide feedback and make changes accordingly.

5. Repeat this entire process every year.

Conducting usability evaluations and tests does not have to be either complex or expensive. Bottom-line usability is all about the relevancy and ease of access of the content for users. The best way to ensure this occurs is by collaborating with users throughout all phases of any design, development or redesign of your digital environments. Although time-consuming and labour-intensive, developing sites in the absence of user input is akin to walking around in the dark hoping to find the right path to success.

Designing highly usable future pathways: an art and a science

The designers of new office buildings and campuses will, at times, wait several months before putting in sidewalks so that the footsteps of users, slowly but surely creating a well worn pathway from building to building in the grass, have shown them the pathways they choose to tread. Usability evaluation and testing is the same concept. While aesthetic beauty makes a significant first impression, universally true across most products and services, it is the utility and substance beneath that serves as a strong foundation for a long-term, highly satisfying relationship. Strong relationships are also resilient and flexible, as change is a constant cacophony of compromise, exploration and refinement.

Usability evaluation and testing embraces the user, the information-seeker, as the central point for designing and experiencing digital environments. 'How do I know if my site is usable?' is a question that is subjective and ever changing. Representative users must inform the nuances of what is effective, efficient and satisfying for them. To attempt to project onto them what you feel they would like is removing them from the focal point of design, relegating them to a reactionary position to designs offered up through your own paradigm. The context will invariably be framed and articulated in nuances too complex, too sophisticated and too familiar for most novice users to understand and use easily.

In the end digital environments are for human use, and taking a human-centred design with an emphasis on pervasive usability with representative users at the central core of design will help ensure that the digital environment is high on utility and ease of use. Usability is first a state of mind and next a process for continuous improvement, which, collectively, will ultimately lead to highly usable environments for your users. Creating digital environments that are widely usable and popular by an ever diverse group of users is both an art of discovery and a science of implementation and continuous improvement.

Notes

1. User-Centered Design, Usability.gov, retrieved from *http://www.usability.gov/basics/ucd/index.html*.
2. *http://www.w3.org/WAI/redesign/ucd*
3. Notes on User Centered Design Process (UCD), W3C Web Accessibility Initiative, 2004, retrieved from *http://www.w3.org/WAI/redesign/ucd*.
4. International Organization for Standardization 9241-11: 'Ergonomic requirements for office work with visual display terminals (VDTs), Part 11: Guidance on usability'. Geneva, Switzerland, 1998.
5. See note 1.
6. Jakob Nielsen, 'Usability 101: Introduction to Usability', Useit.com, retrieved from *http://www.useit.com/alertbox/20030825.html*.
7. International Organization for Standardization 9241-11: 'Ergonomic requirements for office work with visual display terminals (VDTs), Part 11: Guidance on usability'. Geneva, Switzerland, 1998.
8. Jakob Nielsen, '25 years in usability', Useit.com, 21 April 2008, retrieved from *http://www.useit.com/alertbox/25-years-usability.html*.
9. See note 8.
10. Jakob Nielsen, 'Top 10 mistakes in web design', Useit.com, n.d., retrieved from *http://www.useit.com/alertbox/9605.html*.
11. See note 10.
12. 'Definition of pervasive usability', *Usability First Website*, retrieved from *http://www.usabilityfirst.com/glossary/pervasive-usability/*.
13. Jakob Nielsen, 'Ten usability heuristics', *Useit.com*, n.d., retrieved from *http://www.useit.com/papers/heuristic/heuristic_list.html*.
14. Jakob Nielsen, 'Is navigation useful?', *Jakob Nielsen's Alertbox*, 9 January 2000, retrieved from *http://www.useit.com/alertbox/20000109.html*.
15. Jakob Nielsen, 'Usability of websites for teenagers', *Jakob Nielsen's Alertbox*, 31 January 2005, retrieved from *http://www.useit.com/alertbox/teenagers.html*.
16. See note 14.
17. See note 14.
18. See note 14.
19. See note 13.
20. *http://www.useit.com/alertbox/children.html*
21. See note 15.
22. ADA Accessibility Guidelines for Buildings and Facilities, US Department of Justice, 1991. Appendix A to Part 36 – Standards for Accessible Design, retrieved from *http://www.ada.gov/reg3a.html#Anchor-42424*.
23. Disability Rights Section. A Guide to Disability, US Department of Justice, Civil Rights Division, Rights Laws, 2005, retrieved from *http://www.ada.gov/cguide.htm*.
24. Section 508 website, *Laws*, retrieved from *http://www.section508.gov/index.cfm?fuseAction=Laws*.
25. See note 14.
26. Web Content Accessibility Guidelines 1.0, W3C, 1999, retrieved from *http://www.w3.org/TR/1999/WAI-WEBCONTENT-19990505/wai-pageauth.html*.

References

Bates, M. (1989) 'The design of browsing and berrypicking techniques for the online search interface', *Online Review*, 13: 407–12.

Belkin, N., Oddy, R. and Brooks, H. (1982) 'ASK for information retrieval', *Journal of Documentation*, 38(2): 61–71.

Bilal, D. and Kirby, J. (2002) 'Differences and similarities in information seeking: children and adults as Web users', *Information Processing and Management*, 38: 649–70.

Blowers, H. and Bryan, R. (2004) *Weaving a Library Web: A Guide to Developing Children's Websites*. Chicago: ALA.

Chow, A. (2011) *School Librarians and Web Usability: Why Would I Want to Use That?* Association for Educational Communications and Technology Annual Conference Proceedings, 9–11 November.

Chow, A. and Bucknall, T. (2011) *Library Technology and User Services: Planning, Integration, and Usability Engineering*. Cambridge: Chandos.

Chow, A., Smith, K. and Sun, K. (2012) 'Youth as design partners: age-appropriate web sites for middle and high school students', *Journal of Educational Technology and Society*, in press.

Considine, D., Horton, J. and Moorman, G. (2009) 'Teaching and reading the millennial generation through media literacy', *Journal of Adolescent and Adult Literacy*, 52(6): 471–81.

Cooper, L. (2005) 'Developmentally appropriate digital environments for young children', *Library Trends*, 54(2): 286–302.

Derwin, B. (1992) 'From the mind's eye of the user: the sense-making qualitative-quantitative methodology', *Qualitative Research in Information Management*. Westport, CT: Libraries Unlimited, pp. 61–84.

Druin, A. (2002) 'The role of children in the design of new technology', *Behaviour and Information Technology*, 21(1): 1–25.

Druin, A., Bederson, B., Adrian, A.B., Miura, A., Callahan, D.K. and Plat, M. (1999) 'Children as our technology design partners', in. A. Druin (ed.), *The Design of Children's Technology*. San Francisco: Morgan Kaufmann, pp. 51–72.

Dubroy, M. (2010) 'Building virtual spaces for children in the digital branch', *Australian Library Journal*, 59(4): 211–23.

Garrett, J. (2011) *The Elements of User Experience: User-Centered Design for the Web and Beyond*, 2nd edn. Berkeley, CA: New Riders.

Jordan, P. (1998) *An Introduction to Usability*. Philadelphia: Taylor & Francis.

Kamper, R. (2002) 'Extending the usability of heuristics for design and evaluation: lead, follow, and get out of the way', *International Journal of Human–Computer Interaction*, 14(3&4): 447–62.

Large, A. and Beheshti, J. (2005) 'Interface design, web portals, and children', *Library Trends*, 54(2): 318–42.

Large, A., Beheshti, J. and Rahman, T. (2002) 'Design criteria for children's web portals: the users speak out', *Journal of the American Society for Information Science and Technology*, 53(2): 79–94.

Large, A., Beheshti, J., Nesset, V. and Bowler, L. (2006) *Web Portal Design Guidelines as Identified by Children Through the Processes of Design and Evaluation.* Paper presented at the American Society for Information Science and Technology Meeting, Silver Springs, MD.

Lazar, J., Bessiere, K., Ceaparu, I., Robinson, J. and Shneiderman, B. (2003) 'Help! I'm lost: user frustration in web navigation', *IT and Society*, 1(3): 18–26.

Molich, R. and Nielsen, J. (1990) 'Improving a human–computer dialogue', *Communications of the ACM*, 33(3): 338–48.

Moran, T.P. (1981) 'The command language grammar: a representation for the user interface of interactive computer systems', *International Journal of Man–Machine Studies*, 15(1): 3–50.

Morris, R.C. (1994) 'Toward a user centered information service', *Journal of the American Society for Infomation Science*, 45(1): 20–30.

Morville, P. and Rosenfield, L. (2008) *Information Architecture for the World Wide Web.* Cambridge, MA: O'Reilly Media.

Nielsen, J. and Loranger, H. (2006) *Prioritizing Web Usability.* Berkeley, CA: New Riders.

Pirolli, P. and Card, S. (1999) 'Information foraging', *Psychological Review*, 106(4): 643–75.

Poole, H. (1985) *Theories of the Middle Range.* Norwood, NJ: Ablex.

Read, J., Gregory, P., MacFarlane, S., McManus, B., Gray, P. and Patel, R. (2002) 'An investigation of participatory design with children – informant, balanced and facilitated design', in *Interaction Design and Children.* Eindhoven: Shaker Publishing.

Siegal, D. (1997) *Creating Killer Websites*, 2nd edn. Indianopolis, IN: Haydon Books.

Taylor, R. (1968) 'Question-negotiation and information-seeking in libraries', *College and Research Libraries*, 28: 178–94.

3

The history of *Enquire*: the story of UK public libraries on the Web

Joanne John and John Dolan

Abstract. Formalising the collaboration which public libraries have done for decades with ease has added value in today's budget-stretched times. Building on existing national service models *Enquire* (a public library collaborative virtual reference service) widens the knowledge and expertise available to the customer with no discernible dip in service. This approach is imperative for libraries' success in twenty-first-century information provision.

This chapter shows how *Enquire* enables and delivers the ability to have a national service and – within the same subscription – create additional local services. These additional (no cost) local services add value to the local authority and gain all the same statistics and functionality of the national service. Both national *Enquire* and the additional local services support each other and significantly increase the public library's visibility in an increasingly commercial information world.

The chapter looks at how the national *Enquire* service started and built up local participation, and shows how a suite of local services can be deployed for maximum benefit and be virtually cost neutral too.

Keywords: *Ask-A-Librarian*, *Enquire*, public libraries, reference

Introduction

In this chapter we will show how a mature, successful, highly regarded service – with a pedigree to match – matters to public libraries today. We hope this will also offer lessons for tomorrow. *Enquire*[1] is a collaborative, 24/7 virtual reference[2] service that provides answers in real time to anyone with an information query. *Enquire* is delivered by library staff at over 70 participating public libraries across England and Scotland,[3] and, after hours, by collaborative library partners in the USA. It is an accessible chat-based service that is staffed globally, managed nationally and delivered locally.

The mission of *Enquire* is to connect people with information through libraries at the user's point and time of need. By using live chat and email follow-up, *Enquire* provides library staff with the tools to engage with the public in the digital environment, 24/7. From its inception, librarians and library staff who have supported it have acted as examples to others of its value, both locally and to the library and information sector as a whole. Collaboration heightens the online visibility of libraries and allows users access to information not otherwise available from the local library. *Enquire* epitomises public library collaboration. Libraries participate to increase local value with minimum expenditure, meeting expectations to 'do more, with less, work[ing] collaboratively to provide better value for the public'.[4] It also fulfils the legal requirement for a 'comprehensive and efficient service' delivered to those who want it.[5] *Enquire* has demonstrated that there are three requirements for a quality service: national leadership for vision and motivation; collaborative management; and local political and managerial buy-in.

Enquire was initiated with modest seed funding from the Museums, Libraries and Archives Council (MLA).[6] This offset the early adopters' subscription and funded virtual reference training, the balance of the running costs being funded through subscription. This fully managed service is provided by the OCLC,[7] a non-profit organisation, at a cost that is largely unchanged since 2005. The OCLC provides both day-to-day management and QuestionPoint,[8] the software that underpins the service. The most important ingredients are the libraries that subscribe together with their staffs – both librarians and para-professionals – without whom the service would not exist:

> The reference desk, whether physical or virtual, is one of the most visible library services; and the interaction with librarians, as well as quality and delivery of information provided, can significantly impact a patron's overall perception of the library. (Maximiek et al., 2010)

Enquire answers an average of 88 enquiries per day (year to date January to May 2011) which has risen from 43 in 2007.

History

The success of past thinking

Enquire is a service based upon a strong collaborative heritage. *Enquire* is the next generation of *Ask-A-Librarian*, a webform service founded in 1997 by the former Electronic Access to Resources in Libraries Consortium (EARL)[9] and LASER,[10] whose main aim was to look at collaborative working among libraries. For the latter years of *Ask-A-Librarian*, the service was managed by Co-East[11] and supported via a small grant to Co-East by Resource. EARL's legacy cannot be underestimated since the *Ask-A-Librarian* service was truly pioneering as the timeline in Figure 3.1 illustrates.

Ask-A-Librarian launched in 1997 before the ubiquitous Google, which was not launched until 1998. This puts UK public libraries' collaborative working at the forefront of one of the most ground-breaking periods in the history of information at the beginning of the Internet age. *Ask-A-Librarian* was in fact one of the very first (if not *the* first) national online enquiry service delivered by public library staff that was open to anyone, providing unfettered access to information. *Enquire* is now the most extensive collaborative public library virtual reference service run on the same basis.

The mid-1990s saw the hesitant beginnings of UK local authority websites, many offering limited information. With the help of EARL, libraries were able to create more content, and in some instances even had the expertise to maintain their authorities' websites, as for example at Gateshead (Berube, 2011). While EARL's legacy should be recognised for starting the service, so should that of the Co-East regional library partnership in the East of England. *Ask-A-Librarian* was at a critical juncture, requiring a new home after EARL and needing a similarly strong leadership to take the service forward. This mantle was taken up by Co-East, which developed the national service within its regional partnership,

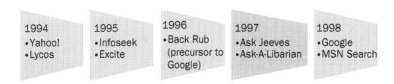

1994	1995	1996	1997	1998
•Yahoo! •Lycos	•Infoseek •Excite	•Back Rub (precursor to Google)	•Ask Jeeves •Ask-A-Libarian	•Google •MSN Search

Figure 3.1   *Ask-A-Librarian* timeline

trialling new technologies so as not to let the service falter. The success of *Ask-A-Librarian* also resulted in the Co-East management raising the profile of UK public library collaboration and virtual collaboration (largely unseen outside the United States) still further by speaking and conducting training across the UK and Europe: Italy, France and also at the British Council in Romania. This success also prompted interest from libraries in Wales, which, with funding from the Welsh National Assembly, invited Co-East to create the first-generation *AskCymru*[12] service, a cross sectoral, bi-lingual webform service, and also to conduct training on the new service's behalf. It was then the success of *Ask-A-Librarian*, *AskCymru* and *Enquire* which prompted Scotland to set up its own cross-sectoral service, *AskScotland*,[13] with initial funding from the Scottish Parliament.

The *Ask-A-Librarian* service was webform only up until 2003 when users were then expecting more instant information. MLA's tender in 2004 for a trio of services for the *People's Network*[14] (Read, Discover and *Enquire*) was timely as *Ask-A-Librarian* had already conducted a virtual reference pilot *Ask Live*.[15] With this experience and library base, Co-East, the service custodians, were uniquely positioned to bid with a technology partner. OCLC's QuestionPoint was selected as it offered the best breadth of functionality and, importantly, an integrated 24/7 Reference Cooperative[16] option and a competitive price. The MLA tender award was underpinned with £50,000 (of £500,000) in seed funding from the *People's Network*, used to offset subscriptions in year one while building the service. The OCLC provided the software and Co-East the management while MLA undertook the governance and promotion of the service. *Enquire* is still part of the *People's Network* suite of services and is open to anyone all day, every day. In 2007, when the Co-East regional partnership was dissolved, management transferred to the OCLC along with one member of staff (Joanne John) to ensure service continuity.

Enquire is now the longest-running full-time, open-to-all web service of its kind, preceding commercial versions, and all delivered by UK public libraries. This demonstrates the pivotal role that libraries have had and continue to play in information delivery, bibliographic search and learning across all ages. It has particular resonance with:

- disengaged and socially excluded communities who find visiting the library difficult, e.g. housebound users, commuters, young people;
- disabled people, notably people with hearing impairment;
- people for whom English is a second language;
- people in education – school children, students, adult learners, teachers, academics.

The OCLC has played a central role in *Enquire*'s evolution and invested in its future since taking over full custodianship in 2007. The OCLC is an organisation adept in cooperative services and information delivery across the world.

Enquire: how it works

Enquire is a browser-based product, requiring no download and minimal PC changes. *Enquire* has effectively been 'in the cloud'[17] before it was *de rigueur* to be there. Collaborative staffing in the emerging reconfiguration of local government is also an important and useful aspect of *Enquire*. Distributed staffing via a rota allows participating libraries to staff the service a minimum of half a day per month (morning or afternoon) on days that are locally achievable while offering local customers 24/7 × 365 access to information, thereby effectively sharing their reference desks. *Enquire*'s software allows complex analysis of transactions and virtual visits for national and regional output reports. The staffing schedule is frequently updated to account for local staffing issues. This schedule is available for participating staff to download on the *Enquire* staff website.[18]

Enquire: value for money

For modest financial input (less than £2,000 p.a. per library authority) subscribers get access to complex back-end functionality which not only permits staff to answer questions, but also allows local library staff and management to:

- report down to individual level on all transactions;
- refer questions within the participating membership, thus enabling the user to make just one contact rather than oftentimes be passed around different services;
- refer out to email contacts (still within the software) who will not have any interaction with the software other than an email, but the answer can be provided back to the librarian (again still within the software) to formulate an answer to the customer;
- obtain a full audit trail of the questions and answers;
- use the chat technology to train staff in different locations;

- report on user demographic information (postcode information, referring URL information);
- use full transcript searching, offering the means to find, via keyword searching, questions and chat transcripts they have answered.

Privacy is important – the software removes customer information (name, email) automatically after 90 days. The software also allows participating libraries to create multiple local services using Chat with page pushing (see Figure 3.2), Chat light using a Qwidget[19] (from a webpage or mobile device – see Figure 3.3) or via email, or even combine all three to provide an all-embracing local offering.

Monitoring chat

Library staff log in to the software on their given shift (there will always be two or more authorities on duty) and pick up questions when they appear in chat. During the session, web pages are pushed to the customer, who is able to see the full webpage in the chat screen. When a chat session comes to an end, it can be finalised in several ways:

- It can be set as answered, indicating no additional follow-up via email is required.

If additional follow-up is required there are three options:

- The chat session is coded as 'follow up by the librarian'. This indicates that within the chat session the customer and the library staff member have entered into an agreement that additional research will be sent to them via email (still within the software) at a later date.
- The chat session is coded as 'follow up by the customer's library'. This indicates that the librarian has advised that additional local research is required and that the customer's local library participates in *Enquire*. The session is then forwarded by the *Enquire* management team the next working day to the local library for them to follow up via e-mail (still within the software).
- If the customer's local library does not participate in *Enquire*, a link is sent to the customer with contact details.

How questions are passed around

Enquire's software has a complex referral mechanism, enabling questions to be transferred within the software to different participating library

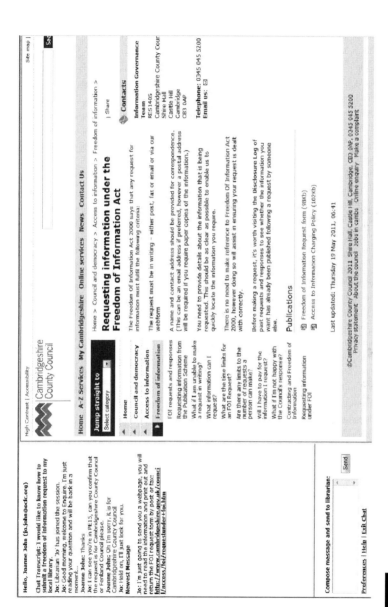

Figure 3.2 Example of full chat with page pushing

The webpage is pushed to the customer within the chat session and is retained to the right of the screen.

Figure 3.3 *Ask-A-Librarian* chat screenshot

Qwidget chat: chat happens within the webpage on which the Qwidget is embedded. Any URLs will not be displayed as full chat; the customer needs to click on them and they open in a new browser session.

authorities. Questions can also be emailed to contacts that may not be accessible to the customer, requiring the customer to make only one contact if they belong to a participating library. For example, a question could be referred from the software out to a planning officer/social worker who will receive a standard email and reply as normal. The answer comes back into the software for the response to be either forwarded as it is or edited as required and sent on to the customer. A full audit trail is always visible within the software, allowing other colleagues to follow these questions up.

For non-participating libraries, the *Enquire* staff in the chat session can offer a webpage with contact details. Even so, it is unfortunate that this two-tiered service exists.

Additional local services available when participating in *Enquire*

An additional benefit from the *Enquire* subscription is the ability to add a local layer to the service and gain all the same statistics and functionality of the national service. This includes full chat, Qwidget and an email form. These chat options can be set for local staffing only or can be set to roll up into the national and international service when local library staff are not available. This way, information-seekers, local and otherwise, always receive an initial human interaction even when their local library staff are not logged into the software. Examples of these local services are:

- full-time local chat services – for general local queries (Calderdale, Cornwall, Essex, Kent, Norfolk, Nottinghamshire, Nottingham City, Sefton, Wigan);
- daily homework helper – homework assistance after school (Essex, Bury, Solihull, Wigan);
- councillor clinics – for elected officials to participate online with the electorate (Bristol, North East Somerset, Nottingham City);
- local heads of service – chat for internal communication regarding cuts, changes to working practices and so on (Cornwall);
- book clinics – for customers to discuss books, genres general and specific: sci-fi and poetry for example (Solihull, Nottingham City, Nottinghamshire);
- chat with an author and publisher (Nottingham City, Sheffield);
- family history (Solihull);
- older people information discovery – in association with Social Services (Norfolk);
- Stay Safe online – aimed at children and parents (Rotherham);
- environmental issues chat for schools – (Somerset);
- Ask an HR Consultant – for customers who are unable to attend local library seminar sessions, the consultant will stay for chat sessions (City of London);
- Ask a Business Consultant – for customers who are unable to attend local library seminar sessions, the consultant will stay for chat sessions (City of London);
- redirectional – Cambridgeshire Library Services used chat when the central library was being redeveloped to direct users to collections and also to inform them about the new building.

In another highly innovative approach Cornwall libraries are delivering remote cross-county staff training to staff on their subscription databases. Here is a little about how the training using their *Enquire* subscription works.[20]

Training sessions take on average 12 minutes per session, and cover several of the libraries' online subscription databases. Costing training the 'chat way' is very efficient, as there are no travel, designing materials or handouts to be printed out, and at the end of the training session the staff have a transcript emailed to them with the whole training chat session, including links. Further analysis has revealed that using *Enquire*'s added value local services for one-to-one training (as well as for their standard local customer chat) each chat training session costs an average of £5, which compared to conventional training means that they save *more* than their *Enquire* subscription in training costs. This saving also allows for more people to be trained locally than their standard training budget would ordinarily allow. Another added benefit is that staff who were aware of chat but who had never used it previously are not just trained on the subscription databases, but experience and gain confidence in chat too – two for the price of one! The social advantages of being able to offer the local service option to customers and also the continued professional development of staff dispersed around the county by virtual means and the savings such provide (more than the national service subscription cost) bring the value of participation much clearer into focus.

While Cornwall currently use this training for online databases, there are already opportunities which can be seen outside the library. There is huge potential within the software and while the local services provided to date are exciting, many other full-time or ad hoc local services could be provided. These 'add on' services can significantly increase the local return on investment (ROI) and provide a great value proposition for engaging locally, still retaining all the benefits of national coverage when local staff are not online. For instance, through remote training, Cornwall has saved more than the annual *Enquire* subscription.

Answers around the clock from around the globe

The *Enquire* Invitation to Tender (ITT) specified that the service should be available 24/7 and QuestionPoint's 24/7 Reference Cooperative enables this. Library staffs from around the world are able to help with very local questions through the software's use of policy pages. Each participating library authority completes a policy page detailing service information along with links (catalogue URL, homepage URL, information about holds, fines, reservation charges, databases subscribed to). This allows responding staff to delve deep into library pages, or to access other authority information, as for example planning or social services. Policy pages provide an immense amount of useful local information for not only the 24/7 Reference Cooperative staff, but also UK staff handling another UK question.

The 24/7 Reference Cooperative staff pick up questions when UK libraries are not online (typically 16 hours daily), or see questions after a delay during *Enquire* staffing hours. This delay enables *Enquire* staff to see UK questions before they are offered to the global partnership. These same delays can be set for libraries offering local services, so when the software detects local staff are online, local questions are seen locally before they are visible to the national *Enquire* service staff. However, when UK or local library staffs are not monitoring chat there is no delay. Monitoring for the 24/7 Reference Cooperative does not mean that staff are inundated with requests from an audience they are not strictly charged with serving; *Enquire* questions take priority at all times. *Enquire* staff reciprocate for other libraries world wide to enable another library's customers to have a human interaction when their local library is closed. This experience cannot be underestimated, as illustrated by the feedback comments shown in Figure 3.4.

When are questions submitted?

Questions are submitted every hour of the day every day, including bank holidays, as shown in Figure 3.5. The 62/38 per cent split illustrates the importance of a 24/7 service to the users and also to the service, and

---

UK user, 9 p.m.: *This is a great service, particularly for us students, who have panics late at night when other services are closed.*

UK user, 10 p.m.: *A lady called Allison helped me here in the UK, and she was over in Wisconsin – amazing! I appreciated the human touch which this chat type of communication permits.*

Irish user, 1.30 a.m.: *I chatted with librarian staff in America who sent me in Dublin Ireland information for a Bradford Yorkshire library in England. Great stuff, nations speaking to and helping other nationalities.*

Figure 3.4   Examples of feedback from after-hours UK customers

Figure 3.5 The times questions are submitted to *Enquire*

further highlights how important *Enquire*'s participation is in the 24/7 Reference Cooperative. With a projected 32,000 questions for January to December 2011, the evidence suggests that 12,000 questions would not get a human response, while a percentage of these users would never be able to submit their question at all.

Service management

One of the important factors for service stability is the continuity of the service management. To date, *Enquire* has continuity of personnel from the EARL days, through Co-East days to the current service management by OCLC personnel. Such continuity provides confidence, trust and an effective advocate for the service, all of which has been of value to both customers and library staff. *Enquire's* service management:

- provide monthly statistics for use locally;
- work to promote the service in as many media as possible;
- report progress via annual reviews to participating authorities and through the Society of Chief Librarians (SCL) who receive a service review and summary;
- monitor the day-to-day staffing requirements and refer out email questions to shift libraries that have been handled by the out-of-hours team the previous evening either to be handled as a general question offline or referred to specific libraries as they require specialist local knowledge;
- provide an ongoing training programme:
  - webinar sessions;
  - slides and notes added to the staff website where webinar technology is not able to be accessed locally;
  - one-to-one telephone training.

Enquire's service management also undertakes periodic surveys of both customers and participating staff to build a service around user needs. Tailored *Enquire* training also benefits local general training objectives. These sessions reinforce on a regular basis what staff have learned and build their confidence to take on new technologies. Used effectively, training around both online and offline activities achieves better service delivery both online and in the library, with staff increasingly confident about information discovery and online working.

Evaluation of customer service, quality and promoting libraries through collaboration

One participating library authority surveyed users to ask which subscription services they valued the most. The staff (as would most) anticipated that the top databases would be those used most frequently. Instead, significantly, the product most valued by the public was *Enquire*.[21]

User testimony is essential. This feedback comes from within the transcripts and also from an exit survey which is sent when a chat session ends. A range of comments on the service is shown in Figure 3.6.

For libraries to be more visible to more people in this digital age the benefits of collaboration are there to see. *Enquire* is now a mature service and the new UK Libraries National Catalogue,[22] a new discovery site for customers to access resources, will further enhance the collaborative library experience.

Staff evaluation and service reporting

The significance of continuous evaluation cannot be underestimated. The quality and customer service reputation that goes hand in hand with libraries should not be any less in the virtual environment than it is in the physical one.

In digital reference, as well as on-site reference, poor skills will out, and in the case of virtual reference they will be quite painfully laid bare for managers, colleagues and users to see (perpetually in the case of transcripts) (Berube, 2004).

For *Enquire*, this evaluation is performed by the Quality Panel. The Panel undertakes two reviews in each subscription year. These transcripts are graded and reported back at an annual service advisory meeting and the *Enquire* Annual General Meeting. As well as reviews by the Panel, *Enquire* encourages staff to submit questions for review and the *Enquire*

'Filling out forms is not one of my usual activities. However, on this occasion I am more than willing to make an exception. This is a truly amazing service. I was looking for some business data in preparation for an interview and thought that the local Cornwall library service might be useful. I then found your resource through an Internet search. I was slightly sceptical as to how long it would take for a real person to respond and nearly missed the chat conversation. I am very glad that I was patient. I have used the Internet for business and at home for over 15 years and cannot recall finding anything that was so useful before. I sincerely hope that this service can continue despite the tough economic conditions and imminent cutbacks.'

'I think this is a great service and should be publicised more. I am thrilled about it and how it quickly dealt with my enquiries within minutes ... I ended up tweeting about it instantly because I think it is very useful. I should have had to wait until 10 a.m. to find the same answers I have here at 1 a.m. Bravo.'

'The librarian was very helpful and struck a pleasant and chatty tone – just right when my eight-year old was chatting with her (via me as the typist).'

'As someone who is unable to get about aged 73, I found this service more helpful than [other genealogy sources] who seem not to have what I want except for lots of money that I don't have.'

Accessibility comments, e.g. 'out of hours', from home, limited IT experience:

'I did not expect to receive such a speedy and efficient answer, particularly on a Friday night.'

'Was impressed that a librarian in Texas answered questions about my local library.'

'I have only just started a computer course and was a bit nervous about using such a service. The staff concerned were brilliant, the answer was almost immediate and it has really boosted my confidence in using such services again.'

Figure 3.6   **Feedback from the exit survey at the end of a chat session**

management also see all customer survey comments. These questions are reviewed (good or bad), added to the Panel shortlist and further reviewed to enable a top five to be compiled. After a final review the 'Best Transcript of the Year' is decided. A prize is awarded at the *Enquire* Advisory Meeting, along with the Panel's report and assessment of the top five 'excellent' transcripts. This allows best practice and exceptional customer service to be disseminated to all subscribing libraries.

While *Enquire* management has no line management responsibility for participating staff, the library authority manager is advised if evaluation and review highlights where a staff member may benefit from specific additional training. This is rare, happening (to date) only three times in six years. Mostly, evaluation highlights where additional service training can be used to tighten up quality and customer service skills. A staff evaluation is also conducted in a biennial staff survey[23] that gathers feedback on the service, including the reasons for subscription and how the service is managed, as well as suggested improvements and enhancements. *Enquire* also provides an annual service report[24] distributed to all stakeholders to demonstrate best practice and how subscribing members are using the software to the full.

One example of feedback from the 2010 survey is as follows:

> Great to be part of a prestigious library initiative – more and more people are discovering the service and benefiting from it ... emphasis on quality is exemplary ... I am staggered by the expertise within the network and that I can tap into it. (Jane Rose, Kirklees)

The last survey conducted in 2010 identified specific areas where staff would like additional training modules to be delivered in 2011. The survey also showed that within the participatory network, *Enquire* is well appreciated. The following comment sums up the rest:

> It is quite humbling to be a small part of this service, but also proves that it is valued amongst the sector and offers a diverse range of benefits, including:
>
> – Value for money
>
> – National collaborative service
>
> – Local service option for *no extra cost*
>
> – Community engagement
>
> – Additional access point for live reference – choice of access point for customers
>
> – Training and skills enhancement
>
> – Higher libraries visibility
>
> – Efficient

Evaluation in a national service is used to maintain quality. This evaluation also informs service quality at the local level to support the wider reference provision (Kern, 2006).

Libraries participate in a collaborative service in order to increase local value with minimum expenditure. In the case of collaborative catalogues, libraries must first expand the technology and then promote and use the technology to its fullest in order to maximise the value of the collaboration. Likewise with *Enquire* collaboration and technology, libraries must first make a financial investment in the technology and staff time, and then promote and use the technology to its fullest in order to see ROI.

Promoting libraries outside normal areas: Yahoo!Answers UK & Ireland

To expand the reach of libraries' participation in information discovery online, *Enquire* participates in the *Yahoo!Answers* community. *Enquire* is a Knowledge Partner[25] in *Yahoo!Answers* UK & Ireland within the categories of Education and Reference and Arts and Humanities. This partnership extends the reach of public libraries outside the usual channels and allows the dissemination of expertise to a wider community, thus highlighting the value of libraries. This participation in a social answers commercial site enables *Enquire* to help people who may never use a public library and perhaps encourage them to do so, showing that public libraries have relevance anywhere. In their December 2010 blog *Yahoo!UK* said this about *Enquire*:

> Enquire are an umbrella organisation for librarians and are one of UK & Ireland Answers' most committed and diligent Knowledge Partners.[26]

What is happening elsewhere in the world

There are many examples of collaborative services and of state-wide services providing information for local library users, but there are few examples of large, open-to-all virtual reference services that are comparable to *Enquire*. Examples of other current European collaborative services are:

- *Ubib.fr* – a collaborating group of French academic institutions (see Figure 3.7). French public library group *bibliosesame* uses QuestionPoint's chat Qwidget for access via chat, as well as providing access via email.

- *Pregunte* – a collaborative chat and webform service supported by the Ministry of Culture in Spain (see Figure 3.8).

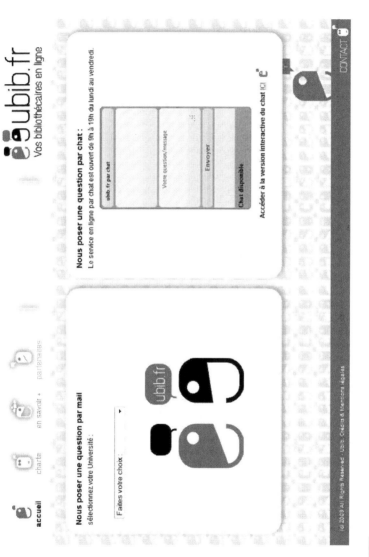

Figure 3.7 Collaborative service – France

Figure 3.8 Collaborative service – Spain

- *QandANJ*[27] – the world-renowned New Jersey state-wide service received over a thousand questions per month and commissioned two high-profile adverts to be shown on MTV. QandANJ is an example of a highly successful service under threat. It has just won a reprieve to continue while a review takes place.[28]

The future

While there is much regard for a national service there must be local ownership. The low subscription cost of *Enquire* makes the service a viable option for almost all library authorities and enables additional local services to be developed, further increasing the value of the local services themselves. *Enquire* has a Twitter page where examples of questions and survey feedback are posted and questions received through the mobile Qwidget. *Enquire* also has a Facebook page, with an embedded Qwidget, which allows users to ask questions without leaving the social networking site. All of this activity in social media allows the message of public libraries to escape the echo chamber (Potter and Woods, 2011)[29] and project the message that library services can help effectively far beyond the physical confines of the sector.

Enquire will form the 'Ask' module in the new public libraries National Catalogue[30] developed by the OCLC in conjunction with The Combined Regions[31] (TCR) which will be a user discovery platform for libraries. This National Catalogue is in its early stages, although there is evidence which shows that libraries understand the need to work together to maximise efficiencies and in this instance are also able to utilise *Enquire* as the embedded chat option.

Enquire is staffed globally, managed nationally and delivered locally; it is open to anyone (by statute as a UK public library service) which is unique in virtual reference services worldwide. It is a successful example of collaboration, efficiency and modernisation with maximum reach, providing universal access to a reliable, independent and accountable learning and information service.

Notes

1.   Anyone can access the service through participating libraries' websites or the national portal at: *http://www.askalibrarian.org.uk*.

2. Virtual Reference – an umbrella term that encompasses chat and e-mail reference as well as emerging reference communication technologies such as voice-over-IP and online videoconferencing. Virtual Reference focuses on the interaction between patron and librarian (operator) whereas *Digital Reference* is a broader term that includes online resources as well as virtual communications. M.K. Kern (2006), 'Looking at the bigger picture: an integrated approach to evaluation on chat reference services', *Reference Librarian*, 46(95/96): 99–112.

3. A list of *Enquire* partners can be found at: *http://enquire-uk.oclc.org/content/view/56/95/*.

4. *http://www.communities.gov.uk/news/corporate/1616208*

5. The 1964 Public Libraries and Museums Act – see *http://www.legislation.gov.uk/ukpga/1964/75*.

6. Museums Libraries and Archives Council (MLA) at: *http://www.mla.gov.uk/about/who*.

7. Founded in 1967, the OCLC is a non-profit, membership, computer library service and research organisation dedicated to the public purposes of furthering access to the world's information and reducing information costs. More than 72,000 libraries in 170 countries and territories around the world have used OCLC services for cataloguing, reference, resource sharing, eContent, preservation, library management and web services. The OCLC and its worldwide member libraries cooperatively produce and maintain WorldCat, making it the world's largest and richest database of bibliographic information. The OCLC publishes the Dewey Decimal Classification system, the most widely used library classification system in the world. The OCLC is headquartered in Dublin, Ohio, USA and has over 1,200 employees worldwide. For more information visit *http://www.oclc.org/*.

8. QuestionPoint is the software used to provide the *Enquire* service: *http://www.questionpoint.org*.

9. *http://www.ariadne.ac.uk/issue5/interface/*: 'Project EARL was established in 1995 with funding from the British Library, the Library Association and participating libraries, with the objective of developing "the role of public libraries in a networked environment, within a collaborative framework".'

10. *http://www.bl.uk/aboutus/acrossuk/workpub/laser/artwork.pdf*

11. *http://www.co-east.net/*

12. *http://library.wales.org/askcymru/en/*

13. *http://askscotland.org.uk/*

14. *http://www.peoplesnetwork.gov.uk*

15. Co-East's virtual reference trial 'Ask Live' 2003, at: *http://www.lirg.org.uk/lir/pdf/article86e.pdf*.

16. *http://wiki.questionpoint.org/w/page/13839418/24-7-Coop-FAQs*.

17. *http://www.infoworld.com*: 'Cloud computing encompasses any subscription-based or pay-per-use service that, in real time over the Internet, extends IT's existing capabilities.'

18. The *Enquire* service staff information website at: *http://enquire-uk.oclc.org*.

19. A widget – or in this instance a Qwidget as it is a widget created using QuestionPoint – is an application that can be embedded into a webpage to allow easy aggregated access to information via chat.

20. A summary of an email written by the author referencing the remote training Cornwall is providing using the *Enquire* local services option.
21. Taken from the *Enquire* biennial survey where members are surveyed on software/management/service.
22. Public Libraries National Catalogue at: *http://www.oclc.org/uk/en/news/ releases/2011/201118.htm*.
23. 2010 biennial staff survey report at: *http://enquire-uk.oclc.org/content/ view/40/74/*.
24. Enquire 2009–2010 Service Report at: *http://enquire-uk.oclc.org/component/ option,com_docman/task,cat_view/gid,47/Itemid,50/*.
25. Yahoo!Answers UK & Ireland Knowledge Partner Programme at: *http:// help.yahoo.com/l/uk/yahoo/answers/partners/partner-01.html;_ ylt=AhVpMzS7b3.Sn0Sv_g_QqcIfDyV4*.
26. *http://www.voicesforthelibrary.org.uk/wordpress/?p=1741*
27. QandANJ.org service ended on 31 December 2011.
28. *http://www.libraryjournal.com/lj/home/890472-264/nj_online_reference_ service_gets.html.csp*.
29. Escaping the Echo Chamber at: *http://www.netvibes.com/nedpotter#The_ Echo_Chamber*.
30. Public Libraries National Catalogue at: *http://www.oclc.org/uk/en/news/ releases/2011/201118.htm*.
31. *http://www.combinedregions.com/*

References

Berube, L. (2004) 'Collaborative digital reference: an Ask a Librarian (UK) overview', *Program: Electronic Library & Information Systems*, 38(1): 29–41.

Berube, L. (2011) *Do You Web 2.0? Public Libraries and Social Networking: Social Networking and Library Services*. Cambridge: Woodhead Publishing.

Kern, M.K. (2006) 'Looking at the bigger picture: an integrated approach to evaluation on chat reference services', *Reference Librarian*, 46(95/96): 99–112.

Maximiek, S., Rushton, E. and Brown, E. (2010) 'Coding into the great unknown: analyzing instant messaging session transcripts to identify user behaviors and measure quality of service', *College and Research Libraries*, 71(4): 361.

Potter, N. and Woods, L. (2011) *Escaping the Echo-Chamber*. Presentation, online at: *http://www.netvibes.com/nedpotter#The_Echo_Chamber*.

4

Children of the cloud

David Vogt

Abstract. How the human brain processes and manages information is a captivating topic within the realm of 'people in the digital age', information science and librarianship. One of the most interesting dimensions of this is how we filter information and either instantly or more gradually forget it, when it is deemed unimportant, mostly because we can't remember and/or usefully apply everything we've experienced. This is our neural 'librarianship', and different people develop vastly different methods and abilities in this regard.

This chapter considers the analogy between the brain and computing science. In the digital age we are about to have an infinitely greater cloud memory at our immediate disposal. Essentially, anything we see or touch digitally – which will be just about everything in our lives from birth forward – will be part of an immensely greater self-referential system, opening to currently unimaginable benefits and opportunities for personal and social growth, all based on individually scaled, primarily unconscious librarianship.

Keywords: apps, brain, Cloud, digital society

The Web's just not that into you ...

At least not yet and not in terms of a committed one-to-one relationship based on trust and fulfilment. This paper dwells on a probable elaboration of the Social Web (which garners indirect benefits for individuals) into a truly Personal Web (concerted individual benefits) and attendant opportunities in public information management. The perspective aligns with the author's career as a scientist, innovator and entrepreneur focused on the cultural dimensions of emerging media.

Wunderkind

It may be difficult to imagine that our digital prodigy, the Internet, is still in its childhood. And that we, with our own experience and promise so deeply coupled to its upbringing, are really siblings, not parents, for humanity is growing apace. As brashly and precociously as any 'digital native' might behave, we are all as unworldly as the Web is unfinished. With no parents, precedents or reliable gurus (including this author), the Web is being reared by unheralded emergence rather than inspired expertise, qualified scholarship or formal research. For entrepreneurs it is a great place and time to be courageous, because no person or entity owns opportunity unequally. And like a gold rush on an endless landscape, this might always be the case.

Yet even the bold can easily feel insecure online. The hyped perils include pirates, thieves, hackers and virus-coders – a faceless, placeless rogues' gallery curiously akin to children's bogeymen. While real and aggressive, however, such dangers are almost certainly manageable. In the real world we protect our children from equivalent threats until they can independently deal with them and confidently go forth in life as adults. Our safeguards (education, street-proofing, social order and so on) rarely eliminate any hazard completely; they merely allow us not to be paralysed by the knowledge of their existence.

Virtual agoraphobia is also unnecessary. Corresponding online safeguards should enable us to assume our full potential in digital society. The Web is growing quickly and there will always be lots of room for innovative safety measures. Yet as important as these are, that is not what this paper is about. Rather, given that we will eventually achieve a mature sense of safety, security, privacy and autonomy, can we imagine what our 'full potential' could be like? This question is particularly exciting because, unlike the real world, the digital world affords us the opportunity to be systematically self-minded and socially engaged. A unique, rich and unfathomed universe of proactive possibility is opening for us.

What could such 'augmented individuality' look like? The Web is a vast experiment in open innovation where we are literally watching ourselves, in real time, learn how to be globally networked citizens. And while this journey is highly unpredictable and its destination unknowable, there are some compelling clues about some next steps within shared eons of natural selection and social development.

Brain apps

Borrowing from Sir Arthur C. Clarke's contention that 'any sufficiently advanced technology is indistinguishable from magic',[1] the software architecture of the human brain is pure magic. We do not fully appreciate this magic because we literally live in it, or are it. Either way, after centuries of scientific investigation we are still trying to decipher all the things the brain can do, leaving alone how it does it.

Pursuing this comparison with computing science, we now know that over the ages natural selection has coded a large number of magically sophisticated neural tools to help us analyse and interpret incoming sensory data in advantageous ways.[2] We do not usually think of the brain as a toolkit because the separate tools all interoperate so seamlessly that we are never aware of them individually. For example, our brains have a permanent, hardwired visual 'app' for recognising and differentiating between human faces. The DNA-driven 'downloading' of this app into the *fusiform gyrus* portion of the temporal lobe delivers obvious social advantages. People born without it, or who lose it through disease or injury, have a condition called *prosopagnosia*, where they might not even be able to identify themselves in a mirror or photograph, let alone close friends, family and myriad acquaintances, even while they can recognise all manner of other objects easily. We have complementary specialised apps for recognising people using our ears, noses and so forth, so when the visual app malfunctions we normally have sufficient redundancy to operate reasonably well in society.

As a further example, the brain has another app (likely a suite of them) that enables us to synthesise everything we know, observe and think about the individuals we care about into dynamic 'models' that facilitate all of our interactions with them, including predicting what they are likely to do in various situations. The social imperative behind these apps is pretty clear as well. The resonances of each of these models with the special model we maintain that is 'myself' likely determines and evolves the concepts we have for 'know', 'like', 'love' and so on in the continuum of our relationships. It is an infinitely more powerful 'friending' system than offered by Facebook. Our model library and other mental apps also give us instant 'like' or 'dislike' feedback on complete strangers, simply through unconscious comparison with the attributes of people we know.

We have no idea how large our cerebral app store is; it could easily be bigger than Apple's. This analogy is far too facile, however, because it is difficult to imagine that any of the brain's apps are stand-alone: they cooperate in fusion and in parallel with a beautiful complexity we could not begin to design now. And even with so much complexity, when one or many apps fail, the system does not crash; it is incomprehensibly good at recovering and regenerating itself. Every person is born with a slightly different set of apps, and this, along with the way we learn to use them, modify them and create other idiosyncratic ones during our lives, probably has a lot to do with incessantly redefining 'myself'.

But if nature can code self-propelling apps, cannot the brain now do the same for itself, bootstrapping its own evolutionary future? What might 'myself' eventually be when enhanced by any number of additional, artificial and exclusively self-focused apps that analyse and interpret available digital information sources in personally advantageous ways? One glib example (warning – deliberately creepy!) could be the application of emerging social media analytic tools to provide each of us with nuanced personal dashboards deducing the emotional status of our family, social and professional spheres. Objectively, is this any creepier than another of our existing, highly advanced brain apps that help us reliably to determine any person's changing emotions by watching for the slightest variations in their facial expression? Another example application of such analytics could be to provide independent feedback on the success (or otherwise) of our ongoing digital activities, essentially conjuring up silent mentors to guide our behaviour. Once again, brain apps already do this very locally in the real world, and our addiction to social media suggests we care about such things online using more brute force tools. How might our natural domain and capacity therefore be expanded onto the Web through such apps? A very few 'smart' phone apps are already trending this way, toward what people might once have termed an extra-sensory perception (ESP). To really get there, if they are modelled on how we believe existing cerebral apps work, they will require our continuing active participation to generate 'strange loop'[3] phenomena – to be genuinely self-reinforcing through self-reference. There are no good examples yet, but there likely will be within a few years.

The central question to register before we go on is that given the creation of such brave new apps is beyond the capacity of any individual either to design or manage, what organ(s) of society can and should step in to do so? An obvious consideration is that while the commercial and government sectors will want to be involved, most individuals may not be comfortable with such intimately personal appendages to be in these hands. So what trustworthy social/community agencies might be able to mediate the healthy tension between 'personal good' and 'sustainability' (if this latter term can conceivably cover social, public, economic and environmental 'goods')?

Ignorance is bliss

Being an astronomer when the first large detector arrays were being developed, this author had early professional experience with digital overload – the requirement for identifying meaningful teaspoons of information within oceans of incoming data. It turns out that our brains do this brilliantly. We devote much of our early life to consuming the world through our senses, learning to process what we ultimately determine to be the 'sense' of it in terms of sounds, tastes and objects that become reliable signals within the colossal noise of consciousness. As remarkable as this capacity might be, we usually overlook the fact that the most remarkable part of it is indeed the ability to overlook. Walking down the street we are actively aware of less than 1 per cent of the visual information we receive, only because the rest has been studiously ignored by subconscious mental processes. Ignorance? We have an app for that. Phenomena earn our attention only when our cognitive software labels them as 'important' because they might be hazardous or resonant with things we care about.

Ignorance is also a highly personalised talent. We cannot ignore something unless at some other time we have made some sense of it, remembered it, and then automatically determined to disregard it at our discretion when we encounter it again. The world is infinitely subtle, so one person can walk by a tree without giving it apparent notice while another person can invest a lifetime gathering further sense and meaning from it. The unique yet changing business rules governing our individual ignorance patterns are a further means by which we continuously regenerate identity and self.

Once again the Web's software in this area is barely in its infancy compared with our brains. We live in a global knowledge economy but the translation of raw information into useful knowledge is distressingly inefficient, and perhaps increasingly so. Essentially every digital age person will tell you they are overwhelmed. The central problem is almost certainly that we are not very good yet at ignoring low-grade information, obliging us to spend far too much of our valuable time paying attention to things that matter little and shovelling mountains of dross to find a few nuggets. No automatic filtering system for digital information can get much better without learning, as our brains have, to apply those individual business rules surrounding ignorance.

The flip side of this challenge is also an unprecedented opportunity, going far beyond the brain's capacity. For example, the Web allows us, figuratively, to walk down every street in the world at once, certainly to discover items of enormous personal interest that we would never encounter in all of our analogue excursions. And by comparing our business rules with those of other very smart people with similar interests, the Web could also act as a wise agent by introducing us to things we ought to care about, even if we have zero awareness of them now.

Search engines are already incredibly fast, and they are getting better. It is more a societal than technical problem that prevents them from generating such extraordinary personal benefits for us. Quite simply, we do not want giant Web companies owning, exploiting and manipulating our personal 'software' more than they already do. They make money now essentially by scraping our behaviour and networks to partially reverse-engineer our software, thereby activating self-referential marketing. They are already putting blinders on our view of the Web based on their concept of personalisation, which involves a dangerous blend of what they think we want to see and what they would like us to see. The prospective benefits and dangers of engaging our full, active interest in this filtering process are orders of magnitude greater than at present. Clearly, these will need to be negotiated within a relationship we can trust. So the same question arises – what organ of society could best step forward to help us realise this potential in a conscientious way?

A cloud of forgotten dreams

Related to how we undervalue the contribution of studied ignorance to good attention, we often fail to appreciate the contribution of strategic memory loss to effective memory. Forgetting stuff is essential for humans. The issue of which stuff, and when, and why, is something we seldom try to manage. And despite the fact that we regularly chastise ourselves when our automatic management system seems to get it wrong, the brain apparently does a great job here as well.

Memory is central to the processes that generate both identity and consciousness. The brain is a deeply self-referential system, a highly tuned inference engine that propels an instantaneous sense of purpose by selectively filtering and learning from the fire hose of incoming sensory data. The brain's methodology seems Bayesian, hosting nested probabilistic models endlessly enhanced by new data. This exceptional capacity for redefinition derived from anticipation is one of humanity's hallmark strengths. It may be that consciousness itself arose as a point of presence on this continuous strange loop of self-reinvention. All of this is made possible by a prodigious biological library and gifted neural librarianship. For example, only by instantaneous, behind-the-scenes reference to vast, well-maintained 'reserve' and 'special' collections are we able to ignore everything that is not pertinent to our focus on the 'current selections' of our existence. Different individuals seem to have a very broad range of inherited and developed abilities in this area – our understanding of the full potential of our internal librarians remains modest.

Meanwhile, forgetting is not essential for computers. In the digital age just about everything in our lives, prenatal to posthumous, is becoming part of an immense 'cloud' memory with quite different characteristics, potentials and pitfalls from our brains. For example, our neural librarians are historians rather than archivists. We remember very few things precisely; everything else becomes somewhat fuzzy as it is 'classified' across multiple personal contexts and woven in a narrative fabric amenable to self-reflection. In contrast, the cloud is a museum that preserves explicit artefacts that seem jarringly real to us years later without the smoothing effect of contextual harmonisation. This is just one reason why the long tail of our digital past can be embarrassing to us.

The expected shelf-life of almost all knowledge and information is waning. Yet the value never disappears completely, it simply decays on a freshness curve with an ever shorter half-life. Therefore the best way to manage an online reputation is not to spend time erasing stale, negative artefacts, but to continuously obscure them by replenishing the pipeline with fresh, positive material. The grand opportunity here is for individuals to develop ways to mine the dispersed, decaying, yet collectively valuable personal wealth available in cloud memory. Our first problem is the lack of an able, self-interested librarian: we are lucky that our subconscious neural librarians are so fastidious because in contrast our conscious selves are too chronically undisciplined to accomplish this task well. The only existing society entities that are diligently building digital libraries about each of us are doing so for administrative reasons (education, health, financial records, etc.) and marketing purposes (Google,[4] Amazon[5]). Each is differentially blind to the entirety of 'us' because they handle separate limbs of our digital elephant.

Once the question of the ownership of these separate libraries is decided (currently a matter of active yet uncoordinated debate), most likely in favour of the individual, the challenge of building effective tools for digital self-librarianship can begin. Whereas it might be easy for any of us to dismiss the prospective value of having our lifelong Web existence in hand, less than a generation ago most of us would have dismissed the value of having a mobile phone in hand. Analogous to the fortune at the bottom of the pyramid,[6] the personal and social value to our most current priorities, via self-referential networking, that could be generated by these seemingly forgotten relics of our existence is probably immense. Even more so now that social networks are providing a form of public contextualisation to the encoding of our Web activities that seems strikingly similar to the 'historian' proficiency of the brain.

You are what you stream

Previous sections have introduced aspects of cognition and memory, but what about me, the active person? Where is the selfish Web? One way to describe an individual is as a set of vectors representing their distinctive interests, knowledge and experience. For example, suppose I am an Asian female podiatrist living in Auckland who plays the violin, is a gourmet cook and loves sailing. Each distinguishing characteristic, area of expertise and special interest is a vibrant component of the mental model I cultivate about 'myself'. Several of these dynamic vectors probably make me unique as a person, but their dynamic sum qualifies me as an unprecedentedly original human being. This originality is easily as rich and valuable to humanity's societal diversity as my DNA is to our biological diversity. And it is typically the serendipitous entanglement of my vectors – such as how some experience while sailing might inspire a new method in podiatry – that can realise my potential value in the most extraordinary way.

Unfortunately, until now I have also been a human bottleneck: the only calculator for the summation and interaction of my interest vectors walks around with me in my head. The Internet will change that as it becomes personal. Right now the Web can only amplify our vectors separately because the dominant paradigm is social. For example, it is easy for me to find a website that enables me to socialise my interest in podiatry, and another for the violin, but as large as the world is I am unlikely to find a site dedicated to violin-playing podiatrists. And there is no way I could reasonably begin to look for another female podiatrist, anywhere in the world, who also loves the violin, cooking and sailing. While this particular search might seem eccentric, the general problem is already acute in an increasingly specialised world: if you need to hire a German-speaking structural engineer with practical experience in jungle environments and sustainable aluminium fabrication, how can you effectively find such a person?

More selfishly, how can every individual aggregate, amplify, cross-fertilise and promote in advantageous ways (exactly as their brain does) all of the separate and collective digital elements of their existence? This is becoming increasingly important as the explosion of Web media technologies continues to fragment the methods and places whereby we express our identity. Like television, there were once only a few channels for self-expression; now there are thousands. The problem is not necessarily psychological (we have a great natural facility to inhabit multiple personas), it is about efficiencies, economies of scale and managing to potential. It is about not burning out.

The active currency of digital age economies involves personal influence, presence, reputation, knowledge, expertise and networks. Facebook[7] is a good example of a tool that bridges personal-social streams. The author has championed an application called Gleanr[8] that similarly enables digital age professionals to leverage their clickstreams and connectedness across multiple channels of expertise and interest. There will be many more tools, operating external to the brain, designed to extend an individual's presence into the digital realm and to help define and maintain a coherent manifestation of identity across our internal, real and digital worlds.

Childhood's End

At the dawn of the digital age people first imagined the Internet as a place; now it seems more like a continuous event – an 'ether' permeating existence, a space that is outer and inner simultaneously. When Arthur C. Clarke penned *Childhood's End*[9] in 1953 the metaphor was humanity leaving Earth's cradle to find adulthood among the stars. Perhaps the stars are truly a 'final frontier' because we have become occupied beforehand with the exploration and civilisation of digital space (something perhaps inadvertently anticipated by Clarke with the presence of HAL in *2001: A Space Odyssey*).[10] As our relationship with the Web personalises it may earn traits of friend, mentor, colleague, partner and alter ego – a disembodied extension of being.

Human culture is a self-referential narrative, a strange loop, essential stories we tell about ourselves to reinvent ourselves. The mythology of preliterate oral cultures evolved very slowly in pace with bucolic contexts. For the past few millennia libraries, schools, museums and similar organisations have augmented a faster and more complex self-referential renewal process by curating meaningfulness within collections, curricula and other entities. These institutions were invented as 'apps' to inspire individual and collective potential in a socially responsible way. They feed human brains which, by incessantly generating and refining models of the world, are voracious story-telling engines.

The Internet is accelerating identity regeneration at a breathtaking rate. This chapter has sketched a few possible dimensions of future personhood that may traditionally have been addressed by community-scaled and community-oriented apps. It is worrisome that the equivalents of libraries are not stepping forward to serve these information management opportunities with anything like the energy and vision of the commercial world, especially when commerce is apparently the wrong home for them. Perhaps it is just a matter of time, or perhaps there are social enterprise solutions on the horizon. Or perhaps we are just at one of those awkward moments of youth where frictions with traditional parenting and social oversight engender a new level of autonomy. The story unfolds.

Notes

1. *http://en.wikipedia.org/wiki/Clarke%27s_three_laws*
2. See, for example, V.S. Ramachandran (2011) *The Tell-Tale Brain*. London: William Heinemann.
3. See, for example, D. Hofstadter (2007) *I Am A Strange Loop*. New York: Basic Books.
4. *http://www.google.co.uk/*
5. *http://www.amazon.co.uk/*
6. C.K. Prahalad (2004) *The Fortune at the Bottom of the Pyramid*. Upper Saddle River, NJ: Pearson Education.
7. *http://www.facebook.com/*
8. *http://www.gleanr.com*
9. *http://en.wikipedia.org/wiki/Arthur_C._Clarke*
10. A.C. Clarke (1968) *2001: A Space Odyssey*. New York: New American Library.

Surviving or thriving? Building an information landscape

Richard Otlet

Abstract. A fundamental good of the Internet is the democratic access to, and sharing of information on, the World Wide Web. The online digital information environment has dramatically changed the way users access information worldwide. However, just as the access to information facilitated by technologies has increased exponentially over the past few years, it is also widely recognised that merely having access to information is not enough.

The author argues that if we are not only to survive but also to thrive in today's digital information environment, we need to look harder at information itself and develop a better knowledge of our information worlds as a part of developing our information literacy skills. In this chapter he considers the changes and challenges of the digital information environment. This is followed by a closer look at the way we stabilise information. Lastly he considers an approach to managing information for the future and the notion of a personal information landscape.

Keywords: digital information environment, information landscape, information literacy, information retrieval

Introduction

You're coming of age in a 24/7 media environment that bombards us with all kinds of content and exposes us to all kinds of arguments, some of which don't always rank that high on the truth meter ... information becomes a distraction, a diversion, a form of entertainment, rather than a tool of empowerment. (Barack Obama addressing graduates at Hampton University in the USA, in Brooks, 2010)

For some decades now we have been talking and speculating about the relationship between information and technology. The press and media as well as many politicians often emphasise that we are digital citizens (BBC, 2005), that we live in an information age (Negroponte, 1995), that we are part of an information society that is located in a digital universe (Beniger, 1986), that we are economically supported by a knowledge economy fuelled by information (Drucker, 1969; Porat, 1977), and that these things are fundamentally reshaping our society (McLuhan and Fiore, 1967). Many believe that the Internet is a force for good as it provides democratic access and allows information to be shared more widely. However, others have been saying that we live in an age that fetishises information (Poster, 1995), that it is changing society and causing more harm than good (Postman, 1992), or even that it is making us ill (Whitworth, 2009) and we are barely surviving. We have been saying these things for some time now; nevertheless, as Ronald Stamper (1973) commented almost 40 years ago, and is still equally relevant today: 'The explosive growth of information technology has not been accompanied by a commensurate improvement in the understanding of information.'

Without doubt, the rise of an online digital information environment over the past two decades has dramatically changed the way we access, retrieve, use and interact with information world wide. This presents many challenges for education and society in general today. For example, it is widely recognised that merely having access to information is not enough. As the Council of Australian University Librarians (CAUL) (2001) commented a decade ago, 'sheer abundance of information and technology will not in itself create more informed citizens without a complementary understanding and capacity to use information effectively' (CAUL, 2001). Information literacy is seen as the solution to the challenges posed. It is a global priority especially for less privileged groups of people and in countries with lower living standards (Lash, 2002; WSIS, 2003; IFLA, 2005). In education information literacy is recognised through a range of strategies, standards and competencies; for example, in the USA, the Association of College and Research Libraries (2000); in Australia, the Council of Australian University Librarians (2001); and in the UK, the Society of College, National and University Libraries' (SCONUL) 'Seven Pillars Model' (2011). Typically, these strategies identify information literacy as a problem that focuses upon a perceived lack of skills on the part of the information user. Undoubtedly, developing information literacy skills plays a key role in meeting many of the information challenges. However, they are generic skills and may appear to be out of context in terms of the many daily information activities that make up our information worlds. Some even say they are completely out of step with users' needs, 'providing an unrealistic and unattainable goal for students' (Bivens-Tatum, 2011).

SCONUL's 'Seven Pillars Model' (SCONUL, 2011) talks about building information literacy skills that are 'founded on an information landscape which comprises the information world as it is perceived by an individual at that point in time.' But how much do we actually know about our information worlds, and does it really matter? Do we really need to look beyond the near instant 'information gratification' provided by our 'search box'? I argue that if we are not only to survive but also to thrive in today's digital information environment, we need to look harder at information itself and develop a better knowledge of our information worlds as a part of developing our information literacy skills. In this chapter I consider the changes and challenges of the digital information environment. This is followed by a closer look at the way we stabilise information; and lastly I consider an approach to managing information for the future and the notion of our personal information landscape.

Our digital information environment: changes and challenges

The Web is the convergence of various old and new information groupings or information 'presentation layers' with various old and new technologies, and new forms of speech or 'orality'. It is the convergence of these information groupings and technologies that has changed the information environment within which we carry out our information activities and access and use information, from online shopping to in-depth academic research. Websites, wikis and blogs now coexist with older information groupings that have been reformatted for the Web, such as books and academic journals. In our digital environment there are some 'knowns' and 'absolutes' to hold on to with certainty, but conversely there is much uncertainty and many 'unknowns'. These are the changes and challenges that we face in our digital information environments today; examining them further, while they overlap and are intertwined, nine key areas of change are identified.

Disintermediation

The first change lies in the disintermediation of the processes and services that surround traditional information groupings, for example books and newspapers. These include publishers, librarians, bookshops, newsagents and distributors, among many others. Together, they have traditionally provided most of the components of our information environment, whether in the public or the education sector. The disintermediation of the routes to information enables often direct or near direct access for users to increasing amounts of online digital information. The seamlessness of information retrieval means that we no longer have to think about how we are going to complete an information activity. If we think about it at all, we tend to just think about using 'the Web', 'the Internet' or being 'online'. In fact, many people do not even distinguish between the Web browser and the search engine that they are using (Baio, 2011).

Information users across the world increasingly see Google as their new library (Brabazon, 2007; Carr, 2008; Hartman and Mullen, 2008). For example, in UK education, access to electronic resources such as journals is increasing 'dramatically' while access to physical holdings is falling (Nicholas et al., 2011). This also extends to other electronic resources (JISC, 2008; Nicholas et al., 2010). This renders the most visible and physical elements such as the bookshop, the library and the librarian invisible to the end user. Schonfeld and Housewright's (2008) longitudinal study of digital trends in higher education in the USA also highlights this, noting the stark absence of the library in faculty workflows. The disintermediation of the traditional supporting structures surrounding information has dramatically increased the independence of the information user.

Hypertext

The second change is the ability to 'jump' between web pages using hypertext, quickly and easily. A form of hypertext can be observed in twelfth-century books through the use of marginalia (Cahill, 1995). It can also be observed in early modern England in 'commonplace' books. Commonplacing was a form of segmented reading and notation. It involved breaking down texts into fragments and reassembling them 'into new patterns by transcribing them in different sections of their notebooks' (Darnton, 2009). It was used to 'make sense' of their information environments, particularly at a time of information instability in the seventeenth century. The traditional supporting structures surrounding information, particularly those around the book, brought a new level of information stability and the practice of commonplacing declined. The introduction of the novel changed the way we read books and today we have become conditioned to reading from page to page in a predefined order and often from cover to cover (Darnton, 2009). However, the Web brings ease and speed of linking, which marks the difference between then and now; and further, provides greater fluidity or reach to information and texts. As the user 'jumps' between whole groupings of information presentation layers and texts, so they 'surf the Web'. This fluidity heightens the instability of information as users risk losing their way as they move away from their original starting point, unknowingly linking from a trusted to an untrusted site with ease. They may also end up in the depths of a complex text or discussion at their first 'click'. Further, hypertext decentralises the information from one particular grouping to many that are linked. This fluidity also dilutes the traditional notion of an 'information authority' and the older linguistic forms of 'truth bearing' (Lankshear et al., 2000) information layers. It also increases access and if the information is managed and stabilised in some way hypertext enables far greater exploration of information than has ever been possible in the past.

Increasing fluidity

A third observable change lies in the increased fluidity and the decentralisation of information, which is amplified by the reach and speed of access that the Internet and Web technologies enable. Few areas of Western society have been left untouched by the Internet and its reach is global. These technologies facilitate information services that most of us interact with daily. It affects where we can find information and is supranational. We can now connect with remote communities and over huge distances in seconds. We can access services faster – for example, online banking, shopping, accessing academic resources or researching your family tree. Traditional communication channels such as the printed book or the letter are only ever as fast as they can be physically carried. The notion of speed, fluidity and distance beyond physical limitations creates a virtual world that mirrors the physical world. It abstracts information in a way that the physical book and older information environments do not. In turn this develops a sense of information limitlessness and separability that is not possible even in a very large library of books, where there is still a notion of information boundedness. However, the notion of the limitlessness of the Web is an information myth. It is not, and the user needs to know what the limits are; if we have no concept of the online information environment, we may also limit its potential. Typically we already do this by relying on search engines that use algorithms designed to favour nationally based commerce first and the information user second. Search engines give us a false sense of security in terms of stable structures in our information environments and need to be critically appraised in the same way that the information sources and resources they offer us do.

Converging information models

A fourth difference lies in the changing and converging information communications models. The broadcast, or 'one to many', information communications model of television, radio and the media produces a new form of orality that Walter Ong (2002) refers to as 'secondary orality'. Whether it is a speech by a politician on the television, a podcast or a YouTube video, most spoken or oral elements of these media rely on text-based scripts or have some relationship to text to some degree. Further, they may well rely on the context – 'the connected structure of writing' (*Oxford English Dictionary*, 1989) – to aid meaning and comprehension often within a presentation layer such as a website.

Oral cultures are typically more communal and externalise information, as opposed to the more introspective approach common among literate societies; reading is a solitary activity. Secondary orality sits between the contrasting open information experience and the closed solitary one, merging social interactivity with fixed information. As the technologies converge, the 'one to many' becomes 'many to many'. This reconfiguration of the mutable and fluid social model of communication with the fixed information model creating the rise of secondary orality has enabled infinitely greater scope for interactive communication of information than the older broadcast models on their own could achieve; in turn, this allows us to 'reconfigure words, sounds and images so as to cultivate new configurations of individuality' (Poster, 2006). The reach of this interactivity is global and while it is constrained to those that are connected to the Internet, compared to primary oral interactivity it has much greater fluidity, speed and reach. This is because primary oral interactivity has always been limited by physical proximity and organisational factors. For example, a national debate, such as a referendum on a particular topic, would traditionally involve enormous amounts of resources and time. It is now possible to get a feel for the 'mood of the nation' through blogs and wikis in seconds. This was demonstrated to great effect by the Obama presidential campaign in 2008.

Power and control

Related to the rise of social interactivity on the Web, the fifth change concerns Web 1.0 and Web 2.0. The convergence of technologies and orality has enabled the formation of new types of 'information groupings' and 'presentation layers' of information and this has some notable phases. Web 1.0 was marked by a rise in, and proliferation of, new information creators and quasi-publishers at all levels of society. This made information far more fluid, and also unstable, as anybody could publish anything with ease. This undermined the traditional support structures that have arisen around the book where centralisation and standardisation have been at the heart of stabilising information. The continuing disintermediation of information has eroded and in some instances dissolved the boundaries between producers, distributors and consumers of information. However, Web 1.0 is essentially still a broadcast model with one in control broadcasting to the many.

The control of information has always been inextricably linked to power (Headrick, 2000) and the development, alongside Web 1.0, of Web 2.0 and social interactivity has undermined the power base as a decentralised many-to-many information model has emerged. The rise of these open, highly fluid information sources and groupings has moved the locus of control away from small powerful elites to the 'crowd'. These environments 'are poorly under anybody's control and have far-reaching, unexpected effects' (Engeström, 2009). They also represent the movement of the power and control from the single producer, whether individual, institutional, commercial or political, to a socially developed and influenced one. This raises questions of information ownership and intellectual property rights (IPR) (Hargreaves, 2011). It also makes new forms of information outputs possible. These 'new' information groupings are characterised by social and participatory practices on the Web such as Facebook[1] and Wikipedia.[2] Web 2.0 as a single label is misleading

77

because in reality it stands for many different types of information groupings that vary in complexity and stability.

Web 2.0 information sources and groupings are prone to being highly unstable and contain text and other information resources that are highly mutable and fluid. Some groupings are highly democratic and in some instances in the public interest, while in equal measure others may be destructive and even dangerous. They may also be hugely powerful; a recent example of this in the UK was the WikiLeaks scandal. The power of the crowd using Twitter[3] was able to undermine the celebrity gagging orders imposed by the 'legal authority' – as one newspaper headline observed, 'a legal crisis in 140 characters' (Burrell, 2011). An information user can interact and contribute to these sources as well as draw information from them. However, their power to influence may not always be in the best interest of the information user. Further, while there is a perception that they are truly democratic (which in some cases is true), in some cases a relatively small group of elite users may wield most of the power and a have a striking concentration of attention, as a recent study of Twitter found: 'Almost half the information that originates from the media passes to the masses indirectly via a diffuse intermediate layer of opinion leaders, who although classified as ordinary users, are more connected and more exposed to the media than their followers' (Wu et al., 2011). Information users must tread carefully through these online spaces if they are using them as information sources, and must also learn to check the assumptions that are made, based upon what may pass as a democratic and egalitarian information source.

Open or closed?

The sixth change concerns an emerging Web 3.0, which again raises issues of power and the control of information. It is a divided environment. On the one hand, there is the notion of the 'Semantic Web', in which web pages will contain enough metadata about their content to enable software to make informed judgements about their relevance and function, the metadata providing a stabilising influence while still allowing for great information fluidity. On the other hand, another direction is emerging that places the Internet in conflict with the Web, and that is the rise of the app. These are 'walled garden' applications, so called because they are limited or closed, and hold groupings and 'presentation layers' of information. They represent a move from the wide-open Web to semi-closed information platforms. The commercial model is that the customer pays to download the app containing the information. The power and control is held within the app and its creator, owner or publisher. The app is in direct opposition to the notion of an open, free and democratic Web, or 'crowd'-based movements, as it limits and controls information. From the information user's perspective, the notion of 'contained' and 'discrete' information groupings has great appeal as it provides fixity and stability of information in a way that the book does. Some even argue that the Web is now dead (Anderson and Wolff, 2010). It also has great appeal to commercial publishers. However, it may also limit the range of information made available to us and further it is at its core a one-to-many information model.

Information overload

The seventh change is the sheer quantity of information that is now available to us. For two decades our access to information has steadily increased, most notably through access to information that is on the Web with global reach though the Internet, but also through communications technologies such as email and texts. As access has increased and more information is both created and made available online, issues of information overload, information glut and information noise have become increasingly important. According to some, this has reached the point of being a digital tsunami and, looking to the future, how are we going to cope with the 25 quintillion bits of information that we are forecast to have by 2020, when we are struggling now (Gantz and Reinsel, 2010)?

The sheer quantity of information available to us raises the question of effective information retrieval: 'how will we find anything' among all this information? As Dale (2011) asks, at a time when we are already 'awash with data', how are we going to 'tame the beast'? Information retrieval and the way information is structured have long been issues of concern in information science (Urquhart, 1948; Wilson, 1981/2006), where metadata, or data about data, is seen as a key solution. Farhoomand and Drury (2002) argue for creating more digital tools to 'save us', and new ways to add structure to unstructured data, to deal with information overload by creating more information. 'Rather than needing less information, we actually may need lots more, specifically information about information, or metadata.' However, Gantz and Reinsel (2010) also highlight in their forecast that the fastest growing category in the digital universe is metadata itself, which on one level is inadvertently perpetuating the problem of increasing amounts of data. Brown and Duguid (2000) argue that it is a fundamental error to use digital tools on top of digital tools as this proliferates the problem. They highlight the 'human' element in the problem as a part of the solution, and Shirky (2008) argues that we need to filter the information more; that 'it's filter failure', not information overload. What we do know is that increasing amounts of data and information are inevitable, as access increases facilitated by mobile technologies, wireless and cloud solutions, as more analogue information is digitised and as we continue to send emails, write on virtual walls and do virtually all the things that we used to do physically. Against the backdrop of increasing amounts of information and navigating a multitude of complex systems, information sources and 'digital presentation layers', we have to manage and balance our time, money, work and family commitments. The 'human' element would seem to be the vital component in solutions to our information overload dilemmas.

The wider information environment

The eighth change concerns the fact that we too easily forget that offline information sources and resources play a large and important part in our daily lives, and yet we tend to take these for granted, for example oral information such as a question posed to a colleague or a friend perhaps. There are also the many other technologies such as books and other printed artefacts such as magazines and newspapers or a poster in a shop window. In the same way that not all information is online, neither are all the information systems that we access, and some may be a hybrid mix of both. The traditional library is a hybrid model and increasingly in areas such as education these library spaces are evolving (Smith, 2008). We need to understand how they work together as opposed to adopting an 'either/or' stance. Together, all of these information sources and our engagement with them, or 'information experiences', are a part of many interacting activity systems that are the historically and socially formed information environments through which we journey. By combining these sources and resources we develop a better information experience, for example a recommendation from a friend combined with a web search is more likely to help us find that ideal holiday. The secondary orality of Web 2.0 is also useful here; for example, other readers' comments about a book found on the Amazon[4] site may lead us to make a more informed decision about its purchase or download, although this is also open to abuse and again critical skills are needed. For example, according to a Nielsen report (2009), while 70 per cent of people trust recommendations from strangers online, TripAdvisor[5] is also being investigated by the UK advertising watchdog over allegations that not all its reviews are genuine (Singh, 2011).

Human agency

Finally, we too easily assume that because technology impacts our lives, it is the technology that has caused the change. But this is a distracting information myth that suggests we are powerless to do anything about it. This myth is even reinforced by the use of the term 'information technology' and reflects a tendency towards technological determinism (Toffler, 1980; Gates, 1995; Negroponte, 1995; Dertouzos, 1997) that is perpetuated in the media. As early information systems studies such as Orlikowski and Gash's (1994) study of 10,000 office workers demonstrated, our use of technology is determined, not by the intentions of the technology designers or those implementing it, but always within the frame of our knowledge of what we can do with it. Changes to its use will only be achieved by changing our perception of its use, or what we can do with it, rather than the technology itself. A simplistic example is texting; the designers of the mobile phone did not set out to invent a new social phenomenon. It is human agency rather than the technology that leads any change, and in the same way it is human agency that determines technology and information use. It is human agency that will determine how information is stabilised and to what degree, and therefore that determines our information environments.

Information

As we have seen, the information user today accesses a heady mix of stable and unstable information groupings where information can take on any shape as it emerges from the binary soup (Gilster, 1997). Text may be highly mutable, highly fixed or highly fluid, where orality over the Web pushes and users push back through Web 2.0 social channels, with unknown consequences. Regardless of the activity that we are pursuing, information tends to be treated and thought of as a resource. However, because information originates in the mind, it is intangible and therefore has some surprisingly different characteristics that clearly distinguish it from other kinds of resources, for example money or time or indeed information technologies. These characteristics 'make information a very unique resource, the use of which creates some rather unique ethical issues' (Mason et al., 1995). These lie particularly around issues of ownership, control and the stabilisation of information. The problems and issues that surround information and the wish to control information are not new to us, although one could easily be led to believe that they are. As Headrick (2000) argues, 'the information revolution in which we live is the result of a cultural change that began roughly three centuries ago.' The desire and need to stabilise information has long been a priority for governments, commerce and education and in today's information environment it is increasing the responsibility of the information user.

There have been various changes in our information environments brought about by new technologies at various stages of human development – the ages of information. Many today we no longer think of as technology, such as writing or print – they are such a part of the fabric of our society. Ong (2002) identifies three technologies: writing, printing, and computer and electronic communication. Darnton (2009) additionally identifies the codex or book. Postman (1992) identifies the telegraph and the photograph and Poster (1995) the telephone. The latest change in our information environment, digital technologies and electronic communication, in purely temporal terms happened overnight compared to the others (Darnton, 2009). But this temporality belies the fact that the underlying constant and central trait throughout the information ages, information itself, is highly unstable, and this remains unchanged today. A further constant is that there are at least three characteristics to information that impact its stability and its instability. These are its fixity, fluidity and mutability, and they work either positively or negatively, either stabilising or destabilising. For example, if mutability is dominant, the information has a tendency towards the chaotic. An overemphasis on fluidity results in information overload and an overemphasis on fixity results in a 'locked down', stifling information environment. They are not mutually exclusive characteristics – it does not follow that one characteristic on its own is better than another. They are also intertwined so they affect each other. What is desirable is a balance of elements. Balance is dependent on many social and cultural factors emphasising the human element in the stabilising equation.

The instability of information throughout the information ages has traditionally been harnessed and stabilised, at least to some degree, within 'truth-bearing' presentation layers. Latterly the primacy of the printed word elevated the format of the printed book as the 'truth-bearing' information grouping or presentation layer. For over two millennia we have used this controlled and regulated grouping of information for producing and expressing information. Whole institutions and information systems such as the publishing industry have built up around it. As Postman (1992) recognised over a decade ago, 'Western culture had more than two hundred years to accustom itself to the new information conditions created by the press.' The information technologies, and the processes and systems surrounding them, have had little time to evolve and settle in. Further, the methods and processes we have in place today are still largely those based upon and created to support the information age of the printing press. It is hardly surprising that 'the methods by which ... [we] ... have hoped to keep information from running amok are now dysfunctional' (Postman, 1992). Largely it is not a case of simply adopting or modifying the old systems; rather it is more a question of new approaches, some not even developed yet. There are, however, elements of information, as has always been the case, that will never be fully stabilised; for example, misinformation may be deliberate as in propaganda, or accidental.

We are in a time of flux. What we have witnessed for at least the last two decades is the evolution of these traditional 'truth-bearing' information presentation layers and the development of new ones. Part of that evolution is also the decline of the information services associated with the print publishing industry and print-based library services, and the disintermediation of the traditional routes to information. However, we have become so accustomed to the relatively stable traditional formats provided by the book and associated services that we take issues of information stability for granted. We do not tend to think about how to stabilise information and where and how it has been stabilised in the past. If we are to bring any form of stability to information and to maximise its potential, the responsibility for, and ownership of, our information environment lies with us.

Our information landscape

The disintermediation of information support structures and the increasing independence of the information user is perhaps an inevitable part of the changing information environment. Schön (1970), in a lecture about change and the industrial society, highlighted that the enormous increase in the absolute levels of technology has 'done something to human limits and to social limits'. He lists the typical responses that are recognisable in the current discourse on information: firstly, a 'return to the last stable state, to the way it used to be'; secondly, 'the idea of revolt'; and thirdly, 'mindlessness'. However, they are more correctly what he calls 'anti-responses ... [as] ... they are destructive in character.' He argues that constructive responses 'must confront the phenomenon directly ... at the level both of the person and of the institution.' Similarly, there are several camps in the disintermediation debate. Firstly, there are the disintermediationists, or those that 'recognise benefit in the removal of the institutional intermediary in the supply chain' (De Roure, 2011). The futurologists would fall into this group. Secondly, there are the 'antidisintermediationists' (De Roure, 2011), those wanting to preserve the old structures that I have argued are no longer fit for purpose – the technophobes would fall into this camp. The third camp, though, I refer to as the re-intermediationists, those who are striving to build and support new structures around the information sources and resources that comprise our information environment.

Today we must confront our information challenges with constructive responses – we must re-intermediate. Information literacy is clearly a key enabler for active participation and for taking control of information. However, as Whitworth (2009) argues, while information literacy is the favoured solution to problems posed by information, 'any "literacy" risks becoming a passively applied set of skills: a "checklist" that graduates or workers can present as a qualification, without it representing a creative and active relationship with information.' Despite new technologies, information literacy is still at its heart the struggle to stabilise and control and make sense of information, to make the partnership work. New technologies do not provide information literacy and information literacy is not only the mastering of information technology skills. By putting supporting structures around information, we are able to bring about some level of stability although this can never be complete. This is where information literacy needs to be primarily focused.

In the same way that the seventeenth-century practice of commonplacing helped courtiers make sense of their information world and impose their own pattern on their reading matter, we need to take control and own our information environments and impose order on our information experiences in modern times. We need to move beyond being just information 'savvy' and become information literate and information 'wise' (Fieldhouse and Nicholas, 2008). There also needs to be some notion of boundedness if we are going to cope with information and make sense of our information environments. Based upon my research into the information experiences of a group of first-year postgraduate students returning to education in a UK university, the concept of developing an information landscape is presented. The concept is based upon Barnett's (2007) notion of travel metaphors to describe student experiences, which he argues is 'testimony to the voyaging aspect of their studies'. Further, Gilster (1997) describes a journey in relation to digital literacy and also introduces a geographical metaphor to describe the way the Internet has eroded distance and time: we journey through the 'new geography of information' (Gilster, 1997). Finally, Cussins' (1992) theory of 'embodied cognition' and cognitive trails adopts the metaphor of a person moving in a territory, arguing that as they do so they make 'cognitive trails' and 'landmarks' (Cussins, 1992).

Developing an awareness of our information environment enables us to develop our own contextualised information landscape. Our information landscape is formed from the information environment that surrounds us, both virtual and real, and also includes 'all the other things that surround technology and information' (Brown and Duguid, 2000), including offline information and systems. The information landscape creates some boundedness to information and brings some stability to our complex information environments. By thinking about our information environment as a landscape upon which we journey helps us to understand the information and information systems with which we interact and to develop and stabilise information for our own needs and activities. These experiences are profoundly social and historically fashioned, and 'real'. It is our 'will' and human agency that are the driving forces of the journey as we build our landscapes from the information environment we find ourselves a part of. As we carry out an activity, cognitive trails form and once created they can act as guides for future action. It is upon this landscape that we can build our information literacy skills. The impact of information can be increased though the use of 'triggers' that help us build trails to follow across the landscape. These triggers may be learned, come from others around us or come from information professionals who are guiding us.

As much as we have the responsibility for developing this landscape and trails, we have to incorporate and modify existing trails created by others when we embark on any new activity. This means that the responsibility is shared to some extent; our landscape is always unavoidably a co-configured place, whether actively or passively so. For example, entering a work situation or educational environment, our landscape has to incorporate pre-existing trails set by the systems and processes already in place, and these have to be learned. The degree to which trails can be redefined by the users' needs determines the degree to which they are potentially co-configurable. In this sense, the institution or business also needs to be information literate as well, both in its thinking and in its support. The degree to which the 'partner' in this co-configuration wishes to participate may further affect the development of our landscape, which if actively pursued may prove mutually beneficial. Facilitating and supporting this learning as well as developing triggers could be a key role for the librarian and the information professional as they already have a good understanding of the complexity of information and the information environment.

Finally, Postman (1985), writing before the Internet became a commercial proposition, highlighted the insights of two writers in relation to the future of society and technology. Firstly, George Orwell warned that we will be overcome by an externally imposed oppression; he pictured a society where the book was banned. Secondly, Aldous Huxley warned that no externally imposed oppression would be required to deprive people of their autonomy, maturity and history, as there would be no one who wanted to read a book anyway. Postman predicted that Orwell would be right. As he saw it, people will come to love their oppression, to adore the technologies that undo their capacities to think. At the same time, Toffler (1980) argued that the world has been decisively shaped by unstoppable waves of technological innovation, 'which presages a new way of living (which, attests Toffler, will turn out fine if only we ride with the wave)' (Webster, 2006). Whichever the viewpoint, the problems are portrayed as beyond any human control, that technology is now in charge. While there probably is some small degree of truth in both of these positions, I believe that it is human agency and our continuing struggle to stabilise information that is the issue and should be the focus of our attention. To allow technology to control us is to surrender to Google or indeed to the app. This matters because many cannot cope with the quantity of information before them and those that lack information literacy will continue to be further marginalised as more and more information is 'born digital'. It matters because information is central to our society and culture and is essential for our survival. However, it also eats into our resources and threatens to overwhelm us unless we take control. It matters because failure to stabilise and harness information is also to waste the opportunity to exploit what is without doubt one of the greatest information opportunities in information history. By developing our personal information landscapes we may be able to go some way to achieving some information stability and move from merely surviving to thriving.

Notes

1. *http://www.facebook.com/*
2. *http://www.wikipedia.org/*
3. *http://www.twitter.com*
4. *http://www.amazon.co.uk/*
5. *http://www.tripadvisor.co.uk*

References

Anderson, C. and Wolff, M. (2010) 'The Web is dead: long live the Internet', *Wired Magazine*, September. Online at: *http://www.wired.com/magazine/2010/08/ff_webrip/*.

Association of College and Research Libraries (2000) *Information Literacy Competency Standards for Higher Education*. Chicago: American Library Association. Online at: *http://www.acrl.org/ala/mgrps/divs/acrl/standards/standards.pdf*.

Baio, A. (2011) 'A browser is a search engine'. Online at: *http://googlesystem.blogspot.com/2009/06/browser-is-search-engine.html*.

Barnett, R. (2007) *A Will to Learn: Being a Student in an Age of Uncertainty*. Maidenhead: Open University Press.

BBC (2005) 'Are you a digital citizen?' British Broadcasting Corporation. Online at: *http://news.bbc.co.uk/1/hi/talking_point/4678631.stm*.

Beniger, J.R. (1986) *The Control Revolution: Technological and Economic Origins of the Information Society*. Cambridge, MA: Harvard University Press.

Bivens-Tatum, W. (2011) 'The myth of information literacy', *Academic Librarian*. Online at: *http://blogs.princeton.edu/librarian/2011/04/the_myth_of_information_literacy/*.

Brabazon, T. (2007) *The University of Google: Education in the (Post) Information Age*. Aldershot: Ashgate.

Brooks, M.A. (2010) 'Democracy and iPods (and iPads and Xboxes and PlayStations)', *By the People*. Online at: *http://blogs.america.gov/bythepeople/2010/05/11/democracy-and-ipods-and-ipads-and-xboxes-and-playstations*.

Brown, J.S. and Duguid, P. (2000) *The Social Life of Information*, 2nd edn. Boston, MA: Harvard Business School Press.

Burrell, I. (2011) 'A legal crisis in 140 characters', *The Independent*. Online at: *http://www.independent.co.uk/news/media/online/a-legal-crisis-in-140-characters-2281582.html*.

Cahill, T. (1995) *How the Irish Saved Civilisation: The Untold Story of Ireland's Heroic Role from the Fall of Rome to the Rise of Medieval Europe*. New York: Nan A Talese, Doubleday.

Carr, N. (2008) 'Is Google making us stupid?', *The Atlantic*, July/August.

CAUL (2001) *Information Literacy Standards*. Canberra: Council of Australian University Librarians. Online at: *http://archive.caul.edu.au/info-literacy/publications.html*.

Cussins, A. (1992) 'Content, embodiment and objectivity: the theory of cognitive trails', *Mind*, 101(404): 651–88.

Dale, S. (2011) 'Surviving and thriving as a 21st century knowledge and information professional', *Business Information Review*, 28(1): 30–7.

Darnton, R. (2009) *The Case for Books: Past, Present, and Future*. New York: Public Affairs.

De Roure, D. (2011) 'Antidisintermediationarianism and The Cloud', *eResearch*. Oxford: Nature Publishing Group. Online at: *http://blogs.nature.com/eresearch/*.

Dertouzos, M. (1997) *What Will Be: How the New World of Information Will Change Our Lives*. London: Piatkus.

Drucker, P. (1969) *The Age of Discontinuity: Guidelines to Our Changing Society*. New York: Harper & Row.

Engeström, Y. (2009) 'The future of activity theory: a rough draft', in A. Sannino, H. Daniels and K. Gutierrez (eds), *Learning and Expanding with Activity Theory*. Cambridge: Cambridge University Press.

Farhoomand, A.F. and Drury, D.H. (2002) 'Managerial information overload', *Communications of the ACM*, 45(10): 127–31.

Fieldhouse, M. and Nicholas, D. (2008) 'Digital literacy as information savvy', in C. Lankshear, M. Knobel and M. Peters (eds), *Digital Literacies: Concepts, Policies and Practices*. New York: Peter Lang.

Gantz, J. and Reinsel, D. (2010) *The Digital Universe Decade – Are You Ready?* Framingham: IDC.

Gates, B. (1995) *The Road Ahead*. Harmondsworth: Penguin.

Gilster, P. (1997) *Digital Literacy*. New York: Wiley Computer.

Hargreaves, I. (2011) *Digital Opportunity: Review of Intellectual Property and Growth*, an independent report by Professor Ian Hargreaves. Online at: *http://www.ipo.gov.uk/ipreview/ipreview-about.htm*.

Hartman, K.A. and Mullen, L.B. (2008) 'Google scholar and academic libraries: an update', *New Library World*, 109(5/6): 211–22.

Headrick, D.R. (2000) *When Information Came of Age: Technologies of Knowledge in the Age of Reason and Revolution 1700–1850*. Oxford: Oxford University Press.

IFLA (2005) 'Beacons of the information society'. International Federation of Library Associations. Online at: *http://archive.ifla.org/III/wsis/BeaconInfSoc.html*.

JISC (2008) JISC national e-books observatory project. Online at: *http://www.jiscebooksproject.org/*.

Lankshear, C., Peters, M. and Knobel, M. (2000) 'Information, knowledge and learning: some issues facing epistemology and education in a digital age', *Journal of Philosophy of Education*, 34(1): 17–39.

Lash, S. (2002) *Critique of Information*. London: Sage.

McLuhan, M. and Fiore, Q. (1967) *The Medium Is the Massage*. Penguin: Harmondsworth.

Mason, R., Mason, F. and Culnan, J. (1995) *Ethics of Information Management*. London: Sage.

Negroponte, N. (1995) *Being Digital*. London: Hodder & Stoughton.

Nicholas, D., Rowlands, I. and Jamali, H.R. (2010) 'E-textbook use, information seeking behaviour and its impact: case study business and management', *Journal of Information Science*, 36(2): 263–80.

Nicholas, D., Rowlands, I., Williams, P., Brown, D. and Clark, D. (2011) *E-journals: Their Use, Value and Impact*. London: Research Information Network.

Nielsen (2009) 'Global advertising: consumers trust real friends and virtual strangers the most'. Online at: *http://blog.nielsen.com/nielsenwire/consumer/global-advertising-consumers-trust-real-friends-and-virtual-strangers-the-most/*.

Ong, W.J. (2002) *Orality and Literacy? The Technologizing of the Word*. London: Routledge.

Orlikowski, W.J. and Gash, D.C. (1994) 'Technological frames: making sense of information technology in organisations', *ACM Transactions on Information Systems*, 12(2): 174–207.

Oxford English Dictionary Online, 2nd edn. (1989). Oxford: Oxford Unversity Press. Online at: *http://www.oed.com*.

Porat, M.U. (1977) *The Information Economy: Definition and Measurement*. Washington, DC: National Science Foundation.

Poster, M. (1995) *The Second Media Age*. Cambridge: Polity Press.

Poster, M. (2006) 'Postmodern virtualities', in M.G. Durham and D.M. Kellner (eds), *Media and Cultural Studies*, revised edn. Oxford: Blackwell.

Postman, N. (1985) *Amusing Ourselves to Death: Public Discourse in the Age of Show Business*. New York: Penguin Books.

Postman, N. (1992) *Technopoly*. New York: Vintage Books, Random House.

Schön, D. (1970) 'Change and industrial society', *The Reith Lectures*. Online at: *http://downloads.bbc.co.uk/rmhttp/radio4/transcripts/1970_reith1.pdf*.

Schonfeld, R. and Housewright, R. (2008) *Ithaka's 2006 Studies of Key Stakeholders in the Digital Transformation in Higher Education*. New York: Ithaka.

SCONUL (2011) *The Seven Pillars of Information Literacy*. London: Society of College, National and University Libraries. Online at: *http://www.sconul.ac.uk/groups/information_literacy/seven_pillars.html*.

Shirky, C. (2008) *It's Not Information Overload. It's Filter Failure*. Paper presented at the Web 2.0 Expo, 16–19 September, New York.

Singh, A. (2011) 'Watchdog to investigate TripAdvisor reviews', *The Independent*. Online at: *http://www.independent.co.uk/travel/news-and-advice/watchdog-to-investigate-tripadvisor-reviews-2348140.html*.

Smith, R. (2008) 'Technology-rich physical space design: an overview of JISC activities'. Online at: *http://www.jisc.ac.uk/publications/briefingpapers/2008/bpelearnspacesv1.aspx*.

Stamper, R.K. (1973) *Information in Business and Administrative Systems*. London: Batsford.

Toffler, A. (1980) *The Third Wave*. New York: Morrow.

Urquhart, D.J. (1948) 'The distribution and use of scientific and technical information', *Journal of Documentation*, 3: 222–31.

Webster, F. (2006) 'The information society revisited', in L. Lievrouw and D. Livingstone (eds), *Handbook of New Media*, updated edn. London: Sage.

Whitworth, A. (2009) *Information Obesity*. Oxford: Chandos.

Wilson, T.D. (1981/2006) 'On user studies and information needs', *Journal of Documentation*, 62(6): 658–70.

WSIS (2003) The World Summit on the Information Society, Geneva.

Wu, S., Hofman, J.M., Watts, D.J. and Mason, W.A. (2011) 'Who says what to whom on Twitter categories and subject descriptors'. Online at: *http://www.mendeley.com/research/says-whom-twitter-categories-subject-descriptors*.

6

The effect the changing digital landscape is having on the dissemination of e-books and e-journals in a world dominated by Google

Lorraine Estelle

Abstract. This chapter considers why the old models for the dissemination of scholarly information are increasingly under threat. While technological developments mean that search and access are easier and faster than ever before, the role of the library can become invisible, irrelevant or impossibly expensive. The chapter explores the paradox of success: a combination of Google search, authentication technology and a huge spend by libraries on e-journals provides scholars with rapid access to more articles than ever before, and studies have shown a strong correlation between this wide access to e-journals and research excellence. As public-sector cuts bite, and the number of journal articles published each year increases, libraries are struggling to sustain the provision of e-journals. In comparison, library provision of e-books is yet far from successful. The chapter considers the business models employed in scholarly communications, the drivers of emerging technologies and the role of the publishers and libraries.

Keywords: access, business models, challenges, e-books, e-journals, open access, publishing, scholarly information, threats

Introduction

This chapter will consider why the old models for the dissemination of scholarly information are increasingly under threat. While technological developments mean that search and access are easier and faster than ever before, the role of the library can become invisible, irrelevant or impossibly expensive. In a world where a plethora of information is seemingly freely delivered to the desktop (or mobile device), the idea of collection building, to provide 'just-in-case access', can seem oddly quaint. The chapter will also explore paradoxes of success; a combination of Google search, authentication technology and a huge spend by libraries on e-journals, provides scholars with rapid access to more articles than ever before, and studies have shown a strong correlation between this wide access to e-journals and research excellence. Yet this very ease of access means that the user has little idea of the huge cost of e-journals, or in some cases even that the library has paid for them. As public sector cuts bite and the number of journal articles published each year increases, libraries are struggling to sustain the provision of e-journals. In comparison, library provision of e-books is yet far from successful. Although publishers seem to have at last embraced the e-book, the driver has been emerging technologies such as the Kindle and iPad. Amazon provides a 'one-click-buy', which allows the private user to purchase and download a desired e-book in a matter of seconds. However, there is no role for the library in this model, and for certain types of publications, for example e-textbooks, libraries are seen as a threat to the established publishing business model of sales to students. On the other hand, libraries (perhaps aided by Google) may prove the saviour of other declining areas of publishing, allowing for the dissemination of scholarly e-monographs to thousands rather than to hundreds of readers.

New opportunities

In the print era, when the dissemination of information was costly and relatively slow, and when only one person at a time could read a copy of a book or journal, libraries focused on collection building. This meant acquiring, cataloguing and storing a critical mass of print resources in case their users required them. The business models that supported this form of dissemination worked well and largely ensured the sustainability of publishers. The digital age provides new opportunities, giving researchers and students access to more information than ever before. But it is not just the amount of information that has increased: users can now access material whenever and from wherever they wish, providing they have an Internet connection. New technologies and the development of metadata standards mean that searches that would have taken years in the world of print now take seconds in the digital environment. Furthermore, developments in machine-to-machine technologies are enabling data rather than hypotheses-based research. For example, data and text mining allow machines to sift through vast amounts of information to identify relationships and connections hidden within the data reported in scholarly literature.

These previously undreamt of opportunities are emerging all the time and the digital landscape is changing fast. However, the business models that underpin the creation and dissemination of information are firmly rooted in the print era. In the digital era, this presents a challenge to the sustainability of traditional scholarly publishing and the traditional role of the library. This is further complicated because the search engines and Google in particular provide free and unimpeded access to an immense volume of information. Google's mission is 'to organise the world's information and make it universally accessible and useful.' Its very name is a play on words – 'googol' being the term for 1 followed by 100 zeros – reflecting its ambition to provide a vast amount of knowledge.

A recent study (Wong et al., 2009) found that:

> When using freely available Internet resources, Google is top of the list, followed by Google Scholar, Wikipedia, and YouTube. Participants' decisions about which resources to use were based on their prior knowledge and experience with a resource and a belief that resources provided by Google and Google Scholar are reliable and relevant and most of all always return a list of results.

It is against this background that the library community would like to provide its users with collections of scholarly journals and a critical mass of e-books: authoritative material not freely available on the Internet. However, publishers of scholarly material and libraries are struggling to find the business models that provide the widest possible access while proving sustainable for both seller and buyer.

The scholarly journal

Perhaps the most successful transition from print to digital has been the scholarly journal. Since the 1990s, journal publishing has embraced the digital world, and a high proportion of journal articles are now available online: 96 per cent of journal titles in science, technology and medicine, and 86 per cent of titles in the arts, humanities and social sciences (RIN, 2011). This has meant that libraries have largely moved away from a title-by-title selection of journals, and instead license bundles of electronic journal titles. This provides researchers with greatly expanded access at a much lower cost per unit of information. A recent study (RIN, 2011) has found that researchers are proficient when it comes to using electronic journals and quickly find the information they need. The study also indicates a strong and positive correlation between library expenditure on e-journals and numbers of papers published, citation impact, numbers of PhD awards, and research grant and contract income.

> Yet, despite this success, libraries struggle to maintain access to collections of bundled electronic journals in the face of ever-rising costs. Subscription fees for some of the largest publisher journal packages have risen year on year at over twice the rate of inflation for the past decade. (Prosser, 2010)

Publishers point out that the process of scholarly publishing is expensive and that while the use of technology has reduced the cost of some processes, the costs associated with content delivery platforms, search optimisation, XML workflows and so on require considerable investment. Another cost factor is the increase in research outputs, with a growth rate of around 3.5 per cent a year (Mabe, 2003). It is predicted that the increase in research outputs will rise more steeply still as China increases its investment in research. Research funding in China tripled in the ten years from 1998 to 2008, and research output has been doubling every five years since 1980. Scholarly publishing will struggle to cope with this increase in outputs, and libraries already struggling to cope with the ever-rising cost of journals with be challenged even further.

There are concerns about the high cost of the subscription model for journals but many also consider it to be a barrier to equality, creativity and innovation. Thus over the past ten years there has been a growing demand for free to read open access models for journal articles. There are a number of approaches to making journal articles free to read, and many academic institutions have invested in institutional repositories (IRs) as a radical alternative to the traditional model. These repositories provide a mechanism for authors to self-archive their research outputs. However, filling institutional repositories with content can be problematic because, while researchers are highly incentivised to publish in high-ranking journals because of the associated prestige, there is little incentive to deposit papers in IRs. Nonetheless, the aims of IRs impose a longer-term threat to the subscription model, especially as a growing number of institutions are requiring their researchers to deposit all of their work in the local IRs.

The other route to open access is the author pays model, where researchers are funded to pay for the immediate open publication of their papers in journals. In areas such as biomedicine this model is proving successful, and fully open access publishers such as Public Library of Science (PLoS) are becoming financially viable.

> Five years after entering the publishing arena PLoS already had 13,000 peer-reviewers, 26,000 authors and millions of unique visitors.[1]

Perhaps more surprisingly is the marked change in the behaviours of some of the traditional journal publishers, who are beginning to experiment with open access models. Many of them now offer authors the option to pay for immediate open access on publication in their otherwise subscription journals (this is known as the hybrid open access model). More significantly, some traditional publishers are beginning to launch fully open access journals. For example, in early 2011 the Nature Publishing Group and Wiley-Blackwell announced that they are launching fully open access journals. In April 2011, representatives from institutions in the Sponsoring Consortium for Open Access Publishing in Particle Physics (SCOAP3), a global consortium of high-energy physics funding agencies, laboratories and international libraries met to progress an open access initiative. Leading publishers including the American Physical Society, Elsevier, the Institute of Physics and Springer attended and declared their intention to participate in a SCOAP3 tender aiming to convert to open access the high-quality peer-reviewed literature in the field. Funders of research are also pressing for accelerated change as evidenced by the announcement in June 2011[2] that the Howard Hughes Medical Institute, the Max Planck Society and the Wellcome Trust are to support a new, top-tier, open access journal for biomedical and life sciences research.

So, while the subscription model still dominates the marketplace, there are signs that a mixed economy is emerging, particularly in some discipline areas. New technologies are not only making the dissemination of scholarly material possible in new ways, for example through IRs, but are also changing the way in which researchers can use material. Now many researchers not only want to read journal articles but also to run programmes that will mine vast amounts of literature to discover previously latent connections or facts: such as the unrecognised relationship between one protein and another. This use of technology has the potential to provide for rapid innovation, but it is presenting a further challenge in the marketplace because, in order to enable data mining, publishers must expose their entire literature without authentication, and this has led some to argue that data mining is the most important driver for change to an open access model.

E-books

Most UK librarians say that they would like to license a critical mass of e-books at an affordable price and with access terms that are simple and easy to understand. In particular, they would like to provide students with those e-textbooks relevant to their studies, and see this as increasingly important as student expectations are likely to rise with the introduction of higher tuition fees. However, there is confusion and even disagreement about the best business models for the provision of e-books to libraries and in some cases publishers will not make available the e-books and in particular e-textbooks that librarians want, or at least not at an affordable price.

In 2007, JISC Collections undertook the e-Books Observatory Project[3] by licensing a collection of 36 e-books relevant to UK university students in four discipline areas and making the collection freely available across 150 higher education institutions in the UK. All students and staff in those institutions had unlimited access both on and off campus. The project surveyed 52,000 users asking them about their perceptions of e-books and studied users' actual behaviours by looking at the transactional logs of the e-book platform.

The survey results found that students and staff like the convenience of e-books, which allow them to fit work and study more easily into their busy lifestyles. Almost a third of the pages were viewed off campus and at all hours of the day and night. A more recent study, undertaken at the University of Liverpool, also found that:

> eBooks are overwhelmingly preferred in the areas that one would expect: accessibility, availability, currency, and the ability to transfer the information from the text. But where aesthetics are concerned, as in ease and pleasure of reading, print books were clearly favoured.[4]

When studying the actual behaviours of users (as opposed to their perceptions), the JISC Collections' study[5] found that e-books, rather than being read continuously, are used for quick fact extraction and brief viewing, as though they are encyclopedias and dictionaries. The more recent study at the University of Liverpool supports this finding:

> [Users] browsed titles within a certain discipline, but the preferred method for locating material was keyword search, the most direct and efficient method for finding information on a given topic. These findings support a key conclusion: a database of chapters is a highly effective means of acquiring content for a research institution.

The evidence suggests that users like e-books because they can access them whenever they want and wherever they are (rather as they can with Google). Users appear to treat collections of e-books as a huge database which they mine for the facts needed to answer their immediate questions (which again seems similar to the use of Google). If publishers and libraries are to be successful in the digital age, they must work together to ensure that paid 'closed-access' content is as accessible and as readily available as the 'free' content found through a Google search.

In order to protect their intellectual property, publishers of e-books have to put an authentication layer around their collections. This means that in order to use the e-books provided by their library, users need to authenticate via a password, and this can be a tedious barrier leading to frustration that can drive even the most dedicated library user to Google. Additionally, many publishers implement digital rights management systems which prevent the download or printing of e-books, leading to yet further frustration. As Wong (Wong et al., 2009) pointed out, users believe that the resources provided by Google and Google Scholar are reliable and relevant. It is no wonder then that if faced with barriers to accessing the e-books provided by the library users may instead turn to a Google search which provides a quick and good enough way of accessing information on a given subject. Publishers need to improve their platforms, to make authentication easier, to enable fast landing on the search results and most importantly to remove overly restrictive digital resource management. All publishers need to provide free MARC (machine readable cataloguing) records (or the next generation of bibliographic records) to libraries and to expose metadata to the search engines, because if users can see a search result through the library system or Google, they are more likely to be motivated to authenticate to get to it.

However, the technical issues pale into insignificance when compared to finding sustainable business models for the provision of e-books through the library. If publishing as we know it and libraries are to flourish in the digital age, finding such a model is essential and urgent. Some librarians and publishers propose that the 'Big Deal' (or bundled collection) for e-books is the way forward. The idea of libraries acquiring every book published by a particular publisher seems odd, and would be unlikely in a print environment, where librarians would build collections in anticipation of user need rather than publisher output. However, it is a model that has operated in the area of scholarly journals and analysis has demonstrated that the cost per use of e-books in bundled deals can demonstrate good value, even if not all of the titles have been used.

Other librarians argue that in the digital age, libraries should *not* pay for any titles that are not used, and that it no longer makes sense for libraries to build large and expensive 'just-in-case' collections. What makes more sense (particularly in a time of declining library budgets) is to respond to users' needs and eliminate waste by acquiring only the material (books or articles) that they need, through a Patron Driven Acquisitions (PDA) model. Most PDA models work on the basis that a view or number of views by users triggers the library purchase of the e-book. For example, 12 single page views, or one whole chapter view, or one cut and paste, convert the title to a library acquisition.

This leads to a number of problems for publisher and library alike. The publisher, in order to increase income and profitability, needs either to sell more e-books or increase the margin on a fewer number of e-books sold. The first option can be easier because the buyer gets a sense of value for money, even though some of the e-books they buy end up being wasted. The PDA can result in popular e-books having a higher price in order to subsidise those that that are not popular. The PDA model can also be problematic for libraries because, although it eliminates waste, there is a lack of control over budget and a lack of the predictability that comes with library-led collections building. Many experiments with PDA have resulted in the library spending the annual allocated budget too quickly and so having to put a stop to all e-book acquisition for the rest of the year. PDA could work and could provide the library user with access to the e-books they need, when they need them, but the model needs to be calibrated. A method is required to allow the library to control and cap overall costs. This will include control of titles by price limit, date of publication, subject categories and classification, and the library needs to be able to apply constraints when needed.

Mobile devices

A further challenge to publishers and libraries is the mobile device. Increasingly, library users have Kindles, iPads, smart phones and other mobile devices. As these become increasingly ubiquitous, it is likely that users will expect to be able to access e-books on their devices of choice, but it not clear how this will work in practice. Amazon has established a consumer market for e-books, making them easily available for download onto a range of mobile devices. Amazon.com[6] is now selling more Kindle e-books than paperback books. Since the beginning of 2011, for every 100 paperback books sold, the company has sold 115 Kindle books (Adams, 2011). Additionally, during this same time period the company has sold three times as many Kindle books as hardcover books. One reason for this success is that e-books are cheaper than their print counterparts. At the time of writing, the top selling e-book novel on Amazon costs £1 in e-book format as opposed to £8 in paperback format. The same is also true for textbooks. For example (at the time of writing), *Abnormal and Clinical Psychology: An Introductory Textbook* is available in e-book format at £17.37 as opposed to £35 in print format. However, there is no place for the library in this business model, which is firmly directed at individuals as customers. In the UK in February 2011, the publisher HarperCollins announced that new e-book titles licensed to public libraries can only be circulated 26 times before the licence expires (Hardo, 2011). The development has led to much anger among public librarians, who up until now have been able to lend any e-books as often as they like as they do with print copies.

The UK Publishers Association has just announced a clampdown, informing [public] libraries they may have to stop allowing users to download e-books remotely (arguably defeating the objective of an e-book) and instead require them to come to the library premises, just as they do to get traditional print books. The Publishers Association chief executive Richard Mollet said:

> Ultimately, the activities of selling and lending have to be able to co-exist with neither unduly harming the other. If e-book lending were untrammelled (as some comments seem to propose) it would pose an extremely potent threat to the retail market which in the long term would undermine the ability of authors, and the companies which invest in them, to see a reward for their creativity.[7]

The same issues apply in the world of academic libraries. In the UK the dominant business model for textbooks is based on student purchase. On the whole, publishers seem not to believe access, free at the point of use via the library, can coexist or complement the traditional student-purchase model, whether that purchase is a print book or an e-book for download onto a mobile device.

Scholarly monographs

Publishers are understandably reluctant to make some types of e-books and e-text books available via the library because they are fearful that to do so will kill traditional sales to the individual student. However, the scholarly monograph is a completely different type of publication, and one that is not doing well in its traditional markets where print sales are declining rapidly. One reason for this decline is the need for libraries to prioritise the increasing cost of journal subscriptions by cutting back on monograph acquisition. Between 1980 and 2000, a monograph's average library sales plummeted from around 2,000 copies in 1980, to 1,000 in the late 1980s, to 500 in the 1990s, to a little more than 200 in the early years of this century (Gardiner and Musto, 2004, cited in Willinsky, 2009). It would seem that the publishers of humanities and social science (HSS) monographs have been forced to increase the price of the print because of the dwindling hard copy sales. The impact on the scholarly environment is severe, with less research being published and disseminated.

> There is surely no point in institutions supporting huge costs of academic research if there is no means of distributing and accessing monographic content effectively. The current scholarly publishing process is completely illogical from an access point of view. Many academics spend years researching and writing a scholarly book, but then find themselves either without a publishing outlet or with relatively few sales, and commensurate low exposure for their research. (Steele, 2008)[8]

The sharing of knowledge is a critical value of scholarship as is reputation and prestige, both of which are reliant on wide dissemination of the academic monograph. Open access publishing is potentially a model that could simultaneously overcome the demise of the scholarly monograph publishing and increase the dissemination of knowledge in HSS. OAPEN

(Open Access Publishing in European Networks) is a collaborative initiative which aims to develop and implement a sustainable open access publication model for academic books in the HSS. The initiative is based on three fundamental principles:

- that research and dissemination of research results should not be separated but treated as essential elements in the scholarly communication process. We therefore recommend that research funding include the costs of dissemination;

- that academic institutes supporting Open Access should extend their policies to include OA publishing. In other words, they should promote not only OA archiving of existing publications (the 'green road'), but also OA publishing (the 'golden road'). In addition, funds for OA publications should be available for both articles and books;

- that academic publishers should develop OA publishing as a service to the scholarly community. This might be compared to the way many journal publishers grant authors the option of publishing their articles in Open Access within subscription-based journals.

Many scholars in the HSS see this newly developing form of publishing as an important contribution to their ambition to share their knowledge and research results with their peers and other potential readers, provided there is sufficient quality control (OAPEN, 2010).[9]

The position of publishers varies, as highlighted in the OAPEN Report on User Needs:

> Academic presses tend to favour both the development of eMonographs and Open Access, under the condition that a business model will arise that makes this practice feasible and economically viable. Commercial publishers are hesitant, pointing to the existence of a still substantial print market and a few outright refusals by some users in particular disciplines to switch to the digital. Other publishers have brought the present structure of the publishing industry into the discussion as well. They suggest a new role for publishers, as academic content providers and developers of services for the scholarly community in the different fields and disciplines, using the broad array of possibilities digital technology has to offer. None of them expects that the role of the publisher will disappear in a digital future, a position shared by the majority of

other actors in the field of scholarly communication. Organizing independent peer review and performing crucial editing functions remains necessary in the future.

OAPEN is a new initiative, but one which will be interesting to watch, both in terms of how it can help develop the business models that will support the publishing process, and in the impact and reach of the monograph which it makes openly available. Bloomsbury Academic is one publisher that is already experimenting with the model in a commercial way, making all of its publications openly available on the Internet under a Creative Commons Licence. Unlike open-access journals this publisher does not look for authors (or their research funders) to pay for the publishing process, but generates revenue through the sale of print books and e-book formats. This publisher is piloting the model to test if freely available content actually promotes sales and will generate a sustainable business model that supports research and scholarly communications.

Conclusion

'If it doesn't exist on Google, it doesn't exist at all' is an often-quoted phrase. Evidence that suggests most people, including researchers and students, begin their searches on Google supports this idea. In this digital environment the library and the scholarly content that is behind a pay wall is invisible and the role of scholarly publishers and libraries may seem irrelevant. In the case of scholarly journals, the technologies that libraries and publishers have jointly implemented have been successful in providing seamless access to journal articles behind the subscription pay wall for the academic users of a subscribing library. The downside is that academics may be oblivious to the fact that their library has paid a high and ever increasing cost for the articles they access online. In the case of e-books, technology is not so smoothly implemented and users may give up before they ever reach the e-books their library has managed to purchase. Scholarly monographs are still too often confined to print distribution – and thus really do not exist at all in the digital environment.

Despite all of these challenges, the business models employed in scholarly communications are still firmly rooted in the past. There are understandable reasons for this: the wish of journal publishers to maintain a lucrative model, and the fear of book publishers that their sales to the individual might be undermined if access to e-books can be gained through the library. The book publishers are also very aware of the

Internet, and in particular the way in which iTunes[10] has completely disrupted the model for the sale of music. However, there are signs of experimentation in some areas of publishing and some academic disciplines. This experimentation provides for new business models, and to ensure that content does exist on Google. If publishers and libraries do not undertake and develop such experiments, events may overtake them. New technologies can result in the creative destruction of a prior economic order, and in the case of scholarly publishing developments in technology may yet result in a more rapid change than has yet been envisaged.

Notes

1. The official PLoS Blog: *http://blogs.plos.org/plos/2009/06/announcing-the-first-plos-progress-report/*.
2. *http://www.wellcome.ac.uk/News/Media-office/Press-releases/2011/WTVM051897.htm*
3. *http://observatory.jiscebooks.org/*
4. University of Liverpool, Book Study Part 2 (2010) *A Survey of the e-Book Usage and Perceptions at the University of Liverpool.* Online at: *http://www.google.co.uk/url?sa=t&source=web&cd=1&ved=0CBsQFjAA&url=httpp%3A%2F%2Fwww.springer.com%2Fcda%2Fcontent%2Fdocument%2Fcda_downloaddocument%2FV7671%2BLiverpool%2BWhite%2BPaper%2BPart2.pdf%3FSGWID%3D0-0-45-1037538-0&ei=qDdiTrH_C42GhQeUgbGaCg&usg=AFQjCNFLo3FrFz6dIsmScxFfSPsB0RMBzA*.
5. *http://observatory.jiscebooks.org/*
6. *http://www.amazon.com/*
7. The Bookseller.com (2011): *http://www.thebookseller.com/news/pa-moves-calm-unease-over-e-book-lending.html*.
8. C. Steele (2008) 'Scholarly monograph publishing in the 21st century: the future more than ever should be an open book', *Journal of Electronic Publishing*, 11(2).
9. OAPEN Report (2010) 'Digital monographs in the humanities and social sciences: report on user needs'. Online at: *http://www.academia.edu/273623/Digital_Monographs_in_the_Humanities_and_Social_Sciences_Report_on_User_Needs*.
10. *http://www.apple.com/uk/iTunes*

References

Adams, R. (2011) 'Amazon's ebook sales eclipse paperbacks for the first time', *Guardian*, 28 January. Online at: *http://www.guardian.co.uk/world/richard-adams-blog/2011/jan/28/amazon-kindle-ebook-paperback-sales*.

Hardo, J. (2011) *HarperCollins Puts 26 Loan Cap on Ebook Circulations*, Library Journal Free E-Newsletters, Library Journal.com. Online at: *http://www.libraryjournal.com/lj/home/889452-264/harpercollins_puts_26_loan_cap.html.csp*.

Joint Information Systems Committee (JISC) National e-Books Observatory Project (2009) *Key Findings and Recommendations*. Online at: *http://www.jiscebooksproject.org/reports/finalreport*.

Mabe, M. (2003) 'The growth and number of journals', *Serials: The Journal for the Serials Community*, 16(2): 191–7.

Prosser, D.C. (2010) 'Reassessing the value proposition: first steps towards a fair(er) price for scholarly journals', *Serials: The Journal for the Serials Community*, 31(1), 60–3. Online at: *http://uksg.metapress.com/openurl.asp?genre=article&id=doi:10.1629/2460*.

Research Information Network (RIN) (2011) *E-journals: Their Use, Value and Impact – Phase Two Report*. Online at: *http://www.rin.ac.uk/system/files/attachments/Ejournals_part_II_for_screen_0.pdf*.

Willinsky, J. (2009) 'Towards the design of an open monograph press', *Journal of Electronic Publishing*, 12(1). Online at: *http://hdl.handle.net/2027/spo.3336451.0012.103*.

Wong, W., Stelmaszewska, H., Barn, B., Bhimani, N., Barn, S. and Wynne, B. (2009) *User Behaviour in Resource Discovery: Final Report*. Online at: *http://www.jisc.ac.uk/media/documents/publications/programme/2010/ubirdfinalreport.pdf*.

7

Resource discovery

Rachel Bruce and Andy McGregor

Abstract. What would you build if you could start from scratch? This was the question posed to the JISC and RLUK resource discovery taskforce. The taskforce consisted of a group of experts from libraries, museums and archives in the UK higher education sector bought together to discuss how we should work together to develop the UK infrastructure for resource discovery. Resource discovery has always been a challenging issue, but recently we have seen a revolution in user behaviour thanks to massive leaps forward in software and hardware technologies. This chapter starts with a discussion on the background and history of the resource discovery infrastructure in the UK and the broader context of the change in technology and user behaviour before describing how the resource discovery taskforce aims to develop UK infrastructure to meet those challenges. This is related to parallel efforts in other nations and similar initiatives with different types of content such as Europeana, Digital New Zealand, Culture Grid and the Learning Registry.

Keywords: Discovery, information landscape, JISC, Resource Discovery Taskforce

The resource discovery context for higher education

Making resources discoverable, whether books, journals or archives, has been a concern of librarians and information specialists for many years. The driver has been to ensure access to knowledge is maximised. With the move from analogue resources to digital resources and the ubiquity of the Web, it may seem trite to say that there are problems emerging that challenge traditional models of resource discovery, but at the same time there are opportunities whereby the requirements of learners, researchers and the public can be better met. The benefits for end users can be summarised as the ability to have access to resources anytime and anywhere; to be able to re-use and annotate easily; and to recombine and bring a rich range of resources together to meet a wide variety of needs that range from a general search to a specific research question.

The advent of the Web has resulted in a conundrum for libraries and archives with regard to their role and place within this expansive online environment. Should they compete with generic search engines or be part of the Web? Over the past decade, it has eventually become clear that library services need to work with the Web and search engines, thereby ensuring catalogues are indexed by Google and other search engines as a route to users, otherwise they will be left behind. There are opportunities to surface resources at what is termed the 'network level'; this phrase is applied to services that are shared above the organisation. For discovery of academic resources this might mean surfacing resources on the Web or it might mean working in such a way that large-scale sharing, interaction and use can take place. This could, for example, be focused on the creation of metadata descriptions for resources. Working at the 'network level' is about exploiting the benefits of the Web, so more people can use your resources and services and the information provider can, where it makes sense, remove duplication. The JISC (Joint Information Systems Committee) and SCONUL (Society of College, National and University Libraries) Library Management Systems Horizon Scan considered this issue in relation to library catalogues and summarised it as follows:

> Libraries can do much more to open up their catalogue metadata for re-use. Business enterprises (for example, OCLC and Talis[1]) already offer 'platforms' that enable library data to be re-used. OCLC's WorldCat,[2] for example, provides the default platform that enables the 'Find this book in a library' link from Google Scholar. This kind of approach begs the question of the necessity for 180 or so separate OPACs for UK HE alongside union catalogues such as M25 and COPAC. The costs of this duplication must be considerable. The appearance to the user searching globally must be infuriating.[3]

Prior to the developed understanding of working at the 'network level' there have been various initiatives concerned with shared content management and access services with the aim of maximum access. For some time, shared infrastructure to books, journals and archival collections has been provided, for example in some countries there have been national union catalogues. Within UK academia, a number of services have been developed and served as part of JISC's digital infrastructure, namely: COPAC[4] (the National Academic Specialist Library Catalogue), SUNCAT[5] (the Serials Union Catalogue), the Archives Hub[6] and ZETOC[7] (access to the British Library's table of contents). All of these services are developed and served in partnership with academic and research libraries and deal with books, journals and archival collections. It is worth noting that this is a subset of a wider array of discovery services that include multimedia resources, learning materials, mapping data and so on.

To set these developments in context and to demonstrate the long-held belief that shared access needs to be provided at a national level, some of the major developments over the past 50 years are set out in Table 7.1.

Table 7.1   Major developments since the 1960s

1961 The National Lending Library[1] was established in Boston Spa	600 tonnes of research materials are transported from London in 140 rail containers to form the basis of the collection.
1971 WorldCat begins	Online Computer Library Center (OCLC) member libraries begin contributing data from their collections to help create a worldwide library catalogue on the precursor to the Internet; this forms the start of WorldCat.[2]
1973 British Library Lending Division established[3]	The British Library is established by an Act of Parliament and the National Lending Library for Science and Technology (NLL) is merged with the National Central Library to become the British Library Lending Division (BLLD).
1991 WorldCat search opened up	OCLC allows patron searches of WorldCat, available only within public libraries.
1996 COPAC launches[4]	Launch of the Consortium of University Research Libraries (CURL) COPAC service in concert with JISC and Mimas.
1997 Google is developed[5]	The alpha version of Google launches
1999 Archives Hub is born[6]	The JISC Archives Hub service launches.
1999 JISC DNER/ Information Environment born[7]	The DNER (Distributed National Electronic Resource) is a managed information environment which provides secure and convenient access to a range of information services and resources. The Information Environment is the technical architecture of the DNER.

Table 7.1	Major developments since the 1960s (*cont'd*)
2000 OpenURL invented[8]	The work of Herbert Van de Sompel leads to the development of OpenURL.
2001 UKNUC feasibility study[9]	A review of the key issues that impinge on the creation of a National Union Catalogue, or Catalogues, for monographs, serials and other formats for the UK.
2001 British Library (BL) Public Catalogue launched[10]	British Library Public Catalogue goes live and provides simple, free access to over 10 million books, journals, reports, conferences and music scores.
2001 ZETOC launched[11]	Mimas launches the ZETOC database, funded jointly by JISC and the BL. It makes bibliographic records for 20,000 of the BL's most popular research journals available to UK higher education.
2003 SUNCAT project[12]	The JISC project to develop a union catalogue of serials. This was recommended by the UK National Union Catalogue (UKNUC) feasibility study. The project was preceded by a scoping study and moved to service in 2005.
2004 OpenURL Router launches[13]	The JISC-sponsored OpenURL router service administered by the United Kingdom Office for Library and Information Networking (UKOLN) and EDINA launches.
2004 Search engines crawl WorldCat[14]	Web users gain home access to WorldCat through Internet search engines run by Google, Yahoo and Microsoft.
2004 Google Scholar is born[15]	Google Scholar launches.
2005 The JISC Resource Discovery Landscape[16]	A personal reflection on the JISC Information Environment and related activities by Andy Powell of UKOLN. This document provides an opinion piece, looking at the way resource discovery technologies and services are being deployed across the UK HE/FE community. It considers some of the issues being raised by the JISC IE technical architecture, by our current approaches to technologies within that space and by the external trends we see happening around us.
2007 Researchers Use of Academic Libraries and their Services[17]	This study was designed to provide an up-to-date and forward-looking view of how researchers interact with academic libraries in the UK. Harnessing empirical data and qualitative insights from over 2,250 researchers and 300 librarians, the Research Information Network and CURL hope that the results will be useful in informing the debate about the future development of academic libraries and the services they provide to researchers.

Table 7.1	Major developments since the 1960s (*cont'd*)
2008 UK Research Reserve project starts[18]	The UK Research Reserve is an agreement between higher education and the British Library whereby the BL will store journals no longer required by HE libraries, retain them permanently and make them accessible to researchers and others who wish to consult them.
2008 Google Generation[19]	The report, commissioned by JISC and the British Library, counters the common assumption that the Google Generation – young people born or brought up in the Internet age – is the most adept at using the Web. The report by the Centre for Information Behaviour and the Evaluation of Research (CIBER) research team at University College London claims that, although young people demonstrate an ease and familiarity with computers, they rely on the most basic search tools and do not possess the critical and analytical skills to assess the information that they find on the Web.
2009 Creating catalogues: bibliographic records in a digital world[20]	The Research Information Network released a report that mapped the arrangements through which bibliographic records are created and recommended how complexity could be reduced and whether services could be improved through better coordination of effort.

1. *http://www.bl.uk/reshelp/atyourdesk/docsupply/about/history/index.html*
2. *http://www.bizjournals.com/columbus/stories/2008/03/24/story10.html*
3. *http://www.bl.uk/reshelp/atyourdesk/docsupply/about/history/index.html*
4. *http://web.archive.org/web/19990220213054/www.copac.ac.uk/copac/*
5. *http://web.archive.org/web/19990125084553/alpha.google.com/*
6. *http://web.archive.org/web/20001021120157/http://www.archiveshub.ac.uk/*
7. *http://www.ariadne.ac.uk/issue26/dner/*
8. *http://www.dlib.org/dlib/march01/vandesompel/03vandesompel.html*
9. *http://www.lib.gla.ac.uk/Research/uknuc.shtml*
10. *http://catalogue.bl.uk*
11. *http://web.archive.org/web/200101190321/http://zetoc.mimas.ac.uk/*
12. *http://www.jisc.ac.uk/whatwedo/programmes/dlip/suncat.aspx*
13. *http://openurl.ac.uk/doc/*
14. *http://www.bizjournals.com/columbus/stories/2008/03/24/story10.html*
15. *http://scholar.google.com/*
16. *http://www.ukoln.ac.uk/distributed-systems/jisc-ie/arch/resource-discovery-review/*
17. *http://www.rin.ac.uk/our-work/using-and-accessing-information-resources/ researchers-use-academic-libraries-and-their-serv*
18. *http://www.rluk.ac.uk/node/85*
19. *http://www.jisc.ac.uk/news/stories/2008/01/googlegen.aspx*
20. *http://rinarchive.jisc-collections.ac.uk/our-work/using-and-accessing-information- resources/creating-catalogues-bibliographic-records-network*

The timeline in Table 7.1 is not comprehensive and has a UK flavour but it shows some of the major steps that have been taken to deal with the resource discovery issue and the range of material and resource discovery services at a shared level. Over the past five or so years understanding the place of services like COPAC and SUNCAT in the resource discovery landscape and how they should be provided has been a source of deliberation and debate. Throughout this, changes in user behaviour have taken place driven by the user preference for search engines such as Google and the development of Web 2.0 where users expect to have resources in more useable and tailored services on the Web. Responding to this and technical change has been a challenge, not one driven by the vanity of the information provider but by their concern to ensure learners and researchers have access to the 'quality' resources required to underpin scholarship. Lynn Silipigni-Connaway from OCLC undertook research[8] examining user requirements and her conclusions nicely summarise the issues that library services now face in meeting user expectations:

- Patience v. want it now
- Meta-search v. full text
- Complexity v. simplicity
- Logical linear learning v. multi-tasking
- Largely text-based v. multimedia
- Learning from expert v. figure it out yourself

At the same time, user environments have evolved and learning and research takes place on the Web and in online environments that cater for specific needs, for example virtual research or learning environments. Users no longer expect to visit the library or archival catalogue separately but to have it available as part of an integrated experience. This requirement also points to the need to break down silos of information; it is not always appropriate to have to go from a library service to an archival service for example, but rather to be able to access these resources together within the environments that are part of the user's workflow.

The UK shared services, COPAC, SUNCAT, Archives Hub and ZETOC, all have to adjust to this environment, but at the same time such national services have limited resources. In order to inform decisions on the direction that might be taken it is useful to look at how other similar services around the world[9] have evolved to deal with these issues. Three examples that show the sorts of trends and options that can be taken are: Libraries Australia,[10] LIBRIS[11] (the Swedish national union catalogue and related services) and Digital New Zealand.[12] Their strategies are centred around ease of use to meet the requirements of the twenty-first-century information seeker, for example ensuring there is a strong link between finding an item and getting access to that item, so wherever possible access to the full text is offered or users are presented with other options where they can get the item, such as Amazon[13] or Google Books.[14] In the case of Libraries Australia users are able to annotate and collaborate to add context to resources via tagging or reviews taking advantage of user trends in creation and similar to other well used web services such as Flickr.[15] Each of these services seeks to surface resources in other environments through plug-in search boxes, news feeds,[16] via indexing in Google and participation in the WorldCat database or by ensuring they are optimised for mobile interfaces. All three services include resources beyond the union catalogue, for example access to multimedia and image collections. Another trend is to expose the data held in the services. This might be via standard interfaces such as OAI-PMH[17] and z39.50[18] but in the case of LIBRIS the data has been made available as Linked Data.[19] These approaches allow data to be re-used by other services and presented to users in multiple ways. Another approach exemplified in Digital New Zealand is that of iterative and agile development of services, where the service code is developed in 'short sprints' and in consultation with users so the service can adapt quickly and learn what works and what doesn't. It is true to say that the UK services referred to are also adopting similar approaches; for example, the Archives Hub and COPAC have made their data available as Linked Data and all of the services expose data via different protocols to enable re-use and integration into other services. The use of Linked Data is an innovative step and the exact benefits will emerge downstream, but by taking these steps, such services are ensuring they are 'of the Web' and new links and services are possible.

Building on this trend to expose data is the move towards 'open data'. This movement has covered many data types, and in terms of this discussion its application to bibliographic data is relevant. Changing the business and rights models around bibliographic data is believed by many to be more effective and efficient than current models. A number of libraries and services, such as the British Library,[20] the CERN Library[21] and Bibliosnet,[22] are treating bibliographic data as open as it is seen as something often created via the public purse and as an accumulation of facts about books, journals and so on. The case is often made that you might make content available as open access but without open metadata/bibliographic data that resource cannot be easily discovered and found. The recent decision by the British Library to make an extensive collection (14 million records) of metadata available this way is a significant move and means the library makes no claim to copyright in the data and does not apply restrictions on its re-use. The CERN Library records are free to use by any third party and they are provided under the Public Domain Data License[23] that permits liberal use of the data. Jens Vigen, head of the CERN Library, said in the news release when the CERN open records were announced:

> Books should only be catalogued once. Currently the public purse pays for having the same book catalogued over and over again. Librarians should act as they preach: data sets created through public funding should be made freely available to anyone interested. Open Access is natural for us, here at CERN we believe in openness and reuse. There is a tremendous potential. By getting academic libraries world wide involved in this movement, it will lead to a natural atmosphere of sharing and reusing bibliographic data in a rich landscape of so-called mash-up services, where most of the actors who will be involved, both among the users and the providers, will not even be library users or librarians.[24]

The Resource Discovery Taskforce

Collaboration

This complex and shifting resource discovery environment poses problems for researchers and teachers, for information professionals and for those who provide resource discovery services. So it is no surprise that in 2009 JISC and Research Libraries UK (RLUK) independently resolved to act to explore possible ways to address the challenges faced by people seeking to discover resources and by people seeking to enable the discovery of resources. Once JISC and RLUK discovered that both were committed to finding solutions they decided to pool their efforts and work on one joint initiative. After some discussions both organisations felt that what was required was a series of meetings that would bring together experts in resource discovery, give them a clear remit and focus on delivering a vision for ways to improve resource discovery for UK higher education.

JISC and RLUK agreed that the scope for the discussions needed to focus on libraries, archives and museums as they faced similar resource discovery challenges and offered similar services for research and education. JISC and RLUK are both UK higher education organisations so this dictated the scope of the initiative. However, if you look at the big picture this scope is fairly limited. The boundaries were imposed by the nature of the two sponsoring organisations but researchers and teachers do not share those boundaries; they need all sorts of different content from other countries and from other sectors. So JISC and RLUK determined to attempt to transcend the imposed boundaries wherever possible by monitoring and working with developments in other sectors and other countries and by ensuring that any solutions proposed would work with other types of content. So, the initiative had a broad structure, it had an outline scope and it had a desired output. Now it needed a name. JISC and RLUK decided to call it the Resource Discovery Taskforce.

Taskforce

The taskforce ran for a year and in 2010 delivered a vision for JISC, RLUK and partners to implement. The success in delivering the vision was due to a small number of crucial elements:

- *A strong chair*. We were fortunate that David Baker agreed to chair the taskforce. He kept the meetings on track, ensured everyone was heard and maintained the focus on the desired outputs.

- *A committed and expert membership*. The core members of the taskforce were committed to addressing the resource discovery challenges that the sector faced. They came from a range of institutions and roles and brought a real depth of experience and expertise to the discussions. The members were generous with their time with most attending all the meetings and some taking on tasks in between meetings. As well as the core membership, guests were invited to each meeting to represent different viewpoints.

- *Sufficient time*. We decided on a structure of four meetings spread over a year. This gave us the luxury of time to explore issues in detail and produce outputs that all taskforce members were happy with. This time was especially important in ensuring we got the scope right.

- *Clear inputs and outputs*. We put a lot of work into each meeting. Each meeting had a range of inputs taking the form of reports, presentations from guests and visions of the future from influential people.

We were clear from the start that the purpose of the meetings was to produce a vision.

JISC kept a blog about the taskforce that recorded all the meetings, all the decisions over scope and membership and all the documents that served as inputs and outputs for each meeting.[25]

Conflict

Throughout the taskforce meetings the discussions were lively and occasionally crept up to what can only be described as heated. The meetings were full of rich discussions, frank assessments and exciting ideas, but it would not be unfair to sum up the discussions in one sentence. There was complete disagreement over what resource discovery services were required and complete agreement that, no matter what services were required, addressing the issue of metadata had to be the number one priority. This agreement over metadata dictated the focus of the vision that the taskforce was set up to deliver.

Vision

The vision[26] that resulted from the taskforce is essentially very simple. It can be summarised as three steps:

1. Make open metadata available using common formats.

2. Create aggregations of metadata wherever it would be helpful.

3. Use that open metadata to build or improve services that researchers, students, teachers and information professionals can use to do their work more effectively.

This process is illustrated in Figure 7.1.

The vision sets out a broad approach, some implementation guidelines and some targets. It is possible to argue that what the vision excludes is as influential as what it includes. The vision does not set out a clear technical architecture. The vision does not dictate specific tools or standards. The vision does not attempt to imagine the future. These three omissions are intentional. The vision has short timescales and this dictates a practical approach. The resource discovery landscape covers a variety of content types, a wealth of standards and a plethora of software tools. Expecting an elegant and comprehensive technical architecture is impractical, convening around one standard is impractical and developing services that

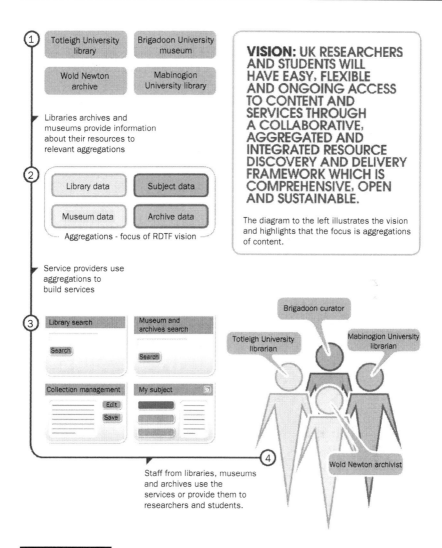

Figure 7.1 The Resource Discovery Taskforce vision

need to be coupled closely to institutional software is impractical. The vision is high level to allow the implementation to address these problems by including a variety of technical approaches and by encouraging the development of solutions that are, as far as possible, agnostic about the standards and tools used by libraries, archives and museums in higher education. This allows the implementation to explore approaches like linked data without committing exclusively to that as the solution.

Consensus

Perhaps the most important element of the vision is that all the members who attended the meetings agreed to add their names as signatories to the vision. This is important, as it represents a consensus between many institutions on a course of action. The support of these people has been incredibly useful in our attempts to implement the vision. Of course, there is still a long way to go but having this support should make it easier to progress. The level of support and involvement in implementing the vision has increased since the publication of the vision with partners such as Collections Trust, EDINA, Eduserv and Mimas involved in steering the implementation.

We have recently sought to expand this even further by producing a set of principles on open metadata and encouraging people to sign up to them.[27] We currently have 30 signatories from a wide range of institutions and we expect this to grow.[28] We are actively seeking further signatories and are keen to hear from anyone who is working with open metadata and is interested in lending their support to the principles. Working with this wide range of people means we have a greater chance of realising the vision and of improving resource discovery for research and education.

Implementation

The vision is ambitious. It focuses on high-level aims that should be realised by the end of 2012. Implementation of the vision is a challenging exercise. To meet this challenge JISC has funded the Discovery programme.[29] A programme is a collection of projects designed to realise a common set of goals. JISC has designed this programme in conjunction with RLUK and other partners and it includes a wide range of work projects each focused on a specific element of the vision. As the programme is broad and varied, it needs a coherent view of all the work that can make it easy for people to see what is happening and to disseminate the useful information and tools produced by the projects. This role is filled by the Discovery website.[30] The site has been established to advocate successful approaches to resource discovery identified by the programme and to ensure that libraries, archives and museums benefit from the investment in Discovery by getting access to the guidance and tools that are developed.

To be able to provide this advocacy and guidance the Discovery programme needs to investigate the key issues that stand in the way of implementing the vision. These include licensing, the business case for open approaches to metadata and technical issues. These investigations have produced a number of useful tools:

- a guide to the implications of open bibliographic data for libraries;[31]

- a discussion of the metadata challenges[32] – this discussion is continuing to develop and the first output of that discussion is a set of draft technical principles;[33]

- a set of open metadata principles to guide the Discovery work[34] – these principles are accompanied by a practical guide to licensing;[35]

- case studies and guides that summarise completed projects and provide guidance on various essential areas – a number are available from the Discovery website[36] with further case studies becoming available from the website in the second half of 2012.

As well as these investigations of key issues we need practical experiments and the development of key tools and services to realise the vision. In the first phase of the implementation, JISC has funded projects that experiment with making open metadata available from libraries, archives and museums and EDINA and Mimas have developed their existing services to make them more open and enhance functionality.[37] Full details of these developments are summarised on the Discovery site[38] but the headline achievements are:

- Cambridge University Library, Lincoln University Library, the Fitzwilliam Museum, the Oxford Text Archive, the Mass Observation Archive, York University and Archives in London and the M25 Consortium have all released open metadata. Each project has also shared lessons on licensing and some have developed tools to help other institutions deal with open and linked data. These lessons and tools are summarised on the Discovery site.[39]

- Mimas has developed a prototype collections management tool for libraries.[40]

- Open linked data is available from SUNCAT and GoGeo.[41]

Perhaps the most important element of the Discovery programme is ensuring that the many people with a stake in resource discovery in libraries, museums and archives are engaged in the project. JISC has been careful to ensure this task is addressed thoroughly by dedicating an entire project to it. This project is charged with engaging with librarians, archivists, curators, vendors, publishers and researchers to understand what they need and how they can help to implement the vision.

The future

Phase 2 of the discovery programme started during September 2011. This phase of work is building on what has been done so far and is starting to move more into developing services for researchers and teachers as well as for librarians, archivists and curators. JISC will continue to fund the Discovery website and the investigative and stakeholder engagement work. In addition, JISC has funded:

- further projects focusing on the release of open metadata about collections essential to teaching and research;
- projects to develop services to address the challenges and needs identified in phase 1 of the implementation;
- exemplar resources on the First World War and Shakespeare that address the needs of researchers and teachers and demonstrate the power and value of open metadata.

These projects are summarised on the JISC website.[42]

The third and final phase of the implementation will begin in the summer of 2012. By that time we hope to be able to glimpse the edges of the resource discovery taskforce vision and to be able to give librarians, archivists and curators the power to offer more effective services to researchers and teachers.

Conclusion

Clearly there has been a significant shift in the resource discovery landscape, one which we would classify as a move from 'service orientated' to 'resource orientated'. What this means is that data and information are key and may be regarded as the way to support a number of different use cases and can be made available so a variety of services can be developed. That is not to say that there are no service-driven requirements – there are. But based on the past 15 years of experience it seems the best way to ensure resources are accessed and used is to make those resources re-useable in a granular way so they can be surfaced via many routes.

This chapter has focused mainly on a sub-set of resource types (library, archive and museum resources), and a more comprehensive and rich resource discovery infrastructure will include research data, reference data sets, open educational resources, multimedia content and more. A resource-orientated approach can be applied across all types of resources and holds promise for supporting an experience that is not hindered by silos of different resource types. However, the socio-technical infrastructure around different resource types is at different states of maturity so how far this completely flexible experience can be supported is not yet proven; for example, research data is nudging its way to become a first-class research output, just as important, or more so, than a research paper. However, research data is complex, so the availability of it and the standards and practice are yet to mature. Other barriers still stand in the way of maximum re-use, for example business models and appropriate licensing; these have shifted, as shown by the work under the Resource Discovery Taskforce and also Europeana, where data is being made available under CC-0.[43] But there is not as yet a wholesale move in this direction.

Resource discovery is only one of many central issues that 'digital libraries' need to support. In order to be complete they also have to deal with curation and management, and it is interesting to see that the resource-orientated, or what might be called a 'data-driven' approach, is applicable in those areas too. For example, recently the JISC, working with SCONUL, has started to implement the Knowledge Base Plus; this is about ensuring there is improved information about the access and licensing of electronic resources so libraries can better manage access and make decisions about collections. The Knowledge Base Plus is built on a foundation of openly available information that is gathered from a number of places. The project states:

> KB+ intends to put in place a foundation of accurate, authoritative, timely, relevant and structured information in support of e-resource management for UK academic institutions.
>
> In addition it will provide tools to aid the analysis, communication, processes and management of e-resources.
>
> All of this will be made available to new and existing service providers, both commercial and open source, as well as other services provided by and for teaching, learning and research globally.[44]

This is not solely a UK-based view. The Andrew W. Mellon Foundation[45] in the USA has also started to look at similar solutions, and there is potential for the data to be shared between the UK and USA.

Resource discovery is global. We can see that by the dominance of Google. Of course there are local needs that must be served; however, it is important that we work within a global context not only so we can learn from each other but also because this can lead to less duplication and further potential for economies of scale and the meeting of research and learning needs. In this context, it will be interesting to see what choices the Digital Public Library of America[46] makes, and it will be important to share our lessons so good practice across borders emerges.

We are beginning to see some really interesting ways to bring a rich array of resources together to meet emerging user needs based on approaches such as Linked Data. Again, this is not fully proven but there is a momentum behind this approach and key shared vocabularies that can link resources across the Web are coming to the fore, for example Friend of a Friend (FOAF).[47] This is part of the move towards resource discovery for research and academic resources being more 'of the Web' than 'on the Web'. 'Of the Web' is a term used to describe tactics used to ensure digital resources and related services are more integrated into the web architecture and experience. Earlier we mentioned LIBRIS, the Swedish union catalogue, and this is precisely what they have done by making the catalogue available as Linked Data, and as part of this they have not used traditional library vocabularies but opted for web-based ones such as FOAF.

Other significant developments need to be accounted for in developing effective resource discovery, one example being that of aggregating activity and usage data and using this to enhance services and user experiences. At JISC we have been investigating this development and it shows promise. A good example is the experimental addition of recommendations to the COPAC interface by mining the circulation data from the John Rylands Library at the University of Manchester.[48] By collecting usage and activity data additional context is available around digital resources. This can help to support personalisation and address what Clay Shirky called 'filter failure',[49] thereby helping to push relevant resources to the right services and users and helping users to pull the resources they will find most relevant to them.

So what is beyond 2012? For the Resource Discovery Taskforce supporting the adoption of the approaches developed during the programme will be essential, but it is also critical that we keep abreast and take advantage of new developments. The digital environment is not static and resource discovery services must be agile in order to respond. A key lesson that has emerged when considering the academic resource discovery infrastructure that JISC provides in the context of the new directions is that we can perhaps split the roles in the provision of resource discovery between 'service providers' and 'data providers'. Data providers do not have to provide services and, likewise, service providers do not have to be data providers. Libraries, archives, museums and infrastructure providers do not have to do everything: when participating in the provision of resource discovery they should choose what they do well and focus on that. The critical aspect to a responsive resource discovery infrastructure is about a commitment to making data (descriptions and content) available in ways that it can be re-used by many.

If you are interested in following the work of the Discovery programme, we recommend you visit the Discovery website and sign up to the regular newsletter.[50]

Notes

1. *http://www.talis.com/*
2. *http://www.worldcat.org/*
3. *http://www.jisc.ac.uk/media/documents/programmes/resourcediscovery/lmsstudy.pdf*
4. *http://copac.ac.uk/*
5. *http://www.suncat.ac.uk/*
6. *http://archiveshub.ac.uk/*
7. *http://zetoc.mimas.ac.uk/*
8. *http://www.oclc.org/research/activities/past/orprojects/imls/default.htm*
9. *http://rdtf.jiscinvolve.org/wp/files/2009/09/jisc-resource-discovery-report-final-20090908.pdf*
10. *http://librariesaustralia.nla.gov.au/*
11. *http://libris.kb.se/?language=en*
12. *http://www.digitalnz.org/*
13. *http://www.amazon.co.uk*
14. *http://books.google.com/*
15. *http://www.flickr.com/*
16. *http://en.wikipedia.org/wiki/RSS*
17. *http://www.openarchives.org/OAI/openarchivesprotocol.html*
18. *http://www.loc.gov/z3950/agency/*
19. *http://www.w3.org/DesignIssues/LinkedData.html*
20. *www.bl.uk/bibliographic/datafree.html*
21. *http://library.web.cern.ch/library/Library/Welcome.html*
22. *http://biblios.net/*
23. *http://opendatacommons.org/licenses/pddl/*
24. *http://newsbreaks.infotoday.com/Digest/CERN-Library-Publishes-Its-Book-Catalog-as-Open-Data-60894.asp*

25. *http://rdtf.jiscinvolve.org/*
26. *http://discovery.ac.uk/vision/*
27. *http://discovery.ac.uk/businesscase/principles/*
28. *http://discovery.ac.uk/businesscase/signatories/*
29. *http://www.jisc.ac.uk/whatwedo/programmes/di_informationandlibraries/resourcediscovery.aspx*
30. *http://discovery.ac.uk/*
31. *http://obd.jisc.ac.uk/*
32. *http://rdtfmetadata.jiscpress.org/*
33. *http://technicalfoundations.ukoln.info/guidance/technical-guidelines-discovery-ecosystem*
34. *http://discovery.ac.uk/businesscase/principles/*
35. *http://discovery.ac.uk/files/pdf/Licensing_Open_Data_A_Practical_Guide.pdf*
36. *http://discovery.ac.uk/projects/*
37. *http://www.jisc.ac.uk/whatwedo/programmes/inf11/infrastructurefor resourcediscovery.aspx*
38. *http://discovery.ac.uk/projects*
39. *http://discovery.ac.uk/projects*
40. *http://mimas.ac.uk/news/2011/07/copac-cmtool/*
41. *http://edina.ac.uk/projects/gold_summary.html*
42. *http://www.jisc.ac.uk/whatwedo/programmes/di_informationandlibraries/resourcediscovery/Phase2.aspx*
43. *http://pro.europeana.eu/web/europeana-project/newagreement*
44. *http://www.jisc.ac.uk/whatwedo/programmes/di_informationandlibraries/emergingopportunities/kbplus.aspx*
45. *http://www.mellon.org/*
46. *http://cyber.law.harvard.edu/dpla/Main_Page*
47. *http://www.foaf-project.org/*
48. *http://salt11.wordpress.com/2011/08/01/final-blog-post/*
49. *http://www.web2expo.com/webexny2008/public/schedule/detail/4817*
50. *http://discovery.ac.uk/news/*

8

Using the Mirrorworld to plan and build better futures for our citizens

Ian Everall and Terrence Fernando

Abstract. The University of Salford THINKlab is a futuristic and spacious research environment with state-of-the-art facilities located within the University of Salford in Greater Manchester. It has an established international reputation in the creative use and application of cutting-edge technologies to provide innovative solutions to meet the needs of industry, commerce and community. Over the last few years, the THINKlab has worked with partners in the public and private sector to develop a dynamic new 3-D Mirrorworld platform capable of creating new interpretations and understandings of local communities. This has started to provide new ways for local public sector stakeholders and decision-makers to engage communities to help communicate the vision for a local area, show how plans for local regeneration and transformation may deliver economic and social benefits for neighbourhood communities and build stronger sustainable futures for citizens and their communities.

This chapter gives an overview of the Mirrorworld platform development over the last few years. It introduces some of the case study work that has helped to shape its present functionality and looks ahead at some of the current challenges driving public sector reform and regeneration which increasingly require smarter, more joined up solutions to deliver benefits for local citizens and businesses.

Keywords: commerce, communities, industry, Mirrorworld platform, regeneration, research, Salford, state-of-the-art, THINKlab

Introduction

The University of Salford THINKlab[1] is a futuristic and spacious research environment with state-of-the-art facilities located within the University of Salford in Greater Manchester. It has an established international reputation in the creative use and application of cutting-edge technologies to provide innovative solutions to meet the needs of industry, commerce and the community. Over the last few years, the THINKlab has worked with partners in the public and private sector to develop a dynamic new 3-D Mirrorworld platform capable of creating new interpretations and understandings of local communities. This has started to provide new ways for local public-sector stakeholders and decision-makers to engage communities to help communicate the vision for a local area, show how plans for local regeneration and transformation may deliver economic and social benefits for neighbourhood communities and build stronger sustainable futures for citizens and their communities.

The Mirrorworld platform is emerging as a joint insight tool that can help local partnerships create a better, more joined-up view of local needs to inform joint planning and shared service delivery. This chapter gives an overview of the Mirrorworld platform development over the last few years. It introduces some of the case study work that has helped to shape its present functionality and looks ahead to some of the current challenges driving public-sector reform and regeneration which increasingly require smarter, more joined-up solutions to deliver benefits for local citizens and businesses.

Developing the Mirrorworld – first steps

The genesis of the Salford Mirrorworld platform has its origins in an Engineering and Physical Sciences Research Council (EPSRC)[2] funded programme in 2003 for the VivaCity2020 project, a consortium within the Sustainable Urban Environment Programme.[3] This provided funding for a five-year programme of research to develop an in-depth understanding of human behaviour in urban environments and to create new practical resources to support urban design professionals with sustainable decision-making.

The VivaCity2020 consortium produced a large and comprehensive Toolkit for a wide range of users concerned with urban design decision-making and city planning. The tools and resources support sustainable and socially responsible urban design decision-making.[4] Part of this Toolkit was a new 3-D visualisation tool developed by the authors, which aimed to support the urban regeneration process by creating new ways of envisioning urban planning and the regeneration of local areas, which could be used to facilitate engagement, consultation and communication with a diversity of stakeholder groups, including local citizens. This tool was subsequently applied as a case study within a real-world urban regeneration setting in the Black Country, supported by the EU CoSpaces programme,[5] a project funded by the European Commission supporting innovative collaborative workspaces for individuals and project teams. This led to the development of an initial Mirrorworld platform prototype.

Black Country case study

The Black Country is a sub-region of the West Midlands in the UK and includes the Boroughs of Dudley, Sandwell and Walsall and the City of Wolverhampton and has a combined population of 1.1 million people. During the last 30 years, the Black Country has suffered a process of decline in many aspects. In 2006, the Black Country was one of only three sub-regions in the UK experiencing net population decline. Since 1990, population had fallen by over 20,000 and net out-migration had approached 4,000 people per annum. Although the area has much social and economic strength, the local economy performed poorly compared to similar sized sub-regions elsewhere in the UK. While it still retained a strong manufacturing sector supporting 22 per cent of total employment, the sub-region had failed to sufficiently attract the new knowledge-based industries that are driving economic growth elsewhere in the UK. The poor quality of the urban environment undermined efforts to attract knowledge industries and their employees to the area.

In order to consider radical change in the sub-region to counter the process of decline over the last 30 years, the Black Country Study had been set up by the Black Country's political and business leaders. The Study aimed to address major spatial challenges in the Black Country and had a number of key aims that included reversing the trend of people leaving the sub-region, raising income levels, attracting and retaining people with higher-level skills and protecting and enhancing the environment. The Study was led by the Black Country Consortium[6] on behalf of the West Midlands Regional Assembly.

The initial aim of the visualisation project was to create a unique spatial reference framework for the Black Country to inform this planning and regeneration process. The University of Salford THINKLab oversaw the creation of the prototype Mirrorworld Black Country platform and provided the research lead. Ordnance Survey (OS)[7] became a partner in the project and provided base mapping data to populate the model. The Black Country Consortium, the sub-regional partnership for the area, provided the regeneration context for the creation of the model. A number of virtual reality (VR) models were also provided by the University of Wolverhampton and enhanced by bespoke VR models commissioned to support an application to the National Lottery Living Landmark's Fund[8] and to support an urban regeneration plan for the Brierley Hill Waterfront and surrounding High Street Area.

What emerged from this collaboration was a new prototype Mirrorworld platform that provided for the first time an interactive immersive 3-D environment for the Black Country. Figure 8.1 shows a helicopter view of the Black Country sub-region. Figure 8.2 shows a more detailed 3-D visualisation of the Brierley Hill area illustrating some of the Action Planning proposals showing how the area may develop over the next 10–15 years.

The Black Country platform integrated OS Mastermap data, terrain data such as aerial photography and light detection and ranging (LIDAR)[9] data, building model footprint and height data, and stereo and oblique imagery. This provided the data for the base platform and

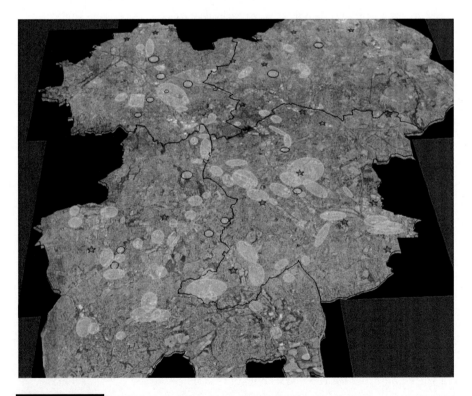

Figure 8.1   Helicopter view of the virtual Black Country

Figure 8.2   Visualisation of Brierley Hill Regeneration Area

enabled the creation of 2½-D models on the fly (without texture) of any building in the Black Country area. The integration of more detailed VR models built to scale, as for example Brierley Hill, enriched the environment considerably and in the hands of a local expert enabled the story of regeneration to be told in a new, more interactive way.

The Black Country platform was subsequently used by the Brierley Hill Regeneration Partnership in local meetings with residents to communicate its vision for the local area, to show how development over the next ten years would help bring skills and job opportunities to the locality, to stimulate debate and to capture feedback to inform the Area Action Planning process. The Regeneration Partnership also presented the Black Country Mirrorworld platform at the annual property developers' conference in Cannes to raise awareness of local plans and encourage inward investment. In addition the Black Country Consortium presented the Mirrorworld platform at its Annual General Meeting in

2007, attended by Black Country leaders and chief executives, in support of its ambitions developed in the Black Country Study, and also used it proactively as a presentation tool in its bid to win significant lottery funding for its ambitions for the Black Country as an Urban Park.

Overall, the initial prototype demonstrated that the platform had great potential to develop as a tool to support the urban planning and regeneration process. In terms of strengths, it clearly demonstrated a novel way of engaging a diversity of audiences from professional stakeholder groups to local communities. In the hands of a local expert it helped to communicate and bring local plans to life and its immersive nature encouraged feedback and debate from participants. It also provided a joint platform to engage diverse stakeholder groups in creating a common vision for a local area and promote collaborative working. The Black Country Mirrorworld also contributed practical support in helping to communicate some of the major regeneration plans and agendas for the sub-region at a challenging time in its history.

The main focus of research in the Black Country had been to understand how the Mirrorworld platform could be used as a tool to visualise and communicate plans for the physical regeneration of areas of the sub-region. However, the technical capability of the Mirrorworld platform to integrate and visualise massive and scattered datasets drawn from local, regional and national government sources meant that it also had great potential to provide a much richer environment to support a wide range of public-sector planning and transformation programmes. This was particularly relevant to the situation where there was a strong collaborative need among local and regional stakeholders to find joined-up solutions to address local needs. A number of these areas are now being explored in more detail as part of the process of creating a Mirrorworld platform for the City of Salford, home of the University of Salford THINKlab, to showcase what the technology is capable of.

Salford Mirrorworld

The City of Salford is a city and metropolitan borough of Greater Manchester and has a population of 219,000 people. The city sits at the heart of the Greater Manchester city region, which in economic terms is the largest city region outside London and accounts for half of the North West's total economic output. Salford makes a significant contribution to the city region's overall economic success. Its location at the hub of motorway and rail networks provides links to the other strong city regions in the north, particularly Leeds and Liverpool, and to Europe and beyond as part of the North West European Trade Axis and as a result of its position approximately ten miles from Manchester airport. While this strategic location puts Salford in an economically strong position, it also impacts on congestion, air quality, environmental sustainability and quality of life for the residents of the city, a challenge which public services in the city must tackle.[10]

According to the national Index of Multiple Deprivation,[11] Salford is the fifteenth most deprived local authority area in the country. This means that when all 354 local authorities are given an average 'score' which shows the level of deprivation in that area, Salford experiences comparatively much higher levels of deprivation than other parts of the country. This reflects some of the significant challenges that public services face in order to improve the quality of life for all Salford residents.

In 2010, Salford commenced a 'Better Life Chances' project led by the city council on behalf of the Greater Manchester city region. The focus of the programme is designed to tackle the economic, social and financial challenges presented by the many areas of high deprivation in the city region. A major emphasis of this work is to establish new models of partnership delivery and improve outcomes while delivering efficiencies in the most challenging areas. There are three pilot areas within Salford, Little Hulton, Winton and a joint cross-boundary pilot with Manchester in the Higher Broughton/Cheetham Hill area. The pilot has led to the development of a 'Place Board' at the local authority level, led by the local authority chief executive. This convenes senior members of all key public services and organisations at local authority level in a group that can take ownership of the pilots, including the chief superintendent of the police, the chief executive of the NHS and other similar organisations. Each pilot area seeks to enable improved partnership working to deliver better joined-up services to a number of deprived neighbourhood communities to help local people optimise their life chances and improve their quality of life, health and well-being.

The THINKlab has worked closely with local partners such as the city council, police, health and housing associations to assemble a range of local data for one of the designated 'Better Life Chance' pilot areas in the Little Hulton area of Salford. Datasets included, for example, numbers of Jobseeker claimants, people claiming out-of-work benefits, lone parents, free school meals, social care data, crime and anti-social behaviour statistics, private and social housing data, health indices and a skills profile of the local area.

The THINKlab had already created a base Salford Mirrorworld platform as part of its ambitions to explore a range of application areas for the technology in partnership with local stakeholders (see Figure 8.3). As with the Black Country platform this approach integrated OS Mastermap data, building model footprint and height data and stereo and oblique imagery to create a visual 'mirror space' of the Salford area. More detailed VR building models of the university campus were also integrated into the base platform (see Figure 8.4). Bespoke aerial photography of Little Hulton providing detailed height and texture data of buildings was also commissioned to enable a more accurate built-to-scale physical representation of the local neighbourhood to be constructed.

Together with the data from partners, this was all integrated into the Salford Mirrorworld platform. What started to emerge from this process was a new joint insight tool that for the first time allowed the city council and partners to visualise or 'mirror' the story of 'reality' in Little Hulton,

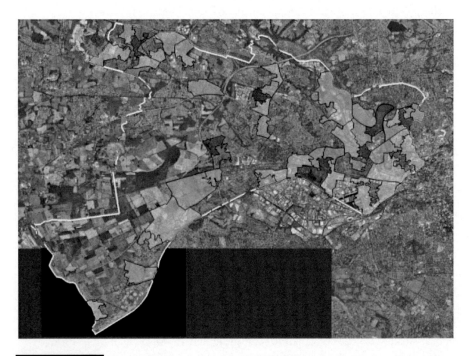

Figure 8.3   Helicopter view of Salford in Greater Manchester

Figure 8.4 Detailed VR model showing the University of Salford Maxwell Campus

which showed the scale of the challenge facing the local community (see Figure 8.5 and 8.6).

The visualisation of Little Hulton as part of the Salford Mirrorworld platform was subsequently demonstrated to the high-level Place Board and was greeted with real enthusiasm. This led to further development of the Mirrorworld as a joint insight tool – focusing in at an even lower level of the street (see Figure 8.6) by visualising how the technology can map, for example, police service use, ambulance call-outs, how much is being spent within a particular street on services and so on. Connections could be identified between the available data when it is mapped in this way and hence attempts may be made to solve the problems causing these demands on services. The 'Better Life Chances' programme is being closely monitored by the UK government and is intended to inform and shape regional and national thinking about how best to improve delivery of joined-up services to local citizens and make a real difference in the lives and life opportunities of local people.

In terms of other policy application areas, projects underway include creating an energy 'heat map' of the city to inform energy management planning, developing a flood simulation tool of the river Irwell to help improve flood defence planning and working with the Greater Manchester

Figure 8.5   Visualisation of performance indicators in Little Hulton

Figure 8.6   Visualisation of social data for Little Hulton

Police to evaluate how the platform can be used to support emergency planning operations. Additionally, current research is focusing on the use of Mirrorworld Technologies to help Greater Manchester Public Health partners tackle key policy challenges in respect of health reform[12] and deliver improved health outcomes for people and places. The THINKlab is also discussing with city council partners how Mirrorworld may support their response to the emerging government agenda for 'Future Cities'[13] as well as tackle key local business priorities such as developing an intelligence-based approach to asset rationalisation and streamlining delivery of locality-based services.

Mirrorworld platform technology overview

Figure 8.7 presents a summary outline of how the technology layers fit together.

- *Data layer/data producers* – comprises an assembly of many datasets which are used to develop the Mirrorworld perspective, including, for example, OS Mastermap, LIDAR, point data, area datasets such as the Index of Multiple Deprivation indices, and local data produced by public sector agencies.

- *Mirrorworld layer* – which manages the integration of the many and scattered datasets.

- *Analytical tools/modelling and simulation layer* – which mirrors the physical/social environment of a city/urban area. To date the main analytical tools that have been used have focused on the visualisation and simulation aspects of the Mirrorworld. However, this is rapidly evolving and new tools highlighted in Figure 8.7 such as data mining are now being investigated in response to emerging and future challenges facing the public sector in the UK – see the section on future developments below.

- *Application layer* – which provides the output of the data assembly, integration, modelling and simulation and is used to tell the stories of place, of reality and of transformation for individual policy planning areas.

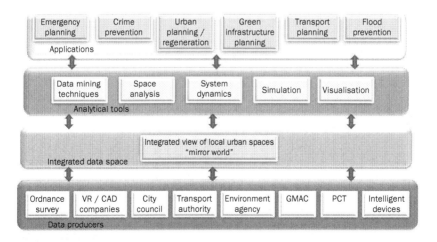

Figure 8.7 Overview of Mirrorworld Technologies platform

Future developments

As we look ahead at the next decade the public sector in the UK faces major challenges. Ongoing public sector spending constraint for the foreseeable future[14] means that public services will need to become more innovative, efficient and outcome focused if they are to continue to improve the quality of life for citizens and support economic growth. Key priorities supporting the sustainable regeneration of local communities,[15] including education, employment and skills, housing, health and social care and the move towards a low carbon economy will continue to drive local planning and shape service delivery agendas. However, these priorities will be further influenced by the emerging policy agendas for localism[16] and the Big Society,[17] which will determine new partnerships between the public, private and voluntary sectors and increasingly drive the need to improve citizen engagement and choices in the decision-making process. With respect to public sector reform and service transformation we can also identify the trend towards co-location and use of front-office shared services by local providers such as the local authority, police and primary care trusts (PCTs).[18] This approach will also combine the use of many channels of delivery to provide improved citizen choice and access with back-office efficiency savings.

It will further drive the need for new partnership models of policy, planning and service delivery which will shape regeneration development, will also impact on governance and decision-making processes and will require new intelligent evidence-based policy models that will enable cities and regions to fast-track decision-making in the face of increasingly complex economic, environmental and societal problems and associated budgetary pressures. The consequence of the global downturn has also heightened the need to find new ways of accelerating the conditions for economic growth, prosperity, health and well-being in communities across England. In a globalised world made up of a diversity of successful economies but with many failing, increasingly volatile market conditions are testing the ability of local and national government to create the right environment for successful sustainable economic growth.

Over the period of the Mirrorworld platform's development it has demonstrated the potential to provide creative joint insight scenarios to address some of the key regeneration and service challenges facing major urban areas in England. The integration and visualisation of new and emerging analytical tools such as data mining (providing pattern analysis, forecasts and predictive scenarios of local regeneration opportunities), and opinion mining (using, for example, social networks to capture emerging views on people's attitudes towards local plans) means the Mirrorworld platform has the opportunity to create further capability to develop new and more powerful tools. These will provide more sophisticated joint insight scenarios and solutions to help tackle the future regeneration and transformation challenges facing the public sector in the next decade.

Over and above the challenges outlined, it is also clear the process of building better futures for our citizens will require an improved capacity to make sense of and more efficiently manage the increasingly vast amounts of data we generate. The Mirrorworld platform is demonstrating how it can support this process. In response to UK and international interest from public, private and voluntary sector agencies in the use of this technology and its application in their own domains, the THINKlab is currently developing a version of the Mirrorworld platform that can be made commercially available. It has developed new technologies capable of integrating many data sources within a dynamic holistic 3-D space. Whatever the future may hold, the Mirrorworld platform has the potential to envision it in novel ways, offering effective solutions for visualising, planning, predicting and managing sustainable urban futures for our communities and citizens.

Acknowledgements

THINKlab

The THINKlab (*http://www.thinklab.salford.ac.uk*) is a futuristic and spacious research environment with state-of-the-art facilities located within the University of Salford in Greater Manchester. It has an established international reputation in the creative use and application of cutting-edge technologies to provide innovative solutions to meet the needs of industry, commerce and community. For further details contact: *t.fernando@salford.ac.uk*.

Mirrorworld Technologies

Mirrorworld Technologies Ltd has been established to help government, business and community leaders in the UK and internationally exploit the potential of the Mirrorworld platform to bring new interpretations, insights and business solutions to some of the most complex, social, economic and environmental challenges facing our cities, regions and communities. For further details contact Ian Everall at: *ian@ mirrorworldtechnologies.co.uk.*

Notes

1. *http://www.thinklab.salford.ac.uk*
2. *http://www.epsrc.ac.uk/*
3. *http://www.urbansustainabilityexchange.org.uk/*
4. *http://www.vivacity2020.eu*
5. *http://www.cospaces.org/index.htm*
6. *http://www.the-blackcountry.com/*
7. *http://www.ordnancesurvey.co.uk/*
8. *http://www.biglotteryfund.org.uk/prog_livinglandmarks*
9. *http://en.wikipedia.org/wiki/LIDAR*
10. *http://www.salford.gov.uk/d/final_scs_15_june_09-2.pdf*
11. *http://www.imd.communities.gov.uk/*
12. *Equity and Excellence: Liberating the NHS*, White Paper, Department of Health, July 2010. Online at: *http://www.dh.gov.uk/en/Publicationsandstatistics/ Publications/PublicationsPolicyAndGuidance/DH_117353.*
13. *https://catapult.innovateuk.org/en_GB/future-cities*
14. *http://cdn.hm-treasury.gov.uk/2011budget_complete.pdf*
15. *http://www.local.gov.uk/programmes*
16. *http://www.communities.gov.uk/publications/localgovernment/ localismplainenglishguide*
17. *http://www.cabinetoffice.gov.uk/big-society*
18. 'Local Government Improvement and Development: Delivering Public Service Transformation 2010: Developing the Financial Case for Front Office Shared Services (FOSS)', at: *http://www.idea.gov.uk/idk/aio/ 24038630.*

9

Beyond the Google generation: towards community-specific usage patterns of scientific information

Chérifa Boukacem-Zeghmouri and Joachim Schöpfel

Abstract. This chapter questions the concept of the Google Generation commonly used to explain information behaviour. The authors try to understand the impact of disciplines on the information behaviour of researchers in science, technology and medicine. A review and analysis of usage studies and empirical results are reported from a qualitative survey with scientists from different disciplines (biology, physics, mathematics, geology and chemistry). Thirty interviews set the information behaviour – information research, reading behaviour, scientific communication and publishing – in the wider framework of scientific activity. Specific attention is paid to new models of academic publishing (open access). Ethnographic observations allow for a reinterpretation of discourse and practice in the information users' work space.

Keywords: attitude, Google generation, information behaviour, researchers, usage patterns

Generation gap and community

Today, researchers can access a wide range of subscription, pay-per-view or open-access digital resources. When invited to evaluate this offer, their answer is unanimous. They wish to be able to access 'more of these resources, at all times and from anywhere'. What do we know about their behaviours and attitudes?

While access to digital scientific information steadily increases, a growing body of empirical studies provides evidence on usage patterns by academic scholars, scientists and students. They usually focus either on information-seeking behaviour as a radical new phenomenon or try to establish a continuum with the 'Gutenberg galaxy' and former research (Tenopir et al., 2009). One of the main questions relates to information literacy and a generation gap between 'digital natives' and 'digital immigrants' (Prensky, 2001). The digital natives or Google generation[1] are defined as 'those born after 1993 ... a cohort of young people with little or no recollection of life before the Web' (Rowlands et al., 2008). A couple of studies strived to confirm the stereotype of this Google generation and to show typical and specific information behaviour performed by those who have 'grown up in a world dominated by the Internet' (Rowlands et al., 2008).

Some examples of real or alleged Google generation behaviour patterns (see OCLC, 2006; Rowlands et al., 2008) include: '89% of college students use search engines to begin an information search ... They prefer visual information over text ... They prefer interactive systems and are turning away from being passive consumers of information ... They think everything is on the web (and it's all free) ...' (Rowlands et al., 2008) and so on. The question about the reality and reliability of these generational patterns is not theoretical but practical because of its impact on teaching programmes, didactics, educational engineering and infrastructure.[2]

Students and younger researchers have also been described as digital natives and as 'Google academics', for example bloggers and tweeters, familiar with social networks and collaborative tools, doing most of their information research online. On the other hand, older scientists are less acquainted with the Internet, unimpressed by Google and more reluctant to engage with information and communications technology (ICT). But does the concept of the Google generation explain the total variation of scholarly information behaviour?

One of the first to express reservations was Schulmeister (2008). In a well-documented working paper he argued for a functional and educational approach to the Internet generation, focusing on socialisation processes, not on media. A recent research project conducted by Education for Change[3] casts doubt on the application of the Google generation concept to research communities. Tomorrow's researchers seem not so very different from researchers today.

We think that the Google generation is a transitional phenomenon and that the research environment or ecosystem, covering the whole spectrum from project team and institution to research community and scientific discipline, and including career and other strategic choices, may have a more structuring impact than age or generation.

This chapter questions the concept of the Google generation commonly used to explain information behaviour. Instead, we try to understand better the impact of disciplines on the information behaviour of researchers in science, technology and medicine (STM). We do not deny possible behavioural convergences and similarities between researchers from different disciplines but we highlight the structuring effect of their specific disciplinary environment, status and social representations of identified practices. Our proposal is to review recent studies on information behaviour in academic environments, to adopt a differential approach and highlight behavioural differences across the range of scientific disciplines.[4] We then report empirical results from a qualitative survey with scientists from five disciplines (biology, physics, mathematics, geology and chemistry). Thirty interviews set the information behaviour – information research, reading behaviour, scientific communication and publishing – in the wider framework of scientific activity. Specific attention is paid to new models of academic publishing, such as open access. Ethnographic observations allow for a reinterpretation of discourse and practice in the information users' work space. The aim is to change the perspective, go beyond the Google generation concept and focus on the community as an ecosystem.

Disciplines and subjects in usage studies

Some studies aggregate findings about information behaviour, without taking into account differences across the demographic characteristics of the respondents. Tenopir et al. (2004) observed how undergraduates, graduates and faculty members performed sessions on ScienceDirect.[5] They distinguished three disciplines (astronomy/physics, chemistry and engineering) but neglected this variable in their interpretation of the results. King et al. (2009) report on a survey with faculty from five United States universities with detailed evidence on information-seeking and reading patterns – as if all scholars behave the same way. Yet the authors are conscious that 'differences in reading patterns result most often from differences in academic disciplines, followed by readers' primary duties (teaching or research), their productivity (faculty who publish more, read more), and their age (older faculty are more likely to read print and to have more personal subscriptions)' (King et al., 2009).

A recent review of literature mentions that 'there were disciplinary differences in methods or use [and] in the use of literature from fields other than searchers' own core interests' (Williams et al., 2010) but then comes to the conclusion that keyword searching in e-journals became the common information behaviour shared by all disciplines. Yet, two studies have focused on the differences in academic disciplines. The 2006 Research Information Network (RIN) report on researchers' usage of discovery services is one of the first studies to apply a disciplinary approach to usage studies. Even though the report states that '[the] similarities are more striking than the differences', it confirms community-specific usage patterns of online services such as library portals and search engines in life sciences, physical sciences, arts and humanities, and social sciences. A follow-up report on the use, value and impact of e-journals (RIN, 2009a) affirms that 'readers in different subjects behave differently' and shows differences in information behaviour related to disciplines. 'E-journal databases ... do not appear to force users into a common style of behaviour. Subjects do!' (RIN, 2009a; see also Nicholas et al., 2010).

A JISC study on e-books provides complementary empirical evidence (JISC, 2009). Students' information behaviour is evaluated by means of deep log analysis of course text e-books in four academic disciplines. In particular, seasonal patterns, access location (sessions off/on campus), page view times and session lengths differ significantly between the four sub-samples. Centre for Information Behaviour and the Evaluation of Research (CIBER) publications introduced discipline-related usage patterns from 2005 onwards. Two studies on usage data from Blackwell (Nicholas et al., 2005) and the OHIOLink consortium (Nicholas et al., 2007) revealed some subject-related differences, especially with regard to the number of sessions and article views and to the format of requested items. The 2008 article on Elsevier's ScienceDirect platform provides a 'detailed and comprehensive subject profile of users' that is meant to improve e-journal systems to become more suitable for users in different disciplines (Nicholas et al., 2008). Some results were as follows:

> Social Scientists conducted ... the highest proportion ... of sessions viewing only abstracts [and] conducted the highest proportion ... of sessions which viewed only articles in press ... Over a quarter of the sessions conducted by Mathematicians included a view to old articles ... Physicists were the most likely to view their own journals – 71% of the journals viewed by them were Physics journals. Computer scientists were the most regular visitors to ScienceDirect. (Nicholas et al., 2008)

After a comprehensive review of log analyses on subject-related usage patterns, Nicholas et al. (2009) compared usage data from history, economics and life sciences collections (Oxford University Press) and concluded that 'subject and institutional differences ... were sometimes considerable, a finding which points to the danger of generalising about usage and information seeking.' A recent study allows for deeper insight into the discipline-related impact on information-seeking behaviour insofar as it draws attention to narrower subject communities within scientific disciplines (Jamali and Nicholas, 2008a, 2008b, 2010). Based on qualitative survey data, the authors describe similarities but also significant differences in methods of finding and using research articles between seven academic sub-fields of astronomy and physics. The findings somehow confirm but then, too, go beyond former results: '... as we can see, different subfields are different and talking of physicists here might be over-generalising the data' (Jamali and Nicholas, 2008a). Table 9.1 gives an overview on eight research projects. The table shows the surveyed disciplines and sub-disciplines, and indicates whether the disciplines were surveyed as characteristics of the community (= the faculty's research field) or of the requested items (= subject of collections, journals or e-books).

What can be learned from these studies?

- The research reviewed covers the whole range of fields of science, including natural sciences, formal sciences, social sciences and applied sciences, with the exception of cognitive sciences. Nevertheless, this coverage is not consistent, and only the publications based on Jamali's PhD thesis (2008a, 2010) take into account sub-divisions and interdisciplinary disciplines (5).

- Four studies (2, 4, 5 and 8) define disciplines through scientific communities, by the research interests and affiliations of academic users (students, scholars). Four other studies (1, 3, 6 and 7) define disciplines through the subject of requested content (collections), as if the theme of an article, journal or e-book was necessarily and always related to the discipline of the user. In all cases, disciplines and/or subjects have not been labelled by the authors/scientists but adopted from the publishers, libraries, institutions or users that were surveyed, weakening coherence and comparability between the different studies.

- The hypothesis of statistically significant differences of information-seeking behaviour related to academic disciplines seems consistent throughout all studies and apparently does not depend on the choice

Table 9.1 Review of academic disciplines in usage studies

	1	2	3	4	5	6	7	8
Community (user)		x		x	x			x
Collection (content)	x		x			x	x	
Science	x		x					
Chemistry				x				x
Materials science				x				
Physics		x		x	x			x
Astronomy					x			
Mathematics				x				
Earth sciences				x				x
Environmental sciences				x				x
Life sciences		x		x		x		x
Medicine	x		x	x			x	
Social sciences	x	x	x	x				
Media studies							x	
Arts & humanities	x	x	x					
History						x		x
Engineering			x	x			x	
Computer sciences				x				
Economics				x		x		x
Business & management							x	

1. Nicholas et al. (2005) 2. RIN (2006) 3. Nicholas et al. (2007)
4. Nicholas et al. (2008) 5. Jamali and Nicholas (2008, 2010)
6. Nicholas et al. (2009) 7. JISC (2009) 8. RIN (2009a) Nicholas et al. (2010)

of research methods (survey, deep log analysis, library usage data, item analysis).

- The observed differences affect several aspects of information-seeking behaviour, such as format, age or status of requested items, number of sessions, visits, searches or retrieved hits, or attitudes to services and tools.

- Nevertheless, the results provide more or less anecdotal evidence, for example a patchwork-like description rather than consistent data on information-seeking behaviour in different scientific communities. In other words, it is not possible, at least for the moment, to draw a consistent picture of specific heuristic patterns related to digital information in history, economics, chemistry or other communities.

Following the studies, a couple of factors impact or moderate discipline-related differences, such as length of experience, academic status of the user group surveyed and type of research conducted, and the research output of institutions in terms of activity and intensity, especially between teaching and research universities. And we can probably add strategic positioning of the researcher and competition within the research environment as systemic variables that interconnect community, discipline and personality (Kurek et al., 2007). We can summarise with a recent JISC-OCLC report on user behaviour projects (Connaway and Dickey, 2010): 'Several studies indicate that some disciplinary differences do exist in researcher behaviours, both professional researchers and students', even if the increasing centrality and integrating effect of e-journals and Google or similar search engines in researchers' behaviour should not be underestimated.

The Google generation concept and French STM researchers

We were offered the opportunity to study French researchers' digital practices and behaviour in the STM fields during a four-year (2006–10) national research project.[6] The combination of methodologies used (qualitative and quantitative) gave us a more complete picture of the manner in which the French academic community appropriated electronic resources and to what degree. The qualitative part of the study provided in-depth understanding of the disciplinary dynamics underlying the practices recorded in the logs. Our challenge was to reconstruct the 'intelligence' of the quantitative part so as to make explicit the meaning and therefore better understand behaviour and usage. The interview structure placed the user's information-seeking behaviour within the discipline's scientific activity. It raised questions relating to the sociology of science and information and communication sciences. The goal was to reconstruct the 'continuum' of scientific activity within each discipline so as to contextualise better behaviour and usage. This methodological approach allowed us to observe closely researchers' everyday way of work. Consequently, we were able to determine whether or not the practices observed were related to the 'Google generation' concept. The researchers we interviewed were members of laboratories from five universities: Paris 6, Lyon 1, Lille 1, Strasbourg 1 and Bordeaux 1.

Cultural differences between fields

The results of our analysis highlight the fundamental importance of social representations in the researcher's practices and usage. Frequently underestimated, or even ignored, this dimension is clearly visible in the interviews we conducted with 30 scholars from five disciplines: biology, physics, mathematics, geology and chemistry. The methodological approach gave us a broad and dynamic view of the researcher's daily work methods, certainly helping to bring this to light. By social representations, we mean 'social knowledge between individuals and groups' (Le Marec, 2001) that is consensual within a discipline and adhered to by researchers. This 'referential reality' was found in both the interviews and in the practices we observed *in situ* (workspace organisation, consultation of editor platforms, consultation of bibliometric databases). During the interviews, social representations were oriented around two spheres. The first was the researcher's perception of his individuality, his place within a larger entity – most often the laboratory. The second was his perception of his community and his place within it.

For the physicists and theoretical mathematicians that we interviewed and observed, the feeling of being an integral part of the community is explained by the community being seen as a place for sharing, discussing, learning and experimenting. The community is capable of stimulating the fundamental nature of research in these fields. It promotes both the sharing of content (articles, data) and technical skills related to the systems used to produce the content. The community is therefore seen as providing the researcher with everything necessary to 'stay in the race': tools to access the latest research (ArXiv)[7] and the latest open and interoperable systems and software. The community appears to be a place where one goes for information and training. The researchers interviewed considered themselves to be integral to this dynamic.

The need to be in constant contact with the community is linked with the need to be aware of the most recent research. These two aspects are self-determined. Consequently, through alerts, spontaneous consultations, word of mouth and online navigation, the researcher is in a state of constant awareness. The feeling of proximity to and integration in the community is reinforced by the fact that the researcher considers it to be a space where research can evolve to the paper stage, in the pre-print sense of the word. The community, through systems such as open archives, enables the researcher to complete the research and scientific communication processes. All the stages are present: reflection, communication, comments and review (first evaluation stage). This explains why repositories, ArXiv in particular, are as important as academic journals. Scientific publications are important for a researcher's career but are not part of the continuum found in the community. This explains the scattered aspect of their informational practices during the scientific communication process. Their screens display the multiple interfaces they use to search for the elements that will allow them to retrace a research path. In addition, their screens also display various word processing programs and other software. They are therefore connected to the Web and multi-tasking out of necessity. They are constantly logged into e-mail which they use to send messages (a question, a request for more information) to the members of their community whether they know them or not. The most remarkable fact was that the institutional membership had no impact on this representation. Claiming to be a big, international, scientific family, institutional considerations are secondary. The status of a researcher, however, was a significant factor in determining 'expert' profiles.

Researchers with the most research experience and responsibilities have practices that are closest to those of the Google generation. In particular, those researchers with important review activities (articles, projects, PhD student advisees) – often the oldest – and who use search engines the most, have practices that most resemble those of the Google generation. The search engine is seen as a harvester meant to 'reconstruct the research environment': PDFs with bibliographic references, home pages of cited authors and so on. The age criterion associated with the Google generation disappears when confronted with the status and nature of review activity. Researchers' informational practices, objective and observable phenomena, are shaped upstream and are based on the idea the researcher makes of his or her choice of action. Multi-tasking, a constant presence on the Web, shared learning experiences, digital forms of communication, the community as a substitute for official authority figures – all are symptoms of a functionality deeply embedded in the social practices of the field. They are exacerbated and revealed on the Web. They cannot, however, be considered as new phenomena.

Among the biologists, chemists and geologists we encountered, proximity with the community is found on two levels: national and international. This dual representation exists because researchers primarily collaborate on the first, more limited, level and frequently publish on the second, broader, level. This dual representation goes hand in hand with a feeling of distance: the experimental nature of research requires the researcher to regularly break with his or her community (small or large).

The researcher is isolated when working in the laboratory. S/he reappears only when there are results to communicate.

The researcher does not suffer from this distance during the experimentation phase. Isolation is necessary in order properly to complete any experiments, as well as to protect the results from the community. Contrary to the earlier discussion, sharing results with the community only occurs when they are published officially in a peer-reviewed journal. Confidentiality and competition interfere in the researcher's rapport with the community. Furthermore, the researcher must also demonstrate the scientific consistency and credibility of their work to this same community. Importantly, it is during the final phase of the scientific communication process (the reviewed article) rather than over time that the researcher's relationship with the community is solidified. The open repositories are seen as irrelevant, a 'Napster of science' for the biologists, or as a 'curiosity' for the geologists and chemists. Hyper Article en Ligne (HAL),[8] the French National Open Archive, is almost unknown among this population. This relationship, built upon 'vigilant distance' is translated and deepened through this population's informational practices. These researchers primarily use specialised databases (PubMed,[9] ScienceDirect,[10] SpringerLink,[11] ...). This distance is slightly altered through the consultation of bibliometric databases (Web of Science,[12] Scopus[13] or Google Scholar[14]). The search results on these databases are 'filtered' based on the reference's impact on the community (number of citations, source of the citation).

The researcher positions his or her research based on the possible response it will receive within this community. This is even truer for interdisciplinary studies, since one must convince the communities of the different fields upon which the study draws. The most active and experienced researchers are the most expert citation arbitrators. They are also the oldest members of the community. When showing us how they proceeded, it was possible to see how these researchers mobilised their knowledge of research themes and their historicity, as well as their understanding of institutional and individual actors. Pertinent articles are identified based on content, but also on their relationship with the community and its referential framework. Based on these informational, communicational and sociological considerations, the meaning of citations is reclaimed.

With this configuration as its basis, Google is an important source of second-hand information. It is useful when a researcher is beginning a new study and wants to get a sense of its Web presence, or when s/he is preparing a class on a specific subject and wants to find illustrative material (images, multimedia texts). Google is also used to access favourite journals or specialised platforms. But scientific publications continue to be crucial. Contrary to what we saw earlier, the social practices of these disciplines prevent researchers from adopting only Google generation practices. The researchers' behaviour and usage continue to be based on the fundamental values that dictate how the field functions.

Convergence and intradisciplinarity

We have just seen that the type of research and the social representation of the researcher generate different practices. These two elements also act to recalibrate the practices. That said, it is important to underline a convergence among the practices identified in our study. We have interpreted this standardisation as being due to the widespread usage of Google (Googlisation). Our most important finding is the total absence of the concept of a library (in the physical and traditional sense) from the researchers' discourse. As access to electronic platforms has become very common, using libraries is no longer part of the researcher's practices. Library websites were almost never consulted. Researchers preferred to access databases directly or via Google. Some of the researchers we interviewed – the youngest – were incapable of identifying who paid the subscription for such and such database (the library, the Centre National de la Recherche Scientifique (CNRS), the laboratory). Furthermore, we observed – and showed in previous studies (Boukacem, 2010) – the widespread adoption of alerts by researchers across disciplines, as well as the dominance of simple searches based on a single keyword. These convergences are symptoms of homogenised infrastructures and technical environments. We focused on the most transversal characteristics and representations in the researchers' discourse in each field. We sought to develop an original way of studying this subject at the preliminary level. Further analyses will allow us to take into account the nuances within each field.

From community to ecosystem and hermeneutics

Our analysis shows that with an increasing sentiment of belonging and integration into their disciplinary community researchers tend to adopt information and communication habits structured by this same discipline. In fact, information behaviour seems mainly to be shaped by the researchers' relationship with and representation of their community, in particular by their adhesion to (or rejection of) community values and principles of the disciplinary culture of science. One of the significant results is that some behaviour patterns commonly associated with the phenomenon of the Google generation seem rooted in specific disciplinary practice and the culture of science. In fact, some typical so-called Googling behaviours may have pre-Web origins in disciplinary search patterns. In these cases, technology, the Internet and the Web rather accelerated and intensified existing routines than created new information behaviours.

The Google generation effect does not explain the whole variation of information behaviour. Job status and position affect search logics and patterns. Also, the specific nature of scientific enterprise (such as applied science or fundamental research) and the intensity and importance of activity seem related to particular behavioural tendencies and profiles. What we mean is that research and information behaviour are part of a scientific ecosystem wherein the scientific discipline plays a major role. Instead of being amazed by ICT and new ways of searching information, we need to understand underlying functional patterns and the interrelation between information consumption and production, communication and research. Age differences should not be over-interpreted as a generational gap but as a variable of communitarian impact on socialisation and learning processes. Research studies that reveal disciplinary variation in behaviour related to information searching seem to confirm our approach – for instance, disciplinary variation has been found in citing behaviour (Zhang, 2011), citation distribution (Radicchi et al., 2008), the adoption of different Web 2.0 tools (RIN, 2009b), and attitudes to the fundamental functions of scholarly publishing (Mulligan and Mabe, 2011) and open access and deposit behaviour (Fry et al., 2009) – and these behaviours can be impacted by language barriers (Monopoli et al., 2002). This last aspect is of particular interest for studies in France where (non-) usage of digital information may be affected by English reading skills generally higher in younger scientists.

About ten years ago, CIBER performed a cluster analysis on information-seeking data (Nicholas et al., 2004). As a result, they distinguished eight different user groups, such as *enthusiastic users* ('used the service frequently, accessed a large number of journals, and generally viewed full text articles'), *gapfillers* ('only accessed a few journals, but did so frequently'), tourists ('used the service, but never viewed a particular journal'), or *exploratory users* ('infrequent users who seldom accessed full text'). The interesting point is that they included demographic data into the clustering and thus were able to relate multifaceted usage patterns to discipline and academic status. For instance, most *enthusiastic users* were social scientists while science staff and students predominated in the *gapfillers* category. This methodology integrates usage assessment, qualitative data collection and complex statistical exploitation. The result seems promising because it allows the researcher to link qualitative studies such as that of Ollé and Borrego (2010) to more concepts of community and discipline. This may be an empirical way to a new and realistic ICT hermeneutics of science.

Coming back to our subject, when we highlight the disciplinary differences of information-usage patterns, we do not deny latent age effects and some Google generation-like phenomena. Nevertheless, we think that this effect may be transitional and a kind of collateral effect of emerging ICT in research work. When all Internet users are digital natives, variation related to the hypothetical generation gap will decrease and disappear, and disciplinary differences will (again) become a central factor, reflecting the richness and diversity of fields of science.

Notes

1. Also called the net generation or generation Y; see overview from Nicholas et al. (2011).
2. ICT in urban development, cf. Menou (2010).
3. Researchers of Tomorrow; see: *http://www.efc.co.uk/projects/researchers_of_tomorrow.jsp*.
4. We understand disciplines as groupings based on their knowledge structures and reputational concerns (Becher, 1994).
5. *http://www.sciencedirect.com/*
6. *http://www.agence-nationale-recherche.fr*
7. E-print archive, covering the fields of physics, mathematics, non-linear science, computer science and quantitative biology; see: *http://arxiv.org*.
8. *http://hal.archives-ouvertes.fr*
9. *http://www.ncbi.nlm.nih.gov/pubmed/*
10. See note 5.
11. *http://www.springerlink.com/*
12. *http://thomsonreuters.com/products_services/science/science_products/a-z/web_of_science/*
13. *http://www.scopus.com/home.url*
14. *http://scholar.google.co.uk/*

References

Becher, T. (1994) 'The significance of disciplinary differences', *Studies in Higher Education*, 19(2): 151–61.

Boukacem-Zeghmouri, C. (2010) 'Pratiques de consultation des revues électroniques par les enseignants chercheurs: les STM en France', *Documentaliste – Sciences de l'Information*, 47(2): 4–13.

Connaway, L.S. and Dickey, T.J. (2010) 'The Digital Information Seeker. Report of Findings from Selected OCLC, RIN and JISC user behaviour projects', *Tech. rep.*, JISC OCLC.

Fry, J., Oppenheim, C., Probets, S., Creaser, C., Greenwood, H. and Spezi, V. (2009) 'PEER Behavioural Research: Authors and Users vis-à-vis Journals and Repositories. Baseline Report', *Tech. rep.*, LISU Loughborough University.

Jamali, H.R. and Nicholas, D. (2008) 'Information-seeking behaviour of physicists and astronomers', *Aslib Proceedings*, 60(5): 444–62.

Jamali, H.R. and Nicholas, D. (2008) 'Intradisciplinary differences in reading behaviour of scientists: case study of physics and astronomy', *Electronic Library*, 28(1): 54–68.

Jamali, H.R. and Nicholas, D. (2010) 'Interdisciplinarity and the information-seeking behavior of scientists', *Information Processing and Management*, 46(2): 233–43.

JISC (2009) 'National E-Book Observatory Project. Key findings and recommendations', *Tech. rep.*, JISC.

King, D.W., Tenopir, C., Choemprayong, S. and Wu, L. (2009) 'Scholarly journal information-seeking and reading patterns of faculty at five US universities', *Learned Publishing*, 22(2): 126–44.

Kurek, K. et al. (2007) 'The research entrepreneur: strategic positioning of the researcher in his societal environment', *Science and Public Policy*, 34(7): 501–13.

Le Marec, J. (2001) 'L'usage et ses modèles: quelques reflexions méthodologiques', *Spirale*, 2: 105–22.

Menou, M.J. (2010) 'Information behaviour of the "Google generation" as a factor in sustainability for Mexican cities', *Aslib Proceedings*, 62(2): 165–74.

Monopoli, M., Nicholas, D., Georgiou, P. and Korfiati, M. (2002) 'A user-oriented evaluation of digital libraries: case study the "electronic journals" service of the library and information service of the University of Patras, Greece', *Aslib Proceedings*, 54(2): 103–17.

Mulligan, A. and Mabe, M. (2011) 'The effect of the Internet on researcher motivations, behaviour and attitudes', *Journal of Documentation*, 67(2): 290–311.

Nicholas, D., Huntington, P. and Watkinson, A. (2005) 'Scholarly journal usage: the results of deep log analysis', *Journal of Documentation*, 61(2): 248–80.

Nicholas, D., Huntington, P. and Jamali, H.R. (2007) 'Diversity in the information seeking behaviour of the virtual scholar: institutional comparisons', *Journal of Academic Librarianship*, 33(6): 629–38.

Nicholas, D., Huntington, P. and Jamali, H.R. (2008) 'User diversity: as demonstrated by deep log analysis', *Electronic Library*, 26(1): 21–38.

Nicholas, D., Huntington, P. and Watkinson, A. (2004) 'Re-appraising information seeking behaviour in a digital environment: bouncers, checkers, returnees and the like', *Journal of Documentation*, 60(1): 24–43.

Nicholas, D., Rowlands, I., Clark, D. and Williams, P. (2010) 'Researchers' e-journal use and information seeking behaviour', *Journal of Information Science*, 36(4): 494–516.

Nicholas, D., Rowlands, I., Clark, D. and Williams, P. (2011) 'Google Generation II: web behaviour experiments with the BBC', *Aslib Proceedings*, 63(1): 28–45.

Nicholas, D., Williams, P., Rowlands, I. and Jamali, H.R. (2009) 'Online use and information seeking behaviour: institutional and subject comparisons of UK researchers', *Journal of Information Science*, 35(6): 660–76.

OCLC (2006) 'College Students' Perceptions of the Libraries and Information Resources: A Report to the OCLC Membership, OCLC, Dublin, OH', *Tech. rep.*, OCLC.

Ollé, C. and Borrego, Ã. (2010) 'A qualitative study of the impact of electronic journals on scholarly information behavior', *Library and Information Science Research*, 32(3): 221–8.

Prensky, M. (2001) 'Digital natives, digital immigrants part 1', *On the Horizon – The Strategic Planning Resource for Education Professionals*, 9(5): 1–6.

Radicchi, F., Fortunato, S. and Castellano, C. (2008) 'Universality of citation distributions: toward an objective measure of scientific impact', *Proceedings of the National Academy of Sciences*, 105(45): 17268–72.

RIN (2006) 'Researchers and Discovery Services: Behaviour, Perceptions, Needs', *Tech. rep.*, Research Information Network.

RIN (2009a) 'E-journals: Their Use, Value and Impact', *Tech. rep.*, Research Information Network.

RIN (2009b) 'Communicating knowledge: how and why researchers publish and disseminate their findings', *Tech. rep.*, Research Information Network.

Rowlands, I., Nicholas, D., Williams, P., Huntington, P., Fieldhouse, M., Gunter, B., Withey, R., Jamali, H.R., Dobrowolski, T. and Tenopir, C. (2008) 'The Google generation: the information behaviour of the researcher of the future', *Aslib Proceedings*, 60(4): 290–310.

Schulmeister, R. (2008) 'Gibt es eine Net Generation?', Working Paper. Universität Hamburg, Zentrum für Hochschul- und Weiterbildung. Available online at: *http://www.zhw.uni-hamburg.de/pdfs/Schulmeister_Netzgeneration.pdf*.

Tenopir, C., King, D.W., Edwards, S. and Wu, L. (2009) 'Electronic journals and changes in scholarly article seeking and reading patterns', *Aslib Proceedings*, 61(1): 5–32.

Tenopir, C., Wang, P., Pollard, R., Zhang, Y. and Simmons, B. (2004) 'Use of electronic science journals in the undergraduate curriculum: an observational study', *Proceedings of the American Society for Information Science and Technology*, 41(1): 64–71.

Williams, P., Nicholas, D. and Rowlands, I. (2010) 'E-journal usage and impact in scholarly research: a review of the literature', *New Review of Academic Librarianship*, 16(2): 192–207.

Zhang, L. (2011) 'Use of web resources in the journal literature 2001 and 2007: a cross-disciplinary study', *College and Research Libraries*, 72(2): 167–79.

10

What we leave behind:
the future of data curation

Aldalin Lyngdoh

Abstract. The term data curation was first formulated for scientific data. Once published, scientific data should remain available forever so that other scientists and researchers can reproduce the results and perform further experiments using this data. Traditionally, researchers have not saved or documented everything for long-term access, as this was neither economical nor feasible. However, it is now becoming possible to store all the data from most experiments and storage and access over the Internet is a reality. But documenting and curating the data is not free.

This chapter's main aim and purpose is only to provide an overview of process in the scientific environment, briefly touching upon the main aspects of data curation and bringing together research on the various technical problems faced by data scientists in a bite-size form. One question this paper aims to answer is what data should be preserved for future use. The issues around data preservation have also been addressed.

Keywords: data curation, interoperability, metadata, preservation, scientific data

Introduction

> What we leave behind is [not] as important as how we've
> lived. After all ... we're only mortal.
>
> (Captain Picard in *Star Trek: Generations*)

This is true not just for 'mortals' but for data as well. It is necessary to preserve what we have learnt in our lifetime or it will be lost forever once we are gone. We need to preserve not just our knowledge but, for the progress of humankind, we need also to save the source of this knowledge – data. Besides enabling us to set up a knowledge base for referencing and research, its safeguarding represents an important milestone in the history of its collection, history and usage.

The University of Illinois at Urbana-Champaign defined data curation as follows:

> Data curation is the active and ongoing management of data through its lifecycle of interest and usefulness to scholarship, science, and education. Data curation enables data discovery and retrieval, maintains data quality, adds value, and provides for re-use over time through activities including authentication, archiving, management, preservation, and representation.[1]

The recognised significance of data curation in science has been brought about by the exponentially increasing volume of primary data in its digital form, generated by its automated collection through experiment, surveys and simulation, as well as derived or compiled data. According to James Farnhill derived/compiled data is 'data that already exists that is used to do something new' (Korn et al., 2007). A good example of derived data is text mining where thousands of papers are put into the machine and at the end you get a précis of the most relevant ones and, potentially, links that have not previously been discovered by researchers (Korn et al., 2007). Data, in itself, has no meaning. For it to assume a value it must be interpreted in its intellectual context. In data curation, context comprises the metadata, which aids the intelligent, efficient and enhanced discovery, retrieval, use and preservation of the data over time. As data is accumulated and its volume perpetually increases, the problem lies not in finding the information but laying one's hand on the relevant bits easily and quickly, as otherwise it may prove time-consuming to the user to sift through the mass of data before finding the pertinent information.

To elaborate and clarify the concept of metadata the example of the Assyrian period, where royal scholars archived important texts like letters, queries and reports for reference purpose, may be used. For ease of access they were organised according to content, using a variety of filing cabinets, leather bags and baskets with clay filing labels attached. This idea survived into the twenty-first century in the form of catalogue cards librarians used to note down the details of books before they were automated and moved onto computers. The actual book constitutes the data and the catalogue card its metadata.

This paper does not aim to give in-depth information on data curation; its main aim and purpose is only to provide an overview of process in the scientific environment, briefly touching upon the main aspects of data curation and bringing together research on the various technical problems faced by data scientists in a bite-size form. A lot of work still needs to be done in this field and it all starts with the researchers' understanding of the need and necessity to preserve the data they accumulate over the years and sharing this information with others.

Selection for preservation

The first and foremost dilemma in data curation is: *what data needs to be preserved?* According to Nystrom (1973): 'One of the consequences of the change [to our modern conception of knowledge] is a movement away from the rigid compartmentalized, uncoordinated specialization in scientific inquiry which characterizes the Newtonian world and a movement toward increasing integration of both the physical and social sciences.' Here, Nystrom examines the growing popularity of the concept of 'interdisciplinarity' or interdisciplinary studies among scholars. This led to the proliferation of data, which then catalysed the need for curation.

However, the problem continues: *what criteria should determine the curation (or not) of data?* Views differ as to the preservation of research data, ranging from determining what we will or will not keep to keeping everything as we never know what might prove useful in the future. According to Gray et al. (2002), some data are irreplaceable and must be saved; other data can be regenerated. He called the two kinds of data 'ephemeral data' and 'stable data'. *Ephemeral data* cannot be replicated or recreated. If we do not record the data today, a decade from now no one will know the rate of inflation, position of stars, pollution at a given time and place or the rites within the paddy ritual of a tribe caught in the confluence of change: this is representative of ephemeral data. 'Metadata about derived data products is ephemeral: the design documents, email, programs and procedures that produce a derived dataset would all be impossible to reconstruct' (Gray et al., 2002). To understand the data collected, later users need metadata. Data by itself is incomprehensible and thus useless and unless there is a detailed and clear description of how, when and where it was gathered, and how the derived data was produced, it would be completely unusable. But, given that metadata, the derived data can be reconstructed from the source data. So one only needs to record the data reduction procedures in order to allow for its reconstruction. Metadata is hence *ephemeral*.

Not all data needs to be saved. Data derived from simulation, from reduction of other data or from measuring phenomena not dependent on time is *stable data* and need not be kept. Let us take an example to illustrate the importance of data and its preservation not just in the world today but in a century not too long ago. The veracity of this story is unclear, but the point it makes is extremely relevant today. According to this legend, Tycho Brahe (a sixteenth-century physicist) observed the positions of the planets, sun and nearly 800 stars to an unprecedented accuracy before the telescope was even invented. He recorded all his observations in hundreds of pages of a *data book* which he was said to have guarded with his life and did not allow anyone to have access. It was not until he became the mentor of Johannes Kepler that he allowed his data to be seen by a second pair of eyes. Kepler's mathematical ability allowed him to analyse Brahe's data and develop his three laws of planetary motion – laws still in wide use today. These laws are now called Kepler's laws. This is just one of the many examples of how vital data is; using the data collected by another scientist Kepler was able to formulate laws that have not only immortalised him but also made a breakthrough in astronomy. Had Tycho Brahe not collected the information and made a painstaking recording of them in his journals, Kepler would never have formulated his planetary laws and the observations that Brahe made would have died with him, causing a major development in astronomy to have taken another century.

Why focus on scientific data when there is a considerable amount of data from the social sciences?

To answer this question one has to look back to the rise of interdisciplinarity. Science is one of the largest disciplines within which there is almost always an interrelation/crossover between the sub-disciplines. This led to the proliferation of compound disciplines such as biophysics, mathematical biochemistry, psychobiology and so on, and this led to the generation of large amounts of data which in turn resulted in the continuing process of scientific discovery. Earlier, scientists were isolated in their research laboratory and only interacted with their peers when things in the lab went well. Most of their information and data were recorded in their notebooks that were inaccessible to anyone but themselves. This data was not published and made public even after the research was completed. Today scientific data is no longer isolated. This rate of proliferation of data and its accessibility changes the very nature of scientific research. Thousands of years ago science was experimental where the scientist actively influenced his area of research to observe the consequences. Hundreds of years later science became theoretical, where the scientist observed but could not control the variables. This was then later replaced by computational science. To put it simply, computational science is the application of computing capabilities to the solution of the problem in the real world. Computational science makes it possible to examine the interplay of processes across disciplinary boundaries (PITAC, 2005).

In 2009, Microsoft published a book of essays, *The Fourth Paradigm: Data-Intensive Scientific Discovery* (Hey, 2009), that argues that a fourth paradigm of scientific discovery is at hand: the analysis of massive data sets. This idea was first pioneered by Jim Gray, a researcher at Microsoft, with the catchphrase: 'It's the data, stupid'. The basic idea is that our capacity for collecting scientific data has far outstripped our present capacity to analyse it, and so our focus should be on developing technologies that will make sense of this 'Deluge of Data' (Hey, 2009). This is due to the ability of modern instrumentation to generate data at rates 100–1,000-fold that of the devices they replaced. A famous example of this would be the next-generation DNA sequencing (Kell, 2009). Although these instruments for the production of data only began to become commercially available in 2004, they are already having a major impact on our ability to explore and answer genome-wide biological questions. These technologies are not only changing our genome-sequencing approaches and the associated timelines and costs, but also accelerating and altering a wide variety of types of biological inquiry that have historically used a sequencing-based readout, or are effecting a transition to this type of readout. Furthermore, next-generation platforms are helping to open entirely new areas of biological inquiry, including the investigation of ancient genomes, the characterisation of ecological diversity and the identification of unknown aetiologic agents. Today, most research in biological science is data driven and one cannot but emphasise the importance of it (Mardis, 2008; Shendure and Ji, 2008).

How should data be preserved?

One of the greatest challenges of twenty-first-century science is how we respond to this new era of data-intensive research (Kell, 2009). Once we have identified what needs to be preserved our next problem arises: *how to preserve the data?* As we all know, the media in which we store information changes constantly – from magnetic tapes to computer to 'cloud' storage and so on – in the endless chain of invention and obsolescence. Not only do the media change but also the format in which they are stored gets updated or transformed. Furthermore, to add to the increasing problem of data preservation is the lack of standards (Gray et al., 2002). What is today a state-of-the-art medium for data storage and preservation can become archaic tomorrow. Ensuring long-term access to this vast universe of data is a huge problem. One of the many key challenges is *media obsolescence*. Obsolescence describes a state of becoming obsolete rather than a state of already being obsolete (Pearson and Webb, 2008). Issues of media failure and obsolescence have received a lot of press coverage over the years. All forms of media are susceptible to failure, be it minor or disastrous.[2] This of course depends on the type of media. Tapes, optical media and hard disk drives in servers are prone to wear and tear over time. For all these media types the consequences of a very small failure can be very significant. Furthermore, these media require specific hardware to read them (Morris and Truskowski, 2003). It is not therefore surprising how quickly they become unavailable or are phased out. In addition, even if we were to overcome the problem of media obsolescence, we are then faced with various *file formats obsolescence*. A file format is the structure of how information is stored or encoded in a computer file. File formats are designed to store specific types of information, such as JPEG and TIFF for image or raster data, Adobe Illustrator (AI) for vector data, or PDF for document exchange. In very simple terms, file format is a particular way of encoding information for storage and use. While the term 'file format' technically refers to the structure and content of a file, the term is also used interchangeably with 'file type', which defines a specific type of file, such as a rich text file or a Photoshop document.[3] Digital content has been and will be encoded in diverse file formats, access to which depends on the availability of the means to understand the encoding.

According to Pearson and Webb (2008), file format obsolescence is related to two often-observed phenomena:

- the development of new format encoding; and

- changes in the availability of presentation tools.

The basic premise of digital preservation is the maintenance of an ability to provide meaningful access. When file formats can no longer be read reliably, access to them is lost and this defeats the purpose of digital preservation.

Interoperability

Our next most contentious issue in data preservation is *interoperability*. According to the World Wide Web Consortium (W3C) 'this new-fangled word is a variant of that other, rather better known new-fangled word, compatibility, and it simply means that something (a document, a program) written according to our specifications should work identically across different applications and different computers/platforms.'[4] There have been many attempts at defining the concept of interoperability in relation to data and data curation. A few examples are given below:

> Interoperability is the ability of multiple systems with different hardware and software platforms, data structures, and interfaces to exchange data with minimal loss of content and functionality. (Hodge and NISO, 2004)

> Interoperability is the ability of two or more systems or components to exchange information and use the exchanged information without special effort on either system. (Committee on Cataloguing: Description and Access, 2000)

> Interoperability: The compatibility of two or more systems such that they can exchange information and data and can use the exchanged information and data without any special manipulation. (Taylor, 1999)

Interoperability is one of the most important principles in metadata implementation, other than simplicity, modularity, reusability and extensibility (Duval et al., 2002; Zeng and Chan, 2004). Data interoperability involves both syntactic and semantic translation. Syntactic interoperability is achieved by marking up our data in a similar fashion so that we can share the data and our machines can understand and take the data apart in sensible ways, for example Extensible Markup Language (XML), Encoded Archival Description (EAD) and Machine Readable Cataloguing (MARC). 'Semantic interoperability is achieved through agreements about content description standards; for example Dublin Core, Anglo-American Cataloguing Rules' (Gehre et al., 2005). However, such content description standards can ensure semantic interoperability only if a domain ontology that suffices a set of basic features is established, in accordance with the following definition based on Gruber (1993): 'An ontology is a formal, explicit specification of a shared conceptualization.'

Both types of translation (syntactic and semantic) are hindered by the lack of standard data models, formats and vocabulary/ontology. Different data sources provide their data in heterogeneous formats. For example, while some data are represented in HyperText Markup Language (HTML) format that can be interpreted by web browsers, other data formats are in flat files. However, according to GENESI-DR EC Grant Agreement (Manzella, 2009), today, different scientific and technological communities are working together to develop federated information systems by applying interoperability solutions and recognising facts such as the following:

- Metadata are critical for recording the provenance of data, including processing steps and quality control certification.

- Auto-harvesting the information, selecting interoperability standards, exchanging metadata and synchronising metadata with evolving standards and needs are important and difficult challenges.

An important reason for creating descriptive metadata is to facilitate the discovery of relevant information. In addition to resource discovery, metadata can help organise electronic resources, facilitate interoperability and legacy resource integration, provide digital identification and support archiving and preservation. Describing a resource with metadata allows it to be understood by both humans and machines in ways that promote interoperability (Noguerasiso et al., 2004). Using defined metadata schemes, shared transfer protocols and crosswalks between schemes, resources across the network can be searched more seamlessly.

Metadata schemes (also called schema) are sets of descriptor types designed for a specific purpose, such as describing a particular type of information resource. The definition or meaning of the elements or descriptor types themselves is known as the semantics of the scheme. Numerous metadata schemes have been developed in a variety of user environments and disciplines, which emerged from the needs of specific interest groups to standardise how they classify information (Gunia and Sandusky, 2010). Some of the most important work on metadata interoperability was done by the W3C, which incorporated metadata activity into the Semantic Web, their initiative to 'provide a common framework that allows data to be shared and reused across application, enterprise, and community boundaries' (Chung and Moen, 2007).

An important prerequisite for achieving semantic interoperability on the Web is the ability to make use of rich computer languages, such as the Web Ontology Language (OWL) to describe the various entities in the computing environment. OWL facilitates greater machine interpretability of Web content than that supported by XML, Resource Description Framework (RDF) and RDF Schema (RDFS) by providing additional vocabulary along with a formal semantics (Herman, 2007). Hence, although XML Document Type Definitions (DTDs) and XML Schemas seem sufficient in the beginning for exchanging data between groups who have previously agreed to some set of shared definitions, their lack of constructs to describe the deeper meaning of these definitions prevents machines from reliably performing this task. For example, when a new XML vocabulary is introduced, the same term may be used with (sometimes subtle) different meanings in different contexts, and different terms may be used for items that have the same meaning (Gehre et al., 2005).

RDF and RDFS addressed this problem by allowing simple semantics to be associated with identifiers. RDF is designed to represent information in a minimally constraining, flexible way. It can be used in isolated applications, where individually designed formats might be more direct and easily understood, but RDF's generality offers greater value from sharing. The value of information thus increases as it becomes accessible to more applications across the entire Internet (Manola and Miller, 2004). RDFS provides information about the interpretation of the statements given in an RDF data model. A schema defines not only the properties of the resource (e.g. title, author, subject, size, colour, etc.) but may also define the kinds of resources being described (books, web pages, people, companies) (Manola and Miller, 2004).

For this to happen, RDF is one of the key enabling standards; it is a standard model for data interchange on the Web (Gehre et al., 2005). RDF extends the linking structure of the Web to use Uniform Resource Identifiers (URI) to name the relationship between things as well as the two ends of the link (this is usually referred to as a 'triple'). Using this simple model, it allows structured and semi-structured data to be mixed, exposed and shared across different applications. The Semantic Web efforts are directed to standards that increase the interoperability of metadata rather than specific metadata schemas (Cardoso, 2009). The World Wide Web has created a revolution in the accessibility of information. The development and application of metadata represents a major improvement in the way information can be discovered and used. New technologies, standards and best practices are continually advancing the applications for metadata (Hodge and NISO, 2004).

The Semantic Web and data curation

Semantic Web technologies aim to define and interconnect data in a way similar to that in which traditional web technologies define and interconnect web pages. In the case of the traditional Web, each web page can be considered a unit of information or entity and pages are explicitly linked using HTML links. The Semantic Web also allows data to be shared using 'linked data' (Berners-Lee, 2009) support where entities can be referenced and their information can be accessed on the Web as part of a linked network of data. One of the appeals of Semantic Web technologies lies in the potential for linking and integrating data from multiple sources and subsequently being able to query and retrieve information across these different sources (Khan et al., 2010).

End note

I have discussed a lot about the few 'technical difficulties' faced when curating scientific data. I have not, however, touched on many topics such as determining the provenance of data, ethical issues, intellectual property issues, funding and many more. These topics are as important as any I have referred to but attempting to squeeze everything into a small paragraph will not do them justice. So, returning to the original topic, with the increasing amount of data being produced in a scientific environment the issue of how we handle this vast generation of scientific data becomes of 'paramount importance' (Berman, 2003). The effort required for the management of and preservation of access to collections of scientific and technical data to be a routine aspect of scientific research and development is substantial. Increasing amounts of scientific data are born digital or become digitised. At the same time, studies show that, in some cases, as many as 20 per cent of Internet addresses become inactive within a year (Dellavalle, 2003). This ephemeral nature of Internet document identifiers will impact the long-term access to scientific data. As Smith (2002) pointed out, 'digital resources will not survive or remain accessible by accident'. Hence, we may suggest that data curation is not just about preservation but about maintaining and adding value (Giaretta, 2005) to data for current and future use. A considerable effort needs to be put into developing continuing information infrastructures for digital materials and into developing the digital curation skills of researchers and information professionals. Without this, current investment in digitisation and digital content will only guarantee short-term rather than long-term benefits.

Dedication

I would like to dedicate this essay to my late Professor Veena Saraf.

Notes

1. *http://www.lis.illinois.edu/academics/programs/ms/data_curation*
2. *http://www.uky.edu/~kiernan/DL/hedstrom.html*
3. *http://www.techterms.com/definition/file_format*
4. *http://www.w3.org/People/Bos/DesignGuide/interoperability.html#Interopera*

References

Berman, F. (2003) *Grid Computing: Making the Global Infrastructure a Reality.* Chichester: Wiley.

Berners-Lee, T. (2009) 'Linked Data – Design Issues', *Linked Data.* Online at *http://www.w3.org/DesignIssues/LinkedData.html.*

Cardoso, J. (2009) 'The Semantic Web: a mythical story or a solid reality?', in M.-A. Sicilia and M.D. Lytras (eds), *Metadata and Semantics.* Boston: Springer US, pp. 253–7. Online at: *http://www.springerlink.com/index/10.1007/978-0-387-77745-0_24.*

Chung, E. and Moen, W.E. (2007) 'The semantics of semantic interoperability: a two-dimensional approach for investigating issues of semantic interoperability in digital libraries', in *Proceedings of the American Society for Information Science and Technology (ASIST)*, 70th Annual American Society for Information Science and Technology Meeting. Online at: *http://digital.library.unt.edu/ark:/67531/metadc36296/.*

Committee on Cataloguing: Description and Access (2000) *ALA/ALCTS/CCS Committee on Cataloging: Description and Access – Task Force on Metadata: Final Report (6/2000)*, Association for Library Collection and Technical Service. Online at: *http://www.libraries.psu.edu/tas/jca/ccda/tf-meta6.html.*

Dellavalle, R.P. (2003) 'INFORMATION SCIENCE: going, going, gone: lost Internet references', *Science*, 302(5646): 787–8.

Duval, E., Hodgins, W., Sutton, S. and Weibel, S.L. (2002) 'Metadata principles and practicalities', *D-Lib Magazine*, 8(4). Online at: *http://www.dlib.org/dlib/april02/weibel/04weibel.html.*

Gehre, A., Katranuschkov, P., Stankovski, V. and Scherer, R.J. (2005) *Towards Semantic Interoperability in Virtual Organisations.* Paper presented at the 22nd Conference of Information Technology in Construction, cibW78, Dresden, Germany.

Giaretta, D. (2005) *DCC Approach to Digital Curation*. Online at: *http://twiki. dcc.rl.ac.uk/bin/view/OLD/DCCApproachToCuration*.

Gray, J., Szalay, A.S., Thaker, A.R., Stoughton, C. and Vandenberg, J. (2002) *Online Scientific Data Curation, Publication, and Archiving*. Redmond, WA: Microsoft Corporation. Online at: *http://research.microsoft.com/apps/pubs/ default.aspx?id=64568*.

Gruber, T. (1993) 'A translation approach to portable ontology specifications', *Knowledge Acquisition*, 52(2): 199–220.

Gunia, B. and Sandusky, R.J. (2010) 'Designing metadata for long-term data preservation: DataONE case study', *Proceedings of the American Society for Information Science and Technology*, 47(1): 1–2.

Herman, I. (2007) 'Web Ontology Language OWL/W3C Semantic Web Activity', *Semantic Web*. Online at: *http://www.w3.org/2004/OWL/*.

Hey, A. (ed.) (2009) *The Fourth Paradigm: Data-Intensive Scientific Discovery*. Redmond, WA: Microsoft Research.

Hodge, G. and National Information Standards Organization (US) (2004) *Understanding Metadata*. Bethesda, MD: NISO Press.

Kell, D. (2009) 'The fourth paradigm of scientific knowledge generation – data-intensive science', Professor Douglas Kell's blog. Online at: *http://blogs.bbsrc. ac.uk/index.php/2009/03/the-fourth-paradigm-of-scientific-knowledge-generation/*.

Khan, H., Caruso, B., Corson-Rikert, J., Dietrich, D., Lowe, B. and Steinhart, G. (2010) *DataStaR: Using the Semantic Web Approach for Data Curation*. Paper presented at the 6th International Conference on Digital Curation, Chicago. Online at: *http://ecommons.cornell.edu/handle/1813/22945?mode= full&submit_simple=Show+full+item+record*.

Korn, N., Oppenheim, C. and Duncan, C. (2007) *IPR and Licensing Issues in Derived Data*. JISC. Online at: *http://www.jisc.ac.uk/media/documents/projects/ iprinderiveddatareport.pdf*.

Manola, F. and Miller, E. (eds) (2004) *RDF Primer*. Online at: *http://www.w3. org/TR/rdf-primer/*.

Manzella, G.M.R (2009) 'Report on Research on Data Curation and Interoperability'. Online at: *http://www.genesi-dr.eu/documents/GENESI-DR-JRA2-DEL-DJRA2.2%20v2.pdf*.

Mardis, E.R. (2008) 'Next-generation DNA sequencing methods', *Annual Review of Genomics and Human Genetics*, 9: 387–402.

Morris, R.J.T. and Truskowski, B.J. (2003) 'The evolution of storage systems', *IBM Systems Journal*, 42(2): 205–17.

Noguerasiso, J., Zarazaga-Soria, F.J., Lacasta, J., Bejar, R. and Muro-Medrano, P.R. (2004) 'Metadata standard interoperability: application in the geographic information domain', *Computers, Environment and Urban Systems*, 28(6): 611–34.

Nystrom, C.L. (1973) *Towards a Science of Media Ecology: The Formulation of Integrated Conceptual Paradigms for the Study of Human Communication Systems*. PhD dissertation, New York University.

Pearson, D. and Webb, C. (2008) 'Defining file format obsolescence: a risky journey', *International Journal of Digital Curation*, 3(1). Online at: *http:// www.ijdc.net/index.php/ijdc/article/view/76*.

President's Information Technology Advisory Committee (PITAC) (2005) *Computational Science: Ensuring America's Competitiveness*. Arlington, VA: National Coordination Office for Information Technology Research and Development (NCO/IT R&D). Online at: *http://www.nitrd.gov/pubs/*.

Shendure, J. and Ji, H. (2008) 'Next-generation DNA sequencing', *Nature Biotechnology*, 26(10): 1135–45.

Smith, B. (2002) 'Preserving tomorrow's memory: preserving digital content for future generations', *Information Services and Use*, 22(2, 3): 133–9.

Taylor, A. (1999) *The Organization of Information*. Englewood, CO: Libraries Unlimited.

Zeng, L.M. and Chan, M.L. (2004) 'Trends and issues in establishing interoperability among knowledge organization systems', *Journal of the American Society for Information Science and Technology*, 55(5): 377–95.

11

The digital curation toolkit: strategies for adding value to work-related social systems

Abby Clobridge

Abstract. Since the mid-2000s, systems, applications, tools and websites that facilitate connecting, collaborating and information sharing – often referred to as 'Web 2.0' – have become the norm throughout much of the Internet. Users expect to be able to connect with information in ways that are different from what was typical in the early or pre-Internet world where people were restricted to playing the role of information consumer. This shift from passive consumption to active interaction has important implications in terms of information and knowledge management.

These implications, particularly when applied to the work environment, have raised new challenges within information and knowledge management – challenges that are best addressed through the application of digital curation. Digital curation is a developing field within information science, situated at the intersection of information management, knowledge management, communication and technology. Digital curation work aims to add value and meaning to digital content.

Keywords: descriptors, digital curation, digital curators, knowledge sharing, metadata, strategies, tagging, tags, user behaviour

Introduction

Since the mid-2000s, systems, applications, tools and websites that facilitate connecting, collaborating and information sharing – often referred to as 'Web 2.0' – have become the norm throughout much of the Internet. Users expect to be able to connect with information in ways that are different from what was typical in the early or pre-Internet world where people were restricted to playing the role of information consumer. This shift from passive consumption to active interaction has the following important implications in terms of information and knowledge management:

- Content creation is no longer the domain of experts.

- Sharing and disseminating information happens in a multitude of ways, many of them far less formal than traditional publishing methods.

- Content is constantly increasing at exponential rates. It is not possible to collect, catalogue and organise all published information in any field, and the concept of 'information overload' is becoming widely accepted.

- There is a difference between findability – that is, the ability to search for and successfully retrieve a specific bit of information – and discoverability – the ability to stumble upon information by browsing or searching through large quantities of information and finding something that meets the requested criteria. For instance, searching for 'flower' in Flickr[1] returns over 18 million results, but it might not be possible to find the exact flower for which someone was searching.

These implications, particularly when applied to the work environment, have raised new challenges within information and knowledge management, challenges that are best addressed through the application of *digital curation*. Digital curation is a developing field within information science, situated at the intersection of information management, knowledge management, communication and technology. Digital curation work aims to add value and meaning to digital content.

The digital curation strategies outlined in this chapter are designed to add value to content and people's experiences interacting with that content, specifically within the work-related context. At the strategic level, digital curation work aims to support digital content within work-related 'social systems'[2] by:

- *adding value*: enhancing, augmenting, showcasing, repackaging and describing information and knowledge;

- *advocating for users*: supporting users' needs, experiences and interactions with digital content, and identifying and anticipating changes in user needs;

- *adding meaning*: taking digital content and elevating it from information to knowledge by providing context, examples, meaning, additional details and connections;

- *supporting resource and content discovery*: linking people with the *right* information – making information findable and retrievable;

- *preparing for the future*: staying abreast of emerging and maturing tools;

- *focusing on the big picture*: emerging issues, trends and themes within the organisation and in the external environment;

- *supporting organisational effectiveness through knowledge management*: establishing ways to collect and make accessible an organisation's lessons learned, best practices and internal expertise.

Digital curation practices take a variety of forms in order to meet the unique needs of each organisation in terms of its culture, values, systems, technology infrastructure, industry and staff. However, the strategies outlined here are intended to be easily adaptable and adoptable based on organisational needs, user needs, corporate mandates, and evolving technologies. Even as technologies or processes are updated, automated or replaced, the mission of digital curation will remain the same: to enhance and add value to digital content in order to best support the people using that information and knowledge – to support how people connect to each other, to knowledge and to information.

Strategies, methods and best practices for digital curation

The strategies and practices outlined here are designed to serve as a starting point rather than a recipe for digital curation. The methods and approaches described have their basis in three key areas:

1. *Information management*: selecting, collecting, organising, describing, disseminating research, data and information.

2. *Knowledge management*: supporting the process of collecting, describing, disseminating insights and knowledge based on information and experiences.

3. *Organisational behaviour*: understanding the needs, value and culture of an organisation as a whole as well as its groups and individuals

Several of the specific practices are related to user-applied tags, taxonomy terms and other types of user-generated metadata as these are the entry points for most digital curation practices.

Strategies are organised into five main clusters of activities:

1. Monitoring, highlighting and showcasing digital content
2. Knowing your users
3. Encouraging knowledge sharing
4. Incorporating technology trends and emerging applications
5. Monitoring and evaluation

These strategies are designed to support social systems in any type of workplace environment including private-sector companies, public-sector organisations, government departments, civil society organisations, schools, universities and research organisations.

Monitoring, highlighting and showcasing digital content

Digital curators are continually looking for new ways to select and draw attention to the most useful information on relevant topics. Practices include:

- creating information bundles;
- trendspotting;
- articulating the 'aboutness' of content.

In a world that is cluttered with information overload, showcasing information and knowledge shared within an organisation is an extremely valuable niche for digital curators to claim.

Create information bundles

One role of digital curation is to monitor the environment – internally produced content as well as relevant parts of the external environment – and then develop ways to highlight and draw attention to a mix of useful, important and interesting content. One approach is to create a daily or weekly 'information bundle' that is disseminated via the system – a package of information pulling together carefully selected news, blog posts, tweets, resources, event listings, videos, images and any other media that might be of use to the community. This approach, when implemented well, helps to attract attention to important content, draw users to the system on a regular basis and keep content fresh.

Likewise, curators can enhance content by developing new components. Curators can prepare summaries of individual articles, blog posts and documents posted to the system, or write overviews of groupings of information, bringing together related items from disparate sources. In either case, the curated portion of the work should include clear links to all referenced items and other related resources such as collections of bookmarks or library-prepared content on the same topic.

Another strategy is to repackage information – take information posted in articles or blog posts and turn it into infographics, infoboxes, or video or audio interviews. As not all individuals are verbal learners, transforming content into an audio or visual format may appeal to other types of learner.

Trendspotting: support emerging trends through hashtags

Platforms such as Twitter[3] build on ways to showcase current trends and tags. This idea of 'trending topics' is extremely popular: Twitter embeds current popular tags directly into its interface. Highlighting these tags serves multiple purposes:

- It serves as an entry point for users to browse content.
- Users are able to discover current popular trends and topics in their field.
- Users are able to learn what makes a good tag for sharing information.
- It demonstrates a way in which tags are used, implicitly encouraging users to apply meaningful tags when they contribute content.

Watching for emerging trends with tags has benefits for both digital curators and users. For digital curators, it is important to spot patterns, emerging themes and ways in which users are applying tags. If useful practices are developing, it is important to highlight them as they emerge. If problematic trends begin to emerge, it is important to spot them and deal with them as necessary as they begin to occur rather than after workflows have been established.

For users, if digital curators showcase tags related to current issues or topics, it provides guidance on how to tag related content and raises awareness of tags. For instance, a graphical information box may be created and placed in a highly visible location for the 'Tag of the Week' or 'Trends of the Week' – a specific tag or group of tags that users are encouraged to apply when relevant to an emerging issue or a hashtag for an upcoming event. The box can also provide scope notes and other suggested terms. As part of the process, curators should also review existing content and apply additional tags if necessary to ensure content that is being used as an example is well tagged. Last, each tag in the infobox should be hyperlinked to a search query for that tag.

Articulate the 'aboutness' of digital content

While most users are able to tag key names of people, objects or events, the meaning and context of digital content is often overlooked – and is critically important. The idea of 'aboutness' includes the 'who, what, where, when and why' of something, but it is particularly important in capturing the underlying ideas, concepts and themes that are not necessarily explicitly articulated and therefore often not clearly described in tags.

Without tags, terms or descriptors describing the 'aboutness' of something, it is extremely challenging for even the best search engines to correctly retrieve results or it is made difficult or impossible for curators to find and showcase content on a particular topic. Reviewing knowledge resources that are of strategic importance is an extremely valuable service for digital curators to perform, one that is closely related to the traditional work of librarians and information professionals. The trick is identifying and sticking to criteria to determine which items are of strategic importance. Some suggestions are as follows:

- summaries, final reports;
- items coming from high-level administrative offices;
- items clicked on the highest number of times;
- items selected for inclusion in information bundles;
- items of current/anticipated importance;
- items related to upcoming organisation-wide meetings.

Knowing your users

Digital curators need to know and understand their users – what their users expect, how they behave, what actions they take, what types of activities they shy away from using within a given system, and what commonly adopted roles there are within an organisation.

User expectations

The reality is that most – although not necessarily all – of Internet-accessible adults have at least some exposure to other social systems such as Facebook,[4] LinkedIn,[5] Yammer,[6] Google+[7] or Ning[8] that they have encountered outside of the work environment. Even if someone does not have an account in a social network, social aspects are being incorporated into news sites such as CNN[9] and the BBC[10] and international shopping sites such as Amazon[11] and eBay.[12] The result is that users' interactions with systems outside of the work environment influence what users expect for *all* web-based systems with social components. Thus, the Web 2.0 hallmarks of engagement, collaboration and information sharing should be the starting point for how a work-related system should function. Digital curators should stay aware of patterns and trends in major web-based systems to be informed of what users expect from work-related systems. Furthermore, curators should be prepared to answer common questions from users such as:

- Why should we use this system instead of LinkedIn or Yammer?
- Why aren't search results as good as Google or Bing?
- Why should we use this to work collaboratively instead of Google Docs?

User behaviour, user needs, user wants

As part of the process to get to know user behaviour as a whole, digital curators should review data on how users behave once in the system, perform usability studies, review individuals' paths once in the system and watch how individuals interact with the system. Data should be collected via a mix of formal and informal techniques and should include both quantitative and qualitative data: informal polls posted within the system, open-ended survey questions, interviews with individuals or small groups and closed survey questions. It can be helpful to start with interviews before drafting survey questions to get a starting point for issues that are most important to users.

In any case, use the results of data to drive decision-making processes: determining which fields to focus cleaning/maintenance efforts on, deciding whether the existing search system and search algorithms are sufficient, how best to reach non-users and so on. (See section on 'Data collection, analysis and reporting' later in this chapter for more practices related to gathering and reviewing data.)

Encouraging knowledge sharing

Knowledge management is the process of extracting, collecting, articulating and disseminating insights, organisational lessons learned, best practices, narrative stories and other forms of knowledge based on information and experiences. Getting users to share knowledge is more challenging than simply sharing bookmarks or posting links to articles. Furthermore, organisational knowledge is often not available in an explicit format. Digital curators should be involved in trying new ways to support knowledge development and sharing within organisations such as capturing storytelling on video or establishing communities of practice across traditional location or organisational unit boundaries.

Support engagement and knowledge sharing at any level

Digital curators can play an important role in supporting engagement and knowledge sharing at any level – from individuals who are just testing the waters to those who are fully embracing the work – and encouraging the organisation to take an active role in incentivising knowledge sharing in general. Digital curators can provide opportunities for all types of users to engage in activities within a knowledge sharing system. For casual users – those who are interested in participating without contributing their own knowledge – establish various easy, informal ways to get engaged:

- post status updates;
- comment on blog posts, articles, bookmarks and other types of content contributed by other users;
- rate materials contributed by others;
- vote in informal polls;
- highlight good examples to be followed by others.

For more engaged users, provide opportunities for deeper forms of knowledge sharing and exchange:

- host or participate in group discussions;

- enable users to create their own communities of practice;

- contribute to organisational content repository – training materials, handouts, marketing materials – and knowledge exchange – slides from PowerPoint decks, links to presentations hosted elsewhere, embedded presentations or interviews;

- use the system for group/project progress reports, project management documents;

- use the system for event planning and management;

- create and post customisable templates for common workflows and organisational practices.

Engage users via tags

Tags have become an essential way to organise content, yet they are often not fully utilised once they are collected. For the most part, tags do not significantly affect search results since typical user tags already match terms already in the content to which they are attached, yet they are opportunities to solicit user engagement and serve as the entry point for many digital curation practices. One way to encourage tagging is to incorporate collaborative, tag-based discussions designed to get users interacting with each other and allow them to become comfortable sharing via the system. For example, the website 43Things[13] asks users to list their goals, which are then converted into tags. The result is a massive, tag-based cloud of goals. Organisations can easily adapt this idea and ask users other questions, questions that are more specific to their organisation or environment.

As users see the benefits of tagging, they are more inclined to invest time in tagging activities. Likewise, as tags are more heavily utilised throughout a system, users become more familiar with the formatting of tags and how to construct useful tags according to current trends. Having general questions not directly related to work activities allows users to become more comfortable with a knowledge-sharing system and sharing personal thoughts within the community.

Incentives for knowledge sharing

A major issue for most work-related systems is a lack of incentive for sharing knowledge. While it is not a digital curator's responsibility to formally review individuals' contributions, curators can serve several related roles:

1. Articulate the importance of knowledge sharing and incentives to administrators and managers. If knowledge sharing is a core value for the organisation, it is important to reiterate to administrators that knowledge sharing should be incentivised and rewarded.

2. Contribute to the development of organisational policies that enable and encourage knowledge sharing.

3. Provide informal recognition through the system – highlight contributions by individuals and departments which are prolific contributors.

4. Share good practices from departments and units with the broader community. Create a feed or channel with screenshots or written summaries of what departments come up with on their own as best practices to encourage contributions and exchange knowledge.

5. In conjunction with an organisational development group, establish a monthly or quarterly award to give to an individual or department who best exemplifies knowledge sharing with the organisation.

Incorporate emerging technologies, tools and applications

The Semantic Web

The underlying theme connecting most of the current work within information management is that of the Semantic Web. The general idea behind the Semantic Web is to create a system in which machines are able to 'understand' information presented on the Internet in the same way that humans can understand or comprehend information – thus allowing machines to better support standard processes such as finding, storing, translating or combining information from disparate sources. In short, the Semantic Web is a vision for the Internet in which more complex human requests are able to be intelligently interpreted by search engines and computers based on the *semantics* of the request – the relationships between words and phrases, their context and their intended meaning.

Three types of Semantic Web applications starting to emerge that are of particular importance to digital curation for work-related systems are as follows:

- *Automated tag extraction.* Automated tag extraction tools are designed to automate the process of extracting concepts, terms and ideas from a specified web page, document or other type of knowledge resource. While many such scripts, programs and tools have existed for years, several more advanced tools have been released that incorporate parts-of-speech (POS) tagging and linguistic analysis.

- *Vocabulary prompting.* Vocabulary prompting applications provide suggestions for other tags/terms for users to consider adding to a particular web page, document or other type of knowledge resource. They can be extremely helpful for users who are new to tagging or are pressed for time. Vocabulary prompting functionality can also suggest alternate preferred versions of tags – for example, 'did you mean "human resources" instead of "HR"?' and cutting down on duplicate and redundant tags.

- *Data visualisation.* Data visualisation tools enable users to create diagrams or other visual representations of concepts, tags or terms within a data set as well as the relationship between terms. Clustering is one such method – individual tags, terms and concepts are displayed in 'clusters' based on their similarities. Concept maps focus on the specific relationships between individual terms rather than groups of terms. Concept maps and clustering techniques are both more advanced versions of tag clouds – the popular Web 2.0 mechanism for displaying tags in a 'cloud' with more often used tags being weighted higher and therefore appearing larger in terms of font size. Clustering and concept maps both provide a more detailed view of a data set rather than a snapshot view.

Table 11.1 provides an overview of selected tools that are currently available.

Monitoring and evaluation

Digital curators should be actively involved in: continuously monitoring and evaluating how people are interacting with digital content and other people via the system; monitoring, reviewing, analysing and improving metadata through routine maintenance; reporting on usage trends, patterns and statistics; and supporting long-term administration and governance.

Table 11.1 Selected Semantic Web tools

Tool	Notes
AlchemyAPI[1]	■ Includes a suite of tools for automated tag extraction and data visualisation ■ Extracts potential tags/terms for a web page or text-based uploaded document ■ Open application programming interface (API) allows for integration with a variety of systems ■ WordPress plug-ins available ■ Drupal modules available ■ Includes advanced capabilities for different languages ■ Includes 'Named Entity' extraction for identifying people, companies, organisations, geographic locations
OpenCalais[2]	■ Includes a growing suite of tools related to various types of Semantic Web applications, including automated tag extraction, vocabulary prompting and data visualisation ■ Semantic analysis of content ■ Identifies 'Named Entities', facts and events
TerMine[3]	■ Automated tag extraction service ■ Online and batch term extractor ■ Hosted on the TerMine server
Topia. TermExtract[4]	■ Automated tag extraction service ■ Advanced semantic automated tagging tool ■ Includes parts-of-speech tagging, date tags, rules and so on ■ Python package

Notes:
1. *http:// alchemyapi.com*
2. *http://opencalais.com*
3. *http://nactem.ac.uk/software/termine/*
4. *http://pypi.python.org/pypi/topia.termextract/*

Data collection, analysis and reporting

As already noted, digital curators should be collecting, reviewing and making decisions based on usage. The exact nature of what data can be easily extracted from the system will depend on the system in use, what data analysis tools are implemented and the level of administrative privileges held by digital curators.

Suggestions for data to collect and present are included in Table 11.2. Whenever possible, share reports and make them available to the entire community.

Table 11.2 Types of data to review

Data	Details
Log-ins	■ How many people log into the system on a daily basis ■ How people are logged in at any given time ■ Log-ins by hour ■ Off-site vs. on-site log-ins ■ For organisations with multiple locations: log-ins by location/office ■ How many new users are added by day, week or month
Searches	■ Number of searches on daily, weekly, monthly basis ■ Number of searches will null results ■ Exact queries from searches with null results ■ Exact queries from all searches – review and create cluster map of type of searches most often conducted
Application of terms from category listings and taxonomies	■ Overall listing of terms and number of times each term has been applied to content ■ Comparison of search queries and number of times each term has been incorporated into a search query ■ Monthly or quarterly changes of term usage ■ Presentation of how terms have been incorporated into curation activities such as how a term has been incorporated into a special feature on the system start page or weekly update email, clicks per term when term was featured in an information bundle
Application of user tags	■ Overall listing of tags and number of times each tag has been applied to content ■ Monthly or quarterly changes in tag usage ■ Most-applied tags for each month or quarter ■ Monthly or quarterly trends in tag usage ■ Comparison of search queries and number of times each tag has been incorporated into a search query ■ Presentation of how tags have been incorporated into curation activities ■ Suggestions of heavily used or frequently searched for tags that should be considered for incorporation into taxonomy

Clean up metadata

Maintaining data is an ongoing process and a necessary role for digital curators. Often, some strategic decision-making along with some simple clean-up techniques can make an immense difference to the usability of data. Not only does well maintained data lend itself to search and retrieval, but well maintained tags are far more useful in supporting browsing, building information packages and creating RSS feeds based on tags. While users create inconsistent yet similar tags while describing their own content, when they are *presented* with information, users expect the content to be presented in a tidy, useful package. When users are presented with a browseable list of tags that includes five variations of the same concept in a row but with different spellings, punctuation, capitalisation, singulars/plurals, it is evident that no one is curating the content – sending the wrong message to users. See Table 11.3 for a list of common issues to look for within a given system.

Some questions to consider based on how data has been entered into fields are as follows:

- Is the purpose of the field clearly articulated? Do users understand what they are expected to enter into that field?

- Does the field type match the data being entered? Example: are user tags being entered into a short text field?

Table 11.3 Common issues to review in metadata for work-based social systems

Issue	Manifestations
Underused fields	■ Fields with minimal data entered when compared to other fields
User input error	■ Typos and spelling errors ■ Extra spaces between words, creating multiple entries for the same concept/phrase ■ Use of commas in sentence structure lists inadvertently separating text into multiple entries
Varying levels of specificity	■ User interpretation varies as to how specific information should be within a particular field ■ Incorporating several concepts into a single field/entry rather than separating tags with commas or using multiple fields
Structural issue – wrong type of field for data being collected	■ Tags vs. categories/taxonomy terms ■ Tags vs. sentence structure/short text field
Formatting and syntax issues	■ Various ways to enter null results – 'not applicable', 'no' or 'nothing' ■ Inconsistencies with abbreviations, acronyms ■ Singulars, plurals, stemming ■ '&' vs. 'and' ■ Composite concepts that appear in different orders

- Too many versions of similar tags? Or are tags on a very wide range of issues?
- Does the field overlap with another field?

Maintaining data does not need to be an intricate process. Identify which fields are most strategically in need of attention and focus efforts on those fields. For instance, if a common field for user tags is incorporated in many places throughout the system and data from the field is prominently displayed on the start page, that field is where maintenance efforts should be focused.

Curators should review all data sorted alphabetically and in descending usage. More time and effort should be put into correcting tags that are common, particularly those that are variations of popular tags. Use a mix of manual changes and batch processes that are stored and can be re-run as new data is added. For changes that will affect large numbers of records or a particular edit that will need to occur in the future, write scripts or batch processes that can be automated. For small quantities of records or one-time fixes, manual edits may be a more efficient way of making changes.

Establish a digital curation coordination group

Even though most digital curation activities are implemented by a single person or a small group of people, it is recommended to establish a digital curation group to help brainstorm new ideas, prioritise activities and coordinate curation work across multiple systems. If the organisation has several organisational taxonomies and/or multiple systems that have interrelated components, it is helpful to establish a group with the right people representing all key areas to serve as a coordinating group.

Possible projects for the group are as follows:

- Document and share best practices for digital curation within and external to the organisation.
- Develop a single taxonomy for the organisation.
- Compare user tags contributed across systems.
- Create an organisational concept map of taxonomies and user tags throughout the organisation, including mapping of how specific terms relate to each other.
- Collect and review data across systems.

- Coordinate reporting mechanisms.
- Develop and implement a plan for selected long-term digital preservation.

Concluding thoughts

Digital curation is becoming an increasingly important application of information science and knowledge management principles within the digital environment. Due to the conflation of user-generated metadata, developments in technology, the growing volume of user-generated digital volume, and the importance of resource discovery and findability, it is anticipated that digital curation will become even more valuable in the coming years. While the entire landscape of digital information is rapidly evolving, it is critically important for organisations of all shapes, sizes and types to incorporate digital curation practices to best support content management, information management and knowledge management. Establishing strategic, formulated digital curation workflows, procedures and best practices now within an organisation will help to best leverage internal resources in the long run.

Notes

1. *http://www.flickr.com/search/?q=flower* returned 18,773,320 results on 3 January 2012.
2. By 'work-related systems' we mean systems utilised in the work environment by an employer to facilitate knowledge exchange, communication, collaboration or management of digital content. Such examples include intranets, extranets, portals, document management systems, digital repositories or digital asset management systems. Other types of systems such as personnel management, customer relationship management (CRM), project management and financial management systems are often linked directly to the work-related systems focusing on communication, collaboration, digital content management and knowledge exchange, but they are not the focus of this chapter except in connection to interoperability as the purpose of the systems is vastly different.
3. *http://twitter.com/*
4. *http://www.facebook.com*
5. *http://www.linkedin.com*
6. *http://www.yammer.com*
7. *http://plus.google.com*

8. *http://ning.com*
9. *http://cnn.com*
10. *http://www.bbc.com*
11. *http://amazon.com*
12. *http://ebay.com*
13. *http://www.43things.com*

The JISC Business and Community Engagement Programme

Abstract. Over the last decade, a consensus within the UK and across Europe has emerged: that the considerable wealth of knowledge and expertise in universities and colleges can and should be harnessed to make a more direct contribution to the economy and society than through graduates alone, and that government support should stimulate this. At the same time, we have experienced an explosion of new web technologies, an increasing amount of business conducted online and a digital world where information is king, but where the kingdom is widely accessible, global and multi-faceted, and the use and context of that information is often more significant than the information itself. In this technology-driven world, open innovation, crowd-sourcing and open access to research are among the key areas of innovation creating new opportunities for universities and businesses alike.

The Joint Information Systems Committee (JISC) Business and Community Engagement (BCE) Programme was designed in 2007 to help UK institutions rise to these challenges and opportunities through the effective use of technology, by supporting and developing their strategic management of relationships with external partners (commercial, public sector including charities and trusts, cultural, social and civic organisations), and providing resources to enable this.

This chapter describes the context and development of the JISC Business and Community Programme 2007–10 and discusses the key achievements.

Keywords: business engagement, collaboration, community engagement, economic benefit, JISC, knowledge exchange, lifelong learning, social benefit

Context and programme development

Simon Whittemore

Establishing the Business and Community Engagement Programme

Over the last decade, a consensus within the UK and across Europe has emerged: that the considerable wealth of knowledge and expertise in universities and colleges can and should be harnessed to make a more direct contribution to the economy and society than through graduates alone, and that government support[1] should stimulate this. At the same time, we have experienced an explosion of new Web technologies, an increasing amount of business conducted online and a digital world where information is king, but where the kingdom is widely accessible, global and multi-faceted, and the use and context of that information is often more significant than the information itself. In this technology-driven world, open innovation, crowd-sourcing and open access to research are among the key areas of innovation creating new opportunities for universities and businesses alike. According to a report[2] by the Boston Consulting Group, the Internet contributed 7.2 per cent of gross domestic product (GDP) to the UK economy in 2009. Information technology and online engagement are therefore vital enablers both of economic growth and of higher and further education institutions' role in the dissemination and enrichment of knowledge and expertise.

The Joint Information Systems Committee (JISC) Business and Community Engagement (BCE) Programme was designed in 2007 to help UK institutions rise to these challenges and opportunities through the effective use of technology, by supporting and developing their strategic management of relationships with external partners (commercial and public sector including charities and trusts, cultural, social and civic organisations) and providing resources to enable this. Institutions would then be better equipped to deliver efficient and effective services that benefit the economy and society, an objective high on the UK government's agenda at the time to increase innovation through knowledge exploitation to enhance the UK's competitiveness.[3]

The programme took as its defining premise the proposal made in an influential 2001 Association of Commonwealth Universities paper *Engagement: A Core Value for Universities*.[4] The term 'engagement' has since gained some purchase as policy-makers, such as the Higher

Education Funding Council for England (HEFCE),[5] analysts and institutions seek to find suitable terminology to describe the new complexity of educational institutions' interactions and constituencies, as Jos Boys and Stephen Hill have noted.[6] 'Engagement' was also the key descriptor for other university activities which also involve communicating to, working in partnership with and managing services for external parties: 'public engagement' and 'employer engagement'.

JISC had brought in Simon Whittemore, a manager with a background both in funding policy for higher education Business and Community activity and in private sector business, to establish, shape and manage the programme. A JISC Advisory Services BCE Team, led by Rob Allen, was subsequently appointed to support the programme manager by coordinating some key projects and acting as change agents for BCE within their constituencies. The programme's conceptual approach placed an emphasis on managing strategic partnerships rather than on the type of interaction (see below) or the type of external partner/client involved. Given JISC's focus on information management, it made sense to adopt an inclusive approach both in terms of institutional areas covered and in terms of external parties.

Defining business and community engagement

Working with key partners and stakeholders across the UK and beyond, JISC supports UK higher and further education institutions in the effective use of technology through cost-effective resources and funding programmes.[7] The BCE programme had an annual budget of £1.9 million to fund projects and provide resources, working with key national stakeholders, to enhance institutions' external engagement.

Higher and further education institutions interact with a wide range of external organisations and in order to inform JISC support for such interaction, the range of those interactions and scope of engagement with externals had to be delineated and the desired outcomes of these engagement activities identified (see Figure 12.1).

As JISC's mission was to 'provide world-class leadership in the innovative use of Information and Communications Technology to support education, research and institutional effectiveness',[8] it was important that the approach to business and community engagement focused on the role of information management in this context. Supporting higher and further education UK-wide as equitably as possible meant that

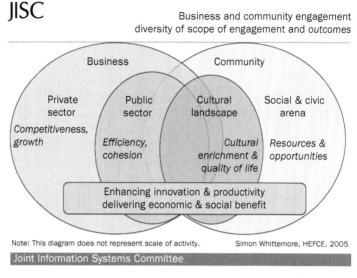

JISC

Business and community engagement
diversity of scope of engagement and *outcomes*

Note: This diagram does not represent scale of activity.　　Simon Whittemore, HEFCE, 2005

Joint Information Systems Committee

Figure 12.1   **Business and Community Engagement: scope of engagement and outcomes**

a synoptic, strategic approach was also required, which recognised the key strategic endeavours around external engagement and the delivery of knowledge and education services. Therefore the scope of business and community engagement activities was defined as encompassing four often overlapping institutional strategic areas:

- knowledge exchange;[9]
- employer engagement;
- public engagement;
- lifelong learning.

The rationale for including these four areas was underpinned by the fact that they had in common, and at their core, some key characteristics which made them particularly challenging to the mainstream of university activity, including:

- working coherently with external partners and clients;
- designing and delivering services, often chargeable, to non-traditional 'customers';
- requiring reliable data to be shared across departments and functions;
- requiring a coordinated approach in order to be credible and sustainable.

The BCE programme had two complementary aims designed to reflect the bi-directional nature of engagement and partnerships:

- to enhance institutions' efficiency, effectiveness and opportunities in BCE activities;
- to improve access to institutions' knowledge and expertise for business and community organisations.

Underpinning these aims, the programme was designed to support a more demand-led approach to all aspects of BCE within institutions, rather than the outward supply of raw research or education. Problem-solving was seen as a key component of this institutional BCE offer, implying a dynamic more akin to a facilitated service. This more client-centred approach reflected an emerging consensus among policy-makers and practitioners on the national skills agenda, reflected in the Leitch Report[10] which identified the need for a more demand-led system and concluded that '... previous approaches to delivering skills have been too "supply driven" ...' Similarly the Confederation of British Industry/Universities UK Report *Stepping Higher*[11] identified several client-focus, capacity-building issues among the '12 key issues for effective workforce development partnerships' including:

- 'recognising both the employer and learners as clients in different ways';
- 'building wider support for employer engagement within universities and recognition of the value of skill enhancement within businesses'.

A demand-led approach was also emerging as a key principle in the knowledge exchange side of BCE in policy initiatives such as the HEFCE-funded South East Coastal Communities Project[12] and the Scottish Funding Council's Call for 'Demand-driven knowledge exchange proposals for Strategic Priority Investments in Research and Innovation Translation' (SPIRIT).[13]

The BCE programme also recognised that for any BCE activity to function most effectively, a fit-for-purpose infrastructure and specific set of skills are required. The recognised role and the associated skills of the BCE practitioner – that is to say the knowledge exchange professional or other 'staff dedicated to assisting external partners and facilitating interactions'[14] – were seen as increasingly critical to the effectiveness of these interactions. The importance of a function empowered to 'translate' between academic research and external needs was becoming widely recognised, as were the requisite attributes of such 'boundary-spanners'

(Kitson et al., 2009) regarded as essential for future UK economic development.

Thus the vision of the JISC BCE programme was to support and empower, through the innovative use of technology, this dynamic, as expressed in Figure 12.2. The interaction would ideally start on the right-hand side – the demand side – with a business/community problem or opportunity. The BCE practitioners – who might be employer engagement or business development staff for example – would facilitate interactions between the external party and the academics, working across departments where combinations of knowledge and skills were required to address the client/partner issue, utilising techniques such as virtual collaboration and customer relationship management processes, for the wider strategic benefit of the institution.

Finally, there was recognition that the realisation of such a vision across the sector constituted a long-term change programme, so the BCE professionals would be agents of change. Traditional processes in institutions were not designed to support this dynamic with externals, so it would need to be integrated into research where publications and peer approval held sway, and teaching where curricula, accreditation and learner support predominated.

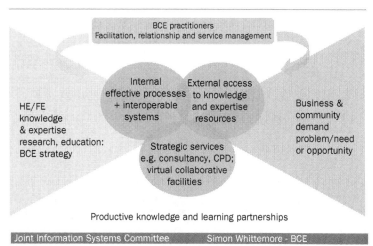

JISC
Business and community engagement – supporting strategic partnerships

BCE practitioners
Facilitation, relationship and service management

HE/FE knowledge & expertise research, education: BCE strategy

Internal effective processes + interoperable systems

External access to knowledge and expertise resources

Strategic services e.g. consultancy, CPD; virtual collaborative facilities

Business & community demand problem/need or opportunity

Productive knowledge and learning partnerships

Joint Information Systems Committee   Simon Whittemore - BCE

Figure 12.2 Business and Community Engagement dynamic: supporting strategic partnerships

Key achievements of the JISC Business and Community Programme 2007–10

Simon Whittemore, Rob Allen and Marc Dobson

The first cycle of the JISC Business and Community Engagement Programme ran from approximately October 2007 to July 2010, and was based primarily on recommendations from a series of studies[15] JISC commissioned for this purpose. It was guided by the strategic advice of the BCE Advisory Group[16] (comprised of senior individuals representing different parts of the BCE landscape within the higher and further education sector), and informed by a series of consultation workshops[17] and the programme manager's own HE and FE policy and private sector experience.

The resultant programme of interventions was structured into six streams[18] (four externally focused, two internally focused), each consisting of several work packages which in turn comprised groups of funded projects. It was designed to achieve improved compatibility and synergy between relevant strategies, processes and systems within institutions via a set of targeted benefits such as:

- easier reporting and more informed, resource-efficient strategic decision-making;
- process and outputs of knowledge better packaged for external impact;
- reduced long-term system costs and enhanced opportunity for shared applications;
- integrated management and exploitation of business-critical knowledge assets for enhanced BCE.

Through these interventions, the BCE programme has supported the higher and further education sectors in the development of 'economic competencies' – such as organisational improvement, market awareness, continuing professional development, knowledge and expertise exploitation – and in the innovative technologies needed to enable effective partnerships, both at individual and institutional levels.

The programme has also delivered a range of online resources (referenced below) designed to support all BCE practitioners and senior managers in institutions in strategically important areas such as relationship management and the promotion of research expertise.

Some of the key achievements of the programme's first cycle are highlighted below in four sections, which reflect the four externally focused streams of the programme:

- enhancing knowledge management (and exploitation of knowledge/ expertise);
- facilitating collaboration;
- enabling change (embedding BCE in institutions);
- enabling the institution–external partner interface.

In each of these areas, the JISC BCE funding and resources provided supported key institutional business and technological change. A fifth stream focused on embedding BCE within and across JISC itself, as this was an entirely new theme and area of intervention for JISC, while the sixth stream comprised evaluation, both of the initial needs and of the resulting outputs and outcomes.

Enhancing the management and exploitation of knowledge and expertise

Customer relationship management

Customer relationship management (CRM) was a core element of a key stream in the programme which aimed to support institutions in developing sustainable systems and ICT strategies for the management and exploitation of their knowledge assets, in order to enable more effective management of strategic partnerships, promotion of resultant knowledge/expertise and related business intelligence. CRM can be described as a business philosophy, or for higher and further education: 'a management strategy to generate enhanced value for the institution, its customers and partners through co-ordinated information management, contact management and marketing, supporting relationship development and bringing enhanced business intelligence and sustainability across the organisation'.[19]

An initial 'User Needs Study[20] into 'how JISC could support Business and Community Engagement' recommended that JISC 'pursue work on Customer Relationship Management (CRM), since this is clearly a sector-wide and immediate need, which will help not only to improve BCE activity but also to integrate it in a more strategic way into the work of institutions.' A subsequent JISC-commissioned study[21] found that CRM usage was generally undeveloped across the HE sector, the main barriers being cultural (resistance to change), operational (multiple narrowly focused operations, multiple partner/client types), and procedural and system/data related (migration/change). The study concluded that if business, employer and community expectations are to be satisfied, institutions need to take up the significant challenge of integrating client-facing systems into a consistent operation. Early work funded resulted in the development of a BCE CRM Self-Analysis Framework (SAF).[22] The SAF allows practitioners to think through the people, process and technology issues before, during and after a CRM implementation which is related to BCE and is supported by an online toolkit.

As part of the JISC BCE Relationship Management programme,[23] from July 2009 to April 2010 13 projects involving 12 universities and one FE college, funded by the aforementioned Grant Call, aimed to improve business processes and to pilot and extend the SAF developed previously. The aim was therefore not to implement CRM software, but to take a more holistic approach to CRM by ensuring that the triumvirate of people, processes and technology was analysed, understood and improvements made where necessary (Perry, 2010).

The Call and the CRM study defined three levels of CRM process maturity: peripheral, tactical and strategic.[24] Of the 13 CRM Process Improvement Pilots, most of the project teams considered that their project had helped the institution to achieve the goal of moving closer to the next level of maturity. Birkbeck, University of London, found their project[25] has enabled the institution to move closer to a strategic level, most notably by automating the functional integration between other institutional systems (such as data from room bookings, sponsored student data) and by increased usage of their existing CRM system, which in turn provided enhanced business intelligence to inform strategy.

Online promotion of research expertise

One of the issues faced by universities in collaborating with business is how to make potential collaborators aware of the range and depth of expertise (intellectual capital) available from subject specialists. A study on engagement models with small to medium enterprises (SMEs) found that the usefulness of institutions' 'services to business' web pages to prospective new business customers varies greatly. Similarly, a year-long study exploring the use of digital communication channels such as websites for the promotion of expertise found that these are generally structured around the internal logic of the organisation and tended to use inward-looking language. Further, external partners expressed difficulty in navigating through the complex array of research expertise available, as most of the websites lacked any coherent information architecture.[26]

Media databases of researchers' expertise are used by many university press offices, mainly aimed at journalists, but representing a small subset of the available expertise. Use of social media is increasing, for example researchers using Twitter[27] to identify research opportunities and organisations using LinkedIn[28] to identify and attract potential recruits, while many institutions produce podcasts aimed at external audiences.

The 'Online Research Expertise' study[29] developed a set of tools to allow universities to benchmark themselves, internally and against others, in their use of digital channels for communication and collaboration and to highlight areas for improvement. It also provided guidance for institutions to better understand the potential for different channels, and to identify 'user journeys' as a way of understanding how businesses might access information.

Employer engagement – developing the UK workforce

As the workforce diversifies, economic pressures intensify and more employees look to combine work and study, work-based learners are an increasingly significant part of the workforce. At the same time the student-worker – and indeed the lecturer-practitioner – is becoming an increasingly significant part of university 'membership', as traditional boundaries become increasingly blurred.[30] Demographic change due to an ageing population and migration is creating more worker-students, most of whom are older than traditional students. The Lifelong Learning and Workforce Development Programme[31] (2009–11) explored how the use of appropriate technologies and processes in universities enables HE-level learning services to meet the needs of institutions, learners in the workplace and their employers.

Thirteen projects were funded which collectively addressed issues in the three key challenging areas of: institutional management and systems to support employer engagement; employers' different culture, technology and business needs; learners' ownership and portability of information.

Most of the projects focused on tools and techniques to bridge these gaps and differences. The University of Gloucestershire developed an online toolkit[32] that supports the development of co-generated higher education courses by universities and employers using language and terminology which is familiar to employers – and the employees who would be acting as learners. The University of Hull, focusing on continuing professional development (CPD) in Engineering, developed a tool[33] to integrate personalised online learning evidence (CPD outputs) into professional frameworks. As with much BCE work, the common theme for these projects was the need to translate effectively between academically defined terms of reference and those used by business and professional bodies.

Facilitating productive collaboration with business and the community

Collaborative online tools

An initial user needs study,[34] undertaken in 2007, recommended that JISC should explore the use of Web 2.0 technologies across BCE. The user needs study noted that many of the respondents had little experience and limited time to investigate new applications, so JISC funded a training programme in 2008, inviting those working across the four BCE dimensions to take part in exploring a range of tools that were already freely available to use. JISC then commissioned a project[35] to trial a number of online collaborative tools across a range of institutions. Key findings included the following:

- *New business opportunities.* Universities across the North East of England used a system to share business opportunities and promote the expertise of others when they themselves were unable to help.[36]

- *Effective sharing of information and knowledge.* Birmingham Metropolitan College found something as simple as having documents in one place helped to improve their response times.

- Savings in time and money as trial projects were spending less time travelling.

- *Enhancement of learning and teaching.* Student surveys at Northumbria University indicated that their perceived learning experience was enhanced by their online engagement with business figureheads.

They are now looking at how other programmes can incorporate cross-institutional activities into their courses.[37]

- *Enhancing research.* The University of the Arts, London, developed an online community of practice around a Master's course in photojournalism. The aim was to enhance the relationship between academics, students and professionals. Not only has it strengthened those relationships, it is also having a major impact on research:

> It brings together a community around shared concerns and breaks down the barriers between theory and practice. Being able to participate in webinars, access material online and benefit from the network's support for our investigations, has helped advance my work. (Prof. David Campbell, Durham University)

Enabling change – embedding BCE in institutional culture and competencies

Embedding BCE

The studies and consultation activities[38] undertaken by JISC referred to earlier highlighted the need to provide further support in the strategic management of BCE operations across HE and FE. While information management, infrastructure and processes were well developed for the long-established strategic missions of Research and Teaching, at most institutions no equivalent infrastructure and processes were in place for the 'third' mission, BCE. In recognition of the fact that this constituted a long-term change agenda, in 2008 JISC commissioned the production of a review process[39] that would help HE and FE to identify their own BCE landscape and assess it in terms of their strategy and vision, objectives and supporting business processes. In line with the resulting *Diagnostic and Self-Evaluation Workbook*[40] institutions can:

- identify strengths, weaknesses and areas for improvement, leading to a development plan for future growth and stronger engagement and relationships both within and external to the organisation;
- better understand the range of BCE activity undertaken, both formally as part of the organisation's formal activities and informally by staff voluntarily and/or outside of their work commitment;

- use the information gathered to promote its impact on local, regional and wider communities for both formal external assessment and to attract wider participation from potential students.

A number of HE and FE institutions field tested the workbook and associated tools in their own context as part of the project. Among these, Shrewsbury College of Arts and Technology highlighted the value of using these resources in helping them to improve their processes and to deliver a 300 per cent increase in income over two years.[41]

BCE professional development (CPD)

JISC, leading a major national project in partnership with a wide range of key stakeholders, is addressing the issue of skills and training for the increasing number of staff working in BCE or external engagement activities. The 'economic competencies' concerned – including 'boundary-spanning' skills, high-level communication, relationship and project management and negotiation – are becoming increasingly vital for the UK economy as it seeks to stimulate innovation and growth, for example by creating new market opportunities from new combinations of knowledge and expertise, rather than compete against far larger, more cost-competitive economies in traditional areas. A pilot online skills diagnostic tool[42] is available which maps skills against the current AURIL (Association for University Research and Industry Links) continuing professional development (CPD) Framework for Knowledge Transfer[43] and guides practitioners to relevant courses and resources from a wide range of providers including JISC. A working group led by JISC and AURIL and comprised of key national representative bodies, including the National Coordinating Centre for Public Engagement (NCCPE)[44] and the New Engineering Foundation as well as institutional representatives, is redeveloping the framework to bring it up to date with current skills needs and also to ensure it encompasses all of the four dimensions of BCE.[45]

Once development of the framework is complete, a new version of the online diagnostic tool will be launched to reflect the revised framework, benefiting a wider range of BCE practitioners and indeed any individual involved in engagement with external partners and clients. The working group is also engaging with institutions' human resources groups and specialist CPD organisations, such as the Chartered Institute of Personnel and Development, to ensure that the framework is embedded as widely as possible across HE and FE human relations (HR) processes, and those of other suitable organisations such as public sector research establishments.

Enabling the institution–external partner interface

Access to resources and open innovation

In 2010 and 2011 the BCE programme addressed issues and opportunities surrounding both Open Innovation and Access to Resources from HE and FE. Initial studies[46] have led to funding a series of pilots and demonstrators in these areas.

In one of the pilots, the University of Bristol has used Open Innovation models to develop mobile applications to provide access to real-time data. In collaboration with Bristol City Council, the MyMobileBristol[47] application provides both university users and members of the general public access to campus-related information together with real-time public transport data, delivering a highly efficient public service.

Mindful of the fact that often businesses are not so much interested in *where* support comes from but rather whether it is useful to them, Queens University Belfast[48] have been working with Belfast Metropolitan College to catalogue their complementary HE and FE 'knowledge assets' and present them online as a single coherent offering to business to the benefit of both the university and the college. It is envisaged that this model could be extended to bring in further partners in Northern Ireland and be replicated elsewhere in the United Kingdom. Indeed, both Cornwall College and South Devon College led similar FE/HE collaborative projects to promote complementary knowledge assets through web channels with Plymouth University and University College Plymouth St Mark and St John (UCP Marjon) respectively. Testing has demonstrated that the online resources from this 'knowledge assets' work are of high interest to the targeted external groups and of high value for the institution.

A key priority of the first phase work (2008–11) in Open Innovation and Access to Resources was to transfer the learning and models of good practice to other regions and sectors. The institutions leading on projects were asked to stage 'transferability workshops' to test the extent to which the model they developed was transferable to another context where an institution or regional group faced similar challenges and opportunities.

The transferee regions are likely to benefit in future, as JISC seeks to build capacity to address these key opportunities nationally.

Developing Community Content

The Developing Community Content[49] programme (2010) has created, enhanced and co-developed digital content with organisations and individuals from outside traditional educational boundaries in a 'two-way engagement'[50] process which could be described as 'crowd-sourcing'. The outputs have delivered direct public benefit; for example, the Lower Severn Community Flood Information Network[51] project at the University of Gloucestershire promotes awareness of local flood histories and flood risk along the River Severn.

SME engagement

SMEs are primarily part of local communities but institutions often struggle to find resource-efficient and cost-effective ways of engaging with them. Institutions will find resources in a JISC BCE-funded toolkit to help them engage with SMEs on the JISC TechDis website and the website, Acumen, of the Higher Education Academy.[52]

Recent activities

Given the progress thus far and the changing HE and FE landscape, in 2010 the initial programme structure was distilled into four strategic priorities for the second programme cycle:

- Organisational Capability and Efficiency for BCE
- Relationship Management
- Public Value and Civic Engagement
- Embedding BCE across JISC.

Recent activities continue to build on work across these themes, with a particular emphasis on three key areas:

- A further set of Access to Resources and Open Innovation projects aim to extend effective models and focus on HE–FE exchange of good practice, in order to develop integrated online information services and help institutions exploit the co-development of their knowledge assets in open innovation online marketplaces.

- In the Transformations Programme, designed to support institutions' organisational change through the use of existing JISC resources, business change champions are invited to participate in a strategic practice group and action learning sets with their peers from other institutions in order to spearhead the enhancement of their own institutions' Organisational Capability for BCE.

- Finally, a portfolio of collaborative projects, facilitated for JISC by the National Coordinating Centre for Public Engagement, brings together BCE user-focused expertise, leading technology practice and a range of research groups in order to help research groups embed the capability and processes for the ongoing identification of impact and benefits of their research, which is essential for their research excellence, future sustainability and funding requirements. BCE 'impact analysts' – expert engagement professionals already in the HE sector – are being deployed to identify and share good practice.

Concluding remarks

In a climate of financial austerity, public accountability and students as 'customers', there is increasing pressure on institutions to demonstrate their value to the economy and society, beyond the provision of graduates. The JISC Business and Community Engagement Programme has provided support and resources for higher and further education institutions in a strategic area of increasing importance, the 'third mission' or external engagement. As institutions become more responsive to these external pressures, such resources help them bridge the gap between their strategy and operations, exploit their knowledge assets and manage their partnerships more effectively, enabling them to create new business opportunities using online services and web technologies. If the UK is to improve its conversion of excellent research into real-life innovation, which is a government objective, then institutions will need to continue to respond to this change agenda, ensuring they develop the infrastructure, processes and distinctive skills needed to embed BCE, as many are already doing. The University of Hertfordshire, for example, found that a 'whole institutional approach'[53] to BCE was needed to harness the combined knowledge and expertise of all individuals effectively. Then coherent, efficient, strategic engagement can be integrated into research and teaching, bringing added benefits to student employability, institutional reputation and impact.

Acknowledgements

Thanks to Caroline Ingram and Andrew Stewart of the JISC Advance Business and Community Engagement team who were also involved in drafting the 'Key Achievements' section.

Notes

1. For example, the Higher Education Innovation Fund: *http://www.hefce. ac.uk/whatwedo/kes/heif.*
2. Boston Consulting Group (2009) *The Connected Kingdom: How the Internet Is Transforming the UK Economy.* Online at: *http://www.connectedkingdom. co.uk/downloads/bcg-the-connected-kingdom-oct-10.pdf.*
3. See the Sainsbury Review of Science and Innovation, UK Government, October 2007, online at: *http://webarchive.nationalarchives.gov.uk/+/http:// www.hm-treasury.gov.uk/independent_reviews/sainsbury_review/sainsbury_ index.cfm*; and Innovation Nation, UK Government, March 2008, online at: *http://www.official-documents.gov.uk/document/cm73/7345/7345.pdf.*
4. *Engagement as a Core Value for the University: A Consultation Document* (2001) London: Association of Commonwealth Universities.
5. Higher Education Funding Council for England: *http://www.hefce.ac.uk/ whatwedo/kes/.*
6. Jos Boys, *eRevolution, Business, Education* (2009) and Professor Stephen Hill, online at: *http://erevolution.jiscinvolve.org/wp/2009/08/20/beyond-the-customermember-divide/.*
7. JISC's core budget was approximately £90 million in 2010–11: *http://www. jisc.ac.uk/aboutus/howjiscworks/finance.aspx.*
8. *http://www.jisc.ac.uk/aboutus/strategy.aspx*
9. Also known as 'knowledge transfer', and sometimes used as the default term for 'third mission' activities.
10. UK Government, December 2006, online at: *http://www.official-documents. gov.uk/document/other/0118404792/0118404792.pdf.*
11. CBI (2008) online, p. 20: *http://www.universitiesuk.ac.uk/Publications/ Documents/Stepping%20Higher%20-%20Final.pdf.*
12. *http://www.coastalcommunities.org.uk/businessCase.html*
13. Scottish Funding Council (2009), online at: *http://www.sfc.ac.uk/web/FILES/ CircularsSFC1909/sfc1909.pdf.*
14. HEFCE (2010) Higher Education and Business Interaction Survey.
15. For example, the BCE Study by B. McCaul, C. Reid, M. McNally and H. Sharifi (2007) 'To Investigate and Produce Guidelines for the Use of

Publicly-funded Infrastructure, Services, and Intellectual Property', online at: *http://www.jisc.ac.uk/media/documents/themes/bce/pubfundinfra.pdf.*

16. *http://www.jisc.ac.uk/aboutus/howjiscworks/committees/workinggroups/bceadvisorygroup.aspx*

17. JISC (2009) BCE Consultation Workshop Series 2008/2009 Report, prepared by C. Dunn and edited by S. Whittemore. Online at: *http://www.jisc.ac.uk/media/documents/programmes/bce/bceconsultationworkshops0409final.pdf.*

18. The six programme streams were: Enhancing Knowledge Management; Facilitating Collaboration; Enabling Change and BCE; Enabling the Interface; Embedding and Communicating BCE; Needs Analysis and Evaluation.

19. S. Whittemore in the JISC Grant Call 05/09: *http://www.jisc.ac.uk/funding opportunities/funding_calls/2009/03/0509bcecrm.aspx.*

20. *http://www.jisc.ac.uk/media/documents/themes/bce/bceuserneedsstudy07.pdf*

21. *http://www.jisc.ac.uk/media/documents/themes/bce/crmstudyfinalre port20070817.pdf*

22. *http://jisc.cetis.ac.uk/crm-tools/*

23. JISC (2009) Relationship Management, online at: *http://www.jisc.ac.uk/whatwedo/programmes/bce/relationshipmanagement.aspx.*

24. Appendix F, paragraph F6.

25. BELS (Birkbeck Employer Link System) Project (Birkbeck, University of London).

26. *http://www.jiscinfonet.ac.uk/tools/research-expertise*

27. *http://twitter.com/*

28. *http://www.linkedin.com/home*

29. *http://www.jiscinfonet.ac.uk/tools/research-expertise*

30. S. Whittemore (2009) 'Business and Community Engagement: Know Your Processes, Know Your Markets: How to Avoid Building Bridges on Quicksand', online at: *http://erevolution.jiscinvolve.org/wp/2009/08/13/technology-and-customer-relationships/.*

31. *http://www.jisc.ac.uk/whatwedo/programmes/institutionalinnovation/workforcedev.aspx*

32. University of Gloucestershire CoGent Online Toolkit: *http://www.pebblepad.co.uk/cogent/.*

33. Further information: *http://www.jisc.ac.uk/whatwedo/programmes/elearning/workforcedev/cpdeng.aspx#downloads.*

34. *http://www.jisc.ac.uk/media/documents/themes/bce/bceuserneedsstudy07.pdf*

35. *http://www.jiscinfonet.ac.uk/infokits/collaborative-tools*

36. *http://www.jiscinfonet.ac.uk/infokits/collaborative-tools/benefits*

37. *http://www.jiscinfonet.ac.uk/infokits/collaborative-tools/benefits-college-university*

38. *http://www.jisc.ac.uk/media/documents/programmes/bce/bceconsutation workshops0409final.pdf*

39. *http://www.jiscinfonet.ac.uk/infokits/embedding-bce/methodology*

40. *http://www.jiscinfonet.ac.uk/infokits/embedding-bce/workbook*

41. Case Study for Embedding Business and Community Engagement, Shrewsbury College, 2009.

42. *http://www.netskills.ac.uk/content/projects/2008/jisc-bce-cpd/index.html*

43. NB: The AURIL KT CPD Framework will be extended beyond traditional knowledge transfer to cater for BCE practitioners in general, including, for example, public engagement.
44. *http://www.publicengagement.ac.uk/*
45. Employer Engagement, Knowledge Exchange/Transfer, Lifelong Learning, Community, Cultural and Public Engagement.
46. *http://www.jisc.ac.uk/media/documents/programmes/bce/stream4 resfinalreport.pdf* and *http://www.jisc.ac.uk/media/documents/programmes/ bce/facilitatingopeninnovationstudyfinalreport.pdf.*
47. *http://www.mymobilebristol.com/*
48. *http://www.qub.ac.uk/sites/engage/*
49. *http://www.jisc.ac.uk/whatwedo/programmes/digitisation/community content.aspx*
50. Batt, C. (2009) JISC, online at: *http://www.jisc.ac.uk/media/documents/ programmes/digitisation/dcatwefinalreport_final.pdf.*
51. *http://www2.glos.ac.uk/severnfloods/*
52. *http://www.jisctechdis.ac.uk/acumen*; *http://www.heacademy.ac.uk/acumen/ contact.*
53. Martin, D. (2009) *Strategic Engagement with Business and the Community.* Online video at: *http://www.jisc.ac.uk/whatwedo/programmes/bce/videos. aspx.*

References

Kitson, M., Howells, J., Braham, R. and Westlake, S. (2009) *The Connected University: Driving Recovery and Growth in the UK Economy.* London: NESTA. Online at: *http://www.nesta.org.uk/library/documents/ Report%2023%20-%20The%20Connected%20Uni%20v4.pdf.*

Perry, S. (2010) *Business and Community Engagement Customer Relationship Management in Higher and Further Education.* University of Bolton.

13

Skills Portal: a study skills and information literacy portal created with Open Educational Resources

Vivien Sieber

Abstract. Skills Portal is an online collection of Open Educational Resources (OER) for undergraduate, master's and doctoral students to use in self-directed learning. This chapter considers the process of identifying, evaluating and adopting resources for inclusion and discusses the reusing and sharing of learning materials.

The main challenge for Skills Portal is getting students to find and use the materials. The main library website was being rebuilt at the same time, giving an opportunity for liaison librarians, learning developers and researcher developers to link to the resources from their information and teaching pages. Skills Portal was demonstrated at every opportunity and, gradually, individuals began to recommend Skills Portal-specific tutorials to their students and ask for items to be included.

Skills Portal continues to grow and develop as new items are added. Google Analytics indicates that use continues to increase both in terms of the number of page requests and the time spent on a particular resource, and that 30 per cent of users revisit the site.

Keywords: Creative Commons, digital repositories, Jorum, OER, Open Educational Resources, Reusable Learning Objects, RLO, Skills Portal

Introduction

The Skills Portal[1] is an online collection of Open Educational Resources (OER) for undergraduate, master's and doctoral students to use in self-directed learning. The collection, initially put together to support postgraduate research students develop the transferable skills outlined in the Roberts Report (Roberts, 2002), and later expanded to include basic study skills and information literacy. The processes of identifying, evaluating, selecting and modifying OER materials, largely from the Jorum[2] repository, to create the collection are described. Creative Commons licences are essential to the OER community as they maintain an author's copyright while allowing the author to determine whether or not derivative works are allowed.

The Roberts review of the supply of science and engineering skills in the UK and the difficulties employers face in recruiting highly skilled scientists and engineers identified the need to develop transferable skills in doctoral research students (Roberts, 2002). The range of skills and competencies required by employers is specified in the 'Joint Skills Statement' (UK GRAD Programme, 2001) and, more recently, in the 'Researcher Development Framework' (RDF) (CRAC, 2009). A programme of face-to-face workshops, mapping to the skills specified by the RDF, has been developed by the Researcher Development Team at the University of Surrey. Workshops are popular with graduate students and we generally receive good feedback. However, the programme does not cover all areas specified by the RDF and some students, particularly part-time and distance learners, find it difficult to attend workshops.

This development began as a 'quick fix' to plug a gap in training provision for postgraduate research students by providing online resources to extend the range of topics covered that would be readily available 24/7, particularly for part-time and distance learners. There was no intention to replace face-to-face workshops, simply to offer an alternative mode of delivery. The intention was to create an open access 'Skills Portal' via a web server for the start of the academic year 2010–11. Time was limited – about three months – and there was no specific budget.

Open Educational Resources

I had already been involved in the Open Educational Resources (OER) movement from the perspective of offering resources for reuse by others via a couple of Higher Education Academy (HEA) subject centre projects: HEA Biosciences[3] and the HEA Medicine, Dentistry and Veterinary Medicine (MEDEV) project Organising Open Educational Resources (OOER).[4] Both projects explored what needs to be done to share online resources: HEA Biosciences concentrated on sharing virtual laboratory or fieldwork resources while MEDEV created toolkits exploring permissions, ethical consent, pedagogy and other information necessary to catalogue and reuse resources. The Skills Portal was an opportunity to experience OER as a consumer.

What is OER?

There have been a number of attempts to promote reusable learning objects (RLOs) over the last ten years with rather limited success. Some define an RLO as didactic subject content plus self-assessment (Boyle, 1997) while others use a considerably broader definition of any digital resource that can be reused. The OER movement really began when the Massachusetts Institute of Technology (MIT) launched the OpenCourseWare (OCW) initiative in 2002 with the aim of making all their teaching materials freely available over the Web.[5] OER can be defined as the sharing and reuse of any digital teaching resource (Hylén, 2007). OER materials range from single files (images, documents), lecture presentations (with and without audio), multimedia and simulations to entire courses. Open educational resources are materials used to support education that may be freely accessed, reused, modified and shared by anyone (Downes, 2011).

Pragmatically an OER is: 'any object (generally file/files) created by one person or group that is subsequently used or modified by another group to promote learning'. The UK government has made significant funding available to universities engaging with OER recently via the JISC, the Higher Education Academy (HEA) and HEA subject centres. In contrast to OCW where whole courses are released, any digital object can be shared via OER. The two initiatives share common fundamental principles and both rely on the same collection of Creative Commons licences.

Historically, there has been limited uptake of third-party teaching materials in the UK and internationally for a number of reasons: the technology has been awkward to use, daunting all but the most tenacious; finding and identifying resources for a specific teaching requirement has been a difficult and time-consuming task. Even when a resource apparently covers a relevant topic, it may contain elements that would not meet the needs or level of the course. Simply not knowing the extent and utility of what is available, let alone how to find and use it, is a major barrier to most academics.

There are many reasons why the reuse and sharing of learning materials are a good idea:

- We can learn how others have approached a particular topic to inform our teaching.

- Creating quality e-resources is time-consuming and expensive – with OER we can avoid reinventing the wheel.

- Increasingly, institutions are unlikely to have active research units across all disciplines, limiting access to real experimental data.

- Teaching is not about giving students a collection of resources, however good, to work through – teaching is about helping students to develop understanding and knowledge through structured learning opportunities and feedback.

Creative Commons licensing

Creative Commons (CC)[6] allows authors to retain their copyright while licensing others to use the materials. CC[7] licences allow authors to control whether or not their materials can be used commercially, how they can be modified and whether or not derivative works must also be shared under the original licence. Ranging from the most permissive, CC[8] licences allow:

Attribution (CC BY) allows any modification and reuse provided the creator is acknowledged.

Attribution-ShareAlike (CC BY-SA) allows modification as above provided the modified resource is released using the same licence.

Attribution-NoDerivs (CC BY-ND) means the resource may be reused provided no changes are made and the originator is credited.

Attribution-NonCommercial (CC BY-NC) offers the same conditions as Attribution for non-commercial use only.

Attribution-NonCommercial-ShareAlike (CC BY-NC-SA) as CC BY SA for non-commercial use only.

Attribution-NonCommercial-NoDerivs (CC BY-NC-ND) is the most restrictive of the licences allowing no change or commercial use.

In many ways Creative Commons underpins both OCW and OER initiatives as these licences enable authors to retain copyright while transparently allowing resources to be shared. From a user perspective adding a CC licence to a web page is remarkably easy as simple check boxes are available to select the desired options, while the HTML code specifying the selection and the icon are generated for copying and pasting into the page (see *http://creativecommons.org/choose/*).

Repositories

Jorum[9]

Following a review of international models for sharing learning resources (Fleming and Massey, 2007), Jorum announced that it would host OER resources to make them freely available to the FE and HE communities. The interface was enhanced to make it somewhat more user friendly and was re-launched in 2010. Depositing in Jorum was strongly encouraged by JISC/HEA for OER projects they funded. One problem with any repository is that the collection it contains must be large enough to be likely to contain materials a typical user would want. This was not initially the case before these initiatives. The Jorum collection is now large enough to make it probable that a search will lead to useful resources. Materials range from rich websites with multimedia (animations, quizzes), to Word documents, presentations and image files. Jorum has recently moved to the University of Manchester and the Mimas service.

Finding materials

It takes a while to identify search terms that are likely to yield useful resources from Jorum. Similarly, where a resource is available as a set of downloadable files, not simply a URL, it is quicker to use the 'View' option than 'download' for initial evaluations. One aspect that has taken me by surprise is the frequency with which new resources are submitted.

For example, over the last six months at least three excellent resources on 'Plagiarism' have been uploaded. To simplify the process and avoid having to repeat searches it is possible to set up an RSS feed or to set up a search, copy that code (Application Programming Interface (API)) and paste it into a web page to automate the search. Widgets that allow searches to display automatically on a web page are currently being beta-tested.[10] Three options are available: search, user and subject. Once the widget has been set up it will automatically update when new resources are added.

Adopting materials

While the CC licences allow you to preview a resource in Jorum without logging in, the Jorum Education Licence requires login with an institutional account verified by Shibboleth/Athens authentication. Login may be required to download a resource; this generates an automatic link to download a zip file. Resources may either be hosted on the depositor's server (a URL) or a collection of files that constitute a resource, along with the metadata describing the resource and licence terms. From my perspective, access to the source files is valuable as they may be edited to meet local requirements and given a local look and feel. It is not always technically possible to edit file formats, as the increasingly popular Flash is only available in the published (.swf) format, while the original (.flv) files are needed to edit the resource. It takes a while to become familiar with the Jorum interface and find efficient ways of using it as it is a little quirky. Differences between 'Export Resource' and 'Download Original Content Package' are not immediately clear. Similarly 'Preview Content Package' can yield a list of files rather than a preview of the resource itself. Jorum teams are working to enhance the user interface, making it more intuitive and easier to navigate. Although most of the resources are web-based, there is considerable variation in the way they have been created. Some have been exported from applications like 'Course Genie'/'Wimba' and 'eXe.exe' or are xml exports while others are long single HTML pages; many have external style sheets. Some include published versions of files with collections of associated files. Some materials are Word files, which can be manually converted to web pages and indexed. All come with baffling amounts of metadata.

My aim was to create a collection of sites that gives students a relatively uniform experience; they should not have to spend time figuring out how to navigate multiple different sites. If you are happy to create indexes, apply style sheets and other minor modifications, this is relatively simple where files are available, but it is not possible where a link to an external site is the only option. A further disadvantage of linking to external sites is that they will continue to need checking on a regular basis. Many of us have spent time creating a web page with useful links to external sites, only to find that it needs checking every few months or it becomes a frustrating collection of broken links. Jorum does guarantee to provide a permanent link to the resources it houses and materials released from recent HEA/JISC projects should be available for at least five years.

Project

Requirement

I moved to the University of Surrey in June 2010. A re-launch of the Researcher Development Programme and associated website was already planned and publicised for October 2010, including the provision of online alternatives for the workshop programme. Neither staff time nor budget had been allocated to developing e-learning resources. I needed a quick fix, something that could be available to students in a couple of months with potential to be developed further. OER was an obvious solution in that large amounts of teaching materials are freely available for sharing and reuse. The Skills Portal was created quickly (July–September 2010) to provide e-learning opportunities for self-directed study and distance learning, initially for doctoral students (see Figure 13.1). It rapidly became clear that these materials would also be useful to wider groups, including undergraduates and taught master's students.

Resources

The process of identifying, evaluating and adopting resources was straightforward:

1. Initial search terms were identified from the Researcher Development Framework (RDF).[11]
2. Jorum Open was the primary repository.[12]

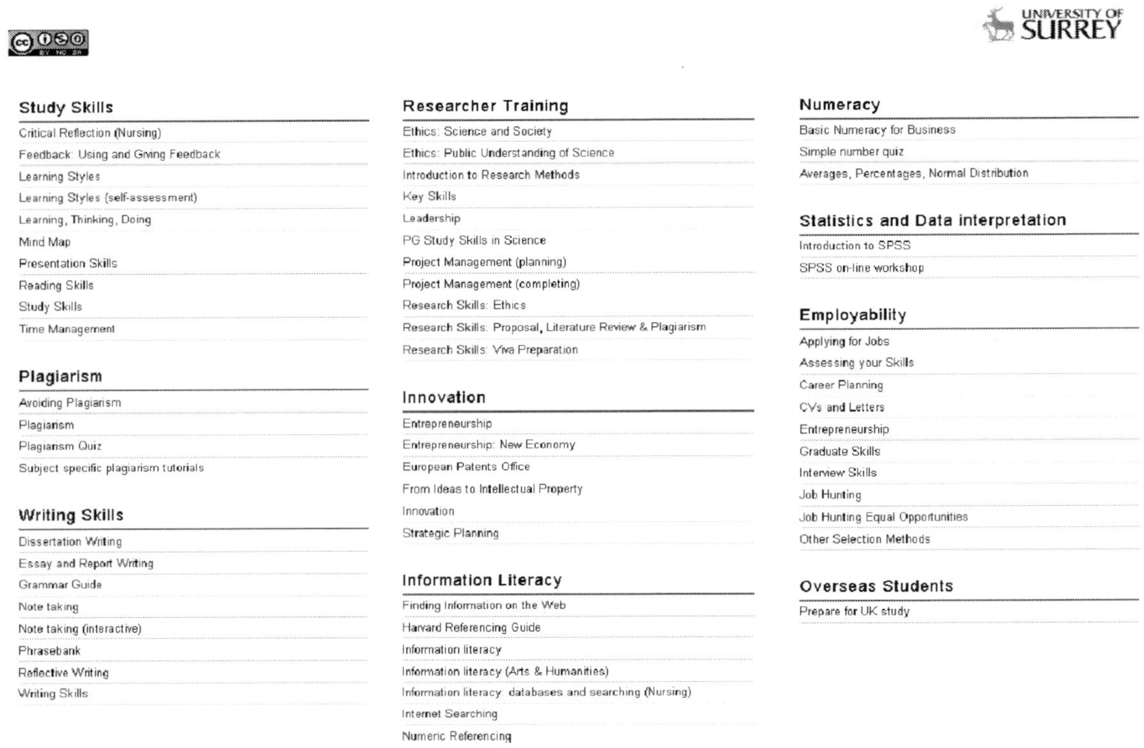

UNIVERSITY OF
SURREY

Study Skills

Critical Reflection (Nursing)
Feedback: Using and Giving Feedback
Learning Styles
Learning Styles (self-assessment)
Learning, Thinking, Doing
Mind Map
Presentation Skills
Reading Skills
Study Skills
Time Management

Plagiarism

Avoiding Plagiarism
Plagiarism
Plagiarism Quiz
Subject specific plagiarism tutorials

Writing Skills

Dissertation Writing
Essay and Report Writing
Grammar Guide
Note taking
Note taking (interactive)
Phrasebank
Reflective Writing
Writing Skills

Researcher Training

Ethics: Science and Society
Ethics: Public Understanding of Science
Introduction to Research Methods
Key Skills
Leadership
PG Study Skills in Science
Project Management (planning)
Project Management (completing)
Research Skills: Ethics
Research Skills: Proposal, Literature Review & Plagiarism
Research Skills: Viva Preparation

Innovation

Entrepreneurship
Entrepreneurship: New Economy
European Patents Office
From Ideas to Intellectual Property
Innovation
Strategic Planning

Information Literacy

Finding Information on the Web
Harvard Referencing Guide
Information literacy
Information literacy (Arts & Humanities)
Information literacy databases and searching (Nursing)
Internet Searching
Numeric Referencing

Numeracy

Basic Numeracy for Business
Simple number quiz
Averages, Percentages, Normal Distribution

Statistics and Data interpretation

Introduction to SPSS
SPSS on-line workshop

Employability

Applying for Jobs
Assessing your Skills
Career Planning
CVs and Letters
Entrepreneurship
Graduate Skills
Interview Skills
Job Hunting
Job Hunting Equal Opportunities
Other Selection Methods

Overseas Students

Prepare for UK study

Figure 13.1 Skills Portal home page (July 2011)

3. About a thousand items were evaluated using the following criteria:
- relevance
- level
- accuracy
- substance
- technology.

4. Objects were downloaded, customised and modified.

5. The modified resource was uploaded to the web server and indexed on the Skills Portal.

I was looking for relatively substantial resources, something that would take students time to work through, rather than handouts. The majority were from the Open University, the University of Leicester, the University of Central Lancashire and Leeds Metropolitan University.

Evaluation

Along with the subject area and topic there is other information that would usefully inform the selection of a particular object:

Target audience
- Intended audience, learning outcomes?

Discipline
- Subject content, activities?
- How the materials were actually used within the course? Were they integrated or stand-alone extras?

Curriculum
- Does the resource contribute to assessment, what is actually assessed and how many marks is it worth? What does it contribute to overall assessment within a module, year or degree?
- Modules are not the same at different institutions nor do they attract similar credits.
- Are there security implications if the item contributes to assessment?

Evaluation
- Has it been evaluated either in terms of academic content or learner experience?

Technology

- Is the technology used to create the resource, file formats, multimedia, plug-ins, VLE, customisable?
- Does it work? Is it free from minor mistakes and accurate? Is it accessible?

Value to users

- Is it something students are likely to value and be prepared to spend time with?

These are complex, often subjective judgements that are difficult to quantify. In an ideal world a panel of 'experts' would be asked to score each resource against a set of defined numerical criteria using a methodology analogous to that of an evidence-based clinical review like the Cochrane Reviews.[13]

Technology

As I preferred to download materials from Jorum to host on a local web server, the majority came as a zip file. Extracting the original files was straightforward and it then took a while to understand how they were related. Generally, once I had identified the index file it became obvious and, as I downloaded more resources, a pattern emerged. To a great extent the technology that was used to create the initial resource determined how it was subsequently modified and customised to give a Surrey look and feel. The Skills Portal is a simple web server without access controls or Sharable Content Object Reference Model (SCORM) player. A single style-sheet (CSS) is used on both the index page and individual resources. The initial simple CSS was modified to accommodate style features from the assorted resources. Resources created with Course Genie/Wimba were particularly easy to restyle and modify once I was familiar with the structure of their exported files.

The 'tracking snippet' code from Google Analytics was added at the end of the index page of each of the new resources.[14] As with Jorum widgets, this is simply a matter of copying and pasting a section of HTML code into the relevant part of the page.

While HTML was all that was needed for much of this development, the Windows editor TextPad[15] was very useful when it came to making the same change in multiple files simultaneously. Where resources were

SCORM compliant, there was an expectation that they would be imported into a virtual learning environment (VLE) which would render the resource. To overcome this limitation, simple 'back | next' navigation was created by adding HTML at the bottom of each page.

A few resources were only available as Word documents. Where they were unique and likely to be particularly useful to students, notably the 'Futures Workbooks' series from Leeds Metropolitan University, they were converted manually. To avoid creating Microsoft's inaccessible HTML, sections from the Word document were copied and pasted into Dreamweaver CS4. This was time-consuming as it was only possible to copy sections of document at a time, and editing and formatting were a manual process with the possibility of introducing additional mistakes and typos. One resource from the University of Leicester, 'Producing Long Documents', was converted from Word to HTML, indexed and short demonstration videos, which were already available from Jorum, added. These examples demonstrate that resources can be modified and enhanced by changing technology but without substantially altering content.

Outcomes

Feedback

Although there is an email link on the Skills Portal inviting suggestions, comments and feedback, none were received over the last nine months. Anecdotally, it appears popular with students who will, when questioned, say that it is useful.

Use analysis with Google Analytics

The main challenge for the Skills Portal is getting students to find and use the materials. The main library website was being rebuilt in parallel to the Skills Portal development which gave an opportunity for liaison librarians, learning developers and researcher developers to link to the resources from their information and teaching pages. I demonstrated it at every opportunity and, gradually, individuals began to recommend either specific tutorials from the Skills Portal to their students or to ask for items to be included on the site.

The Skills Portal continues to grow and develop as new items are added. Google Analytics indicates that use continues to increase both in

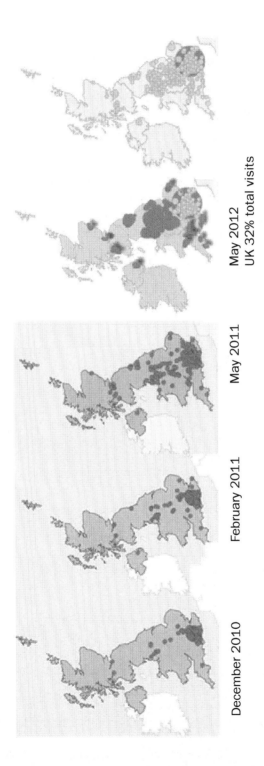

December 2010   February 2011   May 2011

May 2012
UK 32% total visits

Figure 13.2 Geographic distribution of page requests for the Skills Portal, December 2010, February 2011, May 2011 and May 2012

terms of the number of page requests and the time spent on a particular resource while 30 per cent of users revisit the site. Figure 13.2 shows the geographic distribution of requests for Skills Portal pages in the months of December 2010 – May 2012. Initial requests (December 2010) largely came from areas around Guildford; by May 2012 only 32 per cent of requests came from the UK and distribution across the UK had spread.

Google Analytics can give fine-grained information about patterns of use, for example sudden short-lived increases in requests have been correlated with specific activities such as marketing emails to all students or in relation to a face-to-face workshop. Although there is some variation in the most popular resources, 'Harvard Referencing', 'CVs and Letters', 'Applying for Jobs' and 'Introduction to Research and Managing Information' normally top the table. The popularity of the Harvard Referencing tutorial is partially due to academic librarians recommending it to their students. Indeed one librarian now tells students to complete the tutorial before asking for specific help.

Discussion

The Skills Portal began as a quick way of providing e-learning resources to meet a deadline. In little over a month it was possible to create the initial collection of quality resources. Information literacy and study skills development are unusual in that it can be helpful to learners to explore a particular competence, transparently rather than embedded within a subject domain. Although initial resources selected for the Skills Portal were mapped against the RDF, as the collection expanded, generic resources covering an increased range of topics were evaluated and included. Increasingly learning development staff and librarians are asking for resources to be added to the Skills Portal. Librarians have asked that numerical and Vancouver referencing tutorials, used within their faculties, should be included.

A key element in any online resource is whether students will use and engage meaningfully with the resource. There are links to the Skills Portal from multiple, rather deep, parts of the library website which account for approximately 20 per cent of the overall page requests while 70 per cent of requests are from search engines and 10 per cent are direct. The proportion arriving from Google has increased over time as has the global distribution of use. Evidence that users are engaging with resources comes, indirectly, from the time spent with a resource. Average durations (June–July 2011) of 14.5 for 'Science and Society' and 7.5 minutes for 'Producing Long Documents' and 'Leadership' indicate that, at least, some users are finding the materials sufficiently helpful to invest time working with them. Though there is no guarantee that users are using a resource rather than chatting or drinking coffee, times spent on a resource are consistent from month to month. Nor can we tell what a student is learning when they spend time with a book. The time spent on a page will depend on the way a resource has been constructed; users should not need to spend long on a clearly constructed index page. The average time on the Skills Portal itself was nearly two minutes.

We have used a number of approaches to promote the Skills Portal including: all-student emails, RSS feeds, virtual newsletters and so on. We try to recommend relevant resources at appropriate times such as revision techniques at exam time. Google Analytics shows that these efforts can have a detectable effect on page requests as a spike appears in the graph for a couple of days following such an activity. Figure 13.3 shows the profile of Skills Portal requests June 2011 – June 2012. The mean time spent per page is also shown as this is an indication that users find the resources useful and spend time working with them.

The learning development team are piloting using social networking software for master's students using Ning;[16] again it is possible to correlate requests with activity on forums. Students appear to respond to personal recommendations from librarians, as shown with Harvard Referencing, and academic staff, as well as virtual recommendations from Ning and non-specific general publicity (email, RSS). Approximately 40 per cent of requests are from users who have visited the site before.

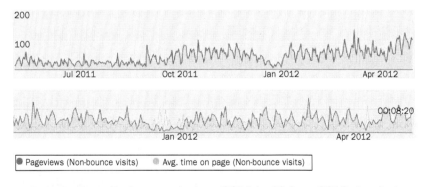

● Pageviews (Non-bounce visits)　　● Avg. time on page (Non-bounce visits)

Figure 13.3 Page requests June 2011 to 19 June 2012 showing both page requests and average time per page

One of the advantages of these OER resources is that they have already been evaluated and modified by their original creators before release. They are substantial resources that have taken time to create, evaluate and modify. It would simply not have been possible to create, let alone evaluate and modify, the wealth of resources available from the Skills Portal *de novo* in the time available. The Skills Portal is, gratifyingly, attracting attention from the OER community as it is an example of reuse with minimal technical intervention. It is evidence that OER can offer value to the community.

A common theme emerging from OER projects is how to identify resources that meet a specific requirement – perhaps a topic included in a specialist curriculum, at an appropriate level, with accurate content and suitable pedagogy? I had to spend time identifying and evaluating resources before adopting them. Information literacy and study skills are generic topics that are, possibly, easier to select than a highly specialised topic in a subject domain. There are a growing number of OER projects that depend on subject specialists evaluating and classifying resources from their subject. Discipline consultants to the HEA Biosciences OERbital project[17] are evaluating resources, giving brief descriptions via a wiki to present their community with a refereed and classified collection. One intention is to save multiple academics from having to repeat similar searches; another, more important, aim is to increase confidence in that resource via a system of peer review. At the start of the HEA-funded Humbox[18] project, academic staff were asked to identify what would make them consider using a third-party teaching resource. Most agreed that they were more likely to consider using an item if someone they respected recommended it. As with OERbital, peer opinion was identified as a key element for resources to be adopted by other academics.

One of the aims reads 'to create an expanding national community of peers committed to sharing and reviewing online resources from a range of subject areas in their own disciplinary contexts, which have a global reach'.[19]

The four Rs of OER

David Wiley (2007)[20] has identified the four Rs of OER as:

- *Reuse*: use the work unchanged.
- *Revise*: modify to meet your particular needs.

- *Remix*: combine original or revised work with other resources.
- *Redistribute*: share the original or modified work with the community via an open website or posting in a repository.

Of the four Rs, reuse and revision are the most common uses of OER resources, much less for remix and redistribution. Revise and remix require technical skills – depending on the technologies involved this might range from editing a Word document or web page to managing videos and multimedia files. Redistribution should be straightforward if a resource is deposited in a repository or on You Tube,[21] possibly less so if access to institutional web servers is required. Although the Skills Portal is still relatively immature some items have progressed through all of the four Rs in that all are reused, while most are revised and redistributed. Word for long documents is an example of remix, where videos have been added to an object created in Word and converted to HTML. Technically all have been revised as a new style-sheet has been applied. This raises a pragmatic question: what constitutes revision? In this example the appearance may have been changed but the content remains unchanged. An analogy might be printing a handout on a different colour of paper or modifying content to match the local context, for example garages in Bradford were replaced by tea shops in Guildford in one resource. Although essentially a trivial change, it might change a student's perception of the material. While there was no major change to content, changing from Word to web produced a significant change in that the resource was then easier to modify and was openly available. Share-and-share-alike is an essential component of Creative Commons licences that underpin the Open Educational movement. The resources on the Skills Portal are under continuous development – at what point should they be re-shared via Jorum?

Future developments

We will continue adding resources to the Skills Portal either as new ones appear or by expanding the range of topics covered. This will cause an immediate problem as the current collection occupies most of an average screen. As users are unlikely to scroll down, those resources that appear below the page are likely to be ignored. We would need to add an index or introduce a search tool; either will change the character of the Skills Portal, and adding an extra click is a deterrent to users. We also need to find ways of collecting user feedback to inform further developments. More importantly, we need to continue to find ways of encouraging both our students and others to use the Skills Portal.

Notes

1. *http://libweb.surrey.ac.uk/library/skills/Learningskills.html*
2. *http://www.jorum.ac.uk/*
3. *http://www.bioscience.heacademy.ac.uk/resources/oer/OER1.aspx*
4. *http://www.medev.ac.uk/static/uploads/MEDEV_OOER_final_report-draft-12-after-HEA-feedback_2010-10.pdf*
5. *http://en.wikipedia.org/wiki/MIT_OpenCourseWare*
6. *http://creativecommons.org/*
7. *http://creativecommons.org/policies*
8. The double C in a circle, the words and logotype 'Creative Commons' and the Creative Commons licence buttons are trademarks of Creative Commons. For more information, see *http://creativecommons.org/policies.*
9. *http://www.jorum.ac.uk/*
10. *http://www.jorum.ac.uk/jorumwidgets*
11. *http://www.vitae.ac.uk/researchers/1272-291181/Researcher-Development-Framework-RDF.html*
12. *http://open.jorum.ac.uk/xmlui*
13. *http://www.cochrane.org/*
14. *http://code.google.com/apis/analytics/docs/tracking/asyncTracking.html*
15. *http://www.textpad.com/*
16. *http://www.ning.com/*
17. *http://www.bioscience.heacademy.ac.uk/resources/oer/*
18. *http://www.llas.ac.uk/projects/3233*
19. *http://www.llas.ac.uk/projects/3233*
20. *http://opencontent.org/blog/archives/355*
21. *http://www.youtube.com/*

References

Boyle, T. (1997) *Design for Multimedia Learning*. London: Prentice Hall.

CRAC (2009) 'Researcher Development Framework Consultation', Careers Research and Advisory Centre Ltd. Available online at: *http://www.vitae. ac.uk/CMS/files/upload/Researcher-development-framework-consultation-briefing-paper.pdf.*

Downes, S. (2011) 'Five Key Questions'. Available online at: *http://www. downes.ca/.*

Fleming, C. and Massey, M. (2007) *Jorum Open Educational Resources (OER) Report*. Available online at: *http://www.jorum.ac.uk/squeezy/cms/docs/ pdf/0707_JorumOERreportFinal.pdf.*

Hylén, J. (2007) *Giving Knowledge for Free*. Paris: OECD Publishing.

Roberts, G. (2002) 'SET for Success: Final Report of Sir Gareth Roberts' Review'. Available online at: *http://webarchive.nationalarchives.gov.uk/+/ http://www.hm-treasury.gov.uk/set_for_success.htm*.

UK GRAD Programme (2001) *Joint Statement of the UK Research Councils' Training Requirements for Research Students*. UK GRAD Programme.

14

Free at last

Susan Myburgh

Abstract. The rate of development of information and communication technologies (ICTs) during the past few decades has been astounding. In many professions, their adoption and use has been fairly straightforward: they have usually accomplished three things. Firstly, ICTs have taken over routine administrative tasks and performed then more quickly than humans were able to do; secondly, they were (generally) able to perform such tasks more accurately; and thirdly, they were able to do things quite differently. In this framework, their effects have perhaps been unremarkable. However, for information professionals – those charged with the collection, management and preservation of information objects to ensure their availability to all – the effects have been both dramatic and, to a large extent, incomprehensible.

This chapter explores the essential characteristics and qualities of a future information professional, with specific reference to the social purpose of the profession and the discipline's teleology, noting that the discipline/profession's theoretical framework must be clarified and enunciated. With the concepts identified, together with the ontology and taxonomy of the information profession, it is clear that ICTs play an effective role in the rejuvenation of librarianship by assuming many technical tasks and allowing practitioners to achieve their professional goals.

Keywords: change, characteristics, future, information behaviour, information professionals

Introduction

This chapter explores the essential characteristics and qualities of a future information professional, with specific reference to the social purpose of the profession and the discipline's teleology, noting that the discipline/profession's theoretical framework must be clarified and enunciated. This shows clearly that information and communication technologies (ICTs) play an effective role in the rejuvenation of librarianship by assuming many technical tasks and allowing practitioners to achieve their professional goals.

Change is an ongoing feature of contemporary life, due to a combination of social, economic, technological and educational trends which bring with them individual, organisational, institutional, social and cultural challenges. The past three decades have been particularly eventful for the information discipline and its practices, with the rapid development of ICTs, the growth of digital documents, increasing globalisation, social networking and interactive, participative document creation.

Library and Information Science (LIS) has, as a result, found itself in a predicament. The literature of LIS is replete with suggestions, whether at the level of the fully developed research report or the illustrative anecdote, that LIS, including the practitioners and the collections of documents they manage, are obsolete, or at the very least will become increasingly redundant because of ICTs.[1, 2] Libraries and information centres are having their funding cut or are being closed down completely.[3] Even more menacing than the closure of libraries is the fact that the academic discipline itself is imperilled. Many educational programmes for LIS have been closed down over the past two decades, particularly in the USA but also in Australia and elsewhere. Others have been reinventing themselves, or at the very least changing their names, dropping 'library' or 'librarianship' (Ostler et al., 1995; Paris, 1988), while, phoenix-like, 'Schools of Information' have been established in the US and Europe.

On today's map of information professions, however, LIS does not feature. The emphasis is on those professions that deal with (design, construct or install) information technologies. Information work is consequently poorly understood, with a lack of distinction between technology and the information itself. LIS is further downgraded by the ignorance which encourages the belief that librarians are old-fashioned, technophobic and unable to cope in a digital world, capable only of performing the most mundane tasks. As part of this image construction, librarians are understood to be concerned with documents as physical objects only. This segues naturally enough into the assumption that if these are digitised, librarians will likewise 'disappear'.

There is little doubt that a previous technology – printing – forced information professionals – librarians, archivists and records managers – to focus on managing the material objects and the spaces in which they were arranged and stored. Because of the necessity to manage the plethora of physical documents through selection, organisation, preservation and provision of access, librarians have, over time, become more concerned with the document as an artefact than the ideas (or content) recorded in the document. The physicality of the documents with which librarians have traditionally worked, which are housed or embodied by the library, has focused the understanding of LIS on the location of professional praxis (for example 'the library'). The library as a place and space has, in many ways, become more important than the work that librarians do there.

But it is not ICTs per se, nor the ways in which they can be used, that have created the predicament of LIS. ICTs are making an increasingly significant difference to the work of librarians: the technical tasks associated with the management of physical objects – cataloguing, classification, organisation, storage, preservation and even access – are changed, reduced or even subsumed by these technologies. The chasm between what librarians had long aimed to achieve (for example education and enculturation) and what they actually do has, by and large, been thwarted by the lack of appropriate technologies. Much of the work of a librarian has been of a rather clerical nature and, indeed, many consider the 'core' knowledge of LIS to revolve around technical issues such as cataloguing rules.

ICTs can, and indeed they should, perform all those tasks which are of a technical, clerical or repetitive nature, leaving professionals free to do what they should do. In this way, the escalation of the development of ICTs provides a welcome moment for the reconceptualisation and rejuvenation of information work, and a reconsideration of the role of cultural custodians. The misperceptions regarding information work – the boundaries, purpose and nature of information work, and how it can be distinguished from the technologies which support it – are still prevalent, and these must urgently be re-examined and elucidated.

For a profession that is constituted to solve society's information problems, there has been remarkable neglect in the practice and purpose of understanding knowledge creation processes and the information flows in communities. Perhaps the most significant changes will be associated with a shift of focus from the library as an institution to the role of librarians and other information workers as professionals: from habitat to performance.

Discipline/profession and need for theory

LIS is not only an area of 'work' in terms of labour or effort: it comprises a discipline as well as a profession, and these two concepts are so closely intertwined that one is tempted to write 'discipline/profession', in the same way that Foucault wrote 'power/knowledge' (Foucault, 1980). A discipline can be characterised, according to Klein, as '[T]he tools, methods, procedures, exempla, concepts and theories that account coherently for a set of objects or subjects' (Klein, 1996). Abbott defines professions as 'exclusive occupational groups applying somewhat abstract knowledge to particular cases', where 'control of an occupation lies in control of the abstractions that generate the practical techniques' (Abbott, 1988). So, while professionals are people who, *inter alia*, have particular knowledge derived from familiarity with an organised body of learning or knowledge domain, their practice has the purpose of helping others in some way. A profession can, therefore, be defined by the role it plays in society and the particular social problems it deals with, whereas a discipline is defined by its theoretical structure.

Neither of these appears to have been resolved. It has long been taken for granted that libraries are 'good' for society, although this 'good' is not articulated. LIS as a discipline has long been criticised for its lack of theory, even though a profession needs a disciplinary or theoretical base to inform its praxis, and thus the discipline/profession suffers from a lack of gravitas in academia. The frequently acknowledged lack of a theoretical framework for LIS[4] has resulted in conceptual confusion concerning the entities and phenomena with which it is involved. Kajberg and Lørring (2005) identified a need 'for devoting more work to the conceptual frameworks and the terminology of the LIS discipline', particularly to explain the terminology where terms frequently have different semantic values.

For example, for a profession that is involved, by all accounts, with 'information' work, it is surprising that there is no operational definition of the term 'information' which enjoys consensus across the field (the interpretation of this term outside of LIS cannot be relevant). The only way in which the term is explained in the LIS literature is through alleged relationships between data, information and knowledge: a hierarchy which is based on a poem written in 1934.[5] This is particularly strange for a social science wishing to be recognised as a 'science'. Shannon and Weaver's 'information theory' (Shannon, 1948; Weaver and Shannon, 1949/1963), which was developed as a transmission model for engineers, is widely regarded as *the* theory for the field, although it does not even begin to connect the purposes and objectives of the profession with the communication of information and meaning, or solve society's information problems. The scope of investigation too remains constrained: only 'information' that is recorded and managed by libraries is considered by those in the field, rather than information that comes from (or is sought for) elsewhere. In particular, indigenous knowledges have been all but ignored until very recently.

Components and purpose of a theoretical framework

A theoretical framework provides a basic, hypothetical, logical, conceptual structure or description of a complex entity or process which can be used to develop theory, by classifying and organising complex information and providing a unified and coherent view. It comprises a set of concepts (*ontology*), and a description of the interrelationships (*propositions* or principles) between them (*taxonomy*). In this case, where the field in question is both a discipline and a profession, the establishment of *teleological* principles for the field is also useful. It is not possible within the confines of this chapter to explore all of the components of a theoretical framework, so there is an emphasis here on the teleology or purpose of the discipline/profession. Why are libraries 'good'? How are they 'good'? Why is reading, as an activity, 'good', regardless of what is being 'read'? Which is more important: the number of people entering a library, or the number of people whose lives have been changed because of the information they encountered – and understood – there? Why and how is the library different and 'better' than Google?

Libraries are social institutions

As disciplines/professions embodied in libraries and other information centres, cultural memory organisations such as libraries, galleries, museums and archives are social institutions. Social institutions are socially constructed, and they can, in turn, shape customs and expected behaviours within a social group. Intrinsically embedded in time, culture and society, they are sometimes considered to be extensions of human nature (for example patriarchy).

Power is inherent in social institutions generally, as social institutions play a key role in 'cultural production'. The two characteristics of librarianship mentioned earlier (dealing with documents as objects and the library as the centre of professional praxis) have resulted in the much ignored, diminished and possibly nearly invisible role of libraries in cultural production, and their potential (or latent) power as political sites, even though information can be considered to be 'messages produced within historical and cultural contexts and specific social interests' (Talja et al., 1999). Hjørland states that 'the ways people are informed are mediated by institutions [such as libraries], by documents, by language and by other cultural products, and the factual content of messages and signs cannot be isolated from these cultural mediators', all of which are associated with power (Hjørland, 1998). The library itself, as a cultural space, is a carrier of meaning, and the fact that particular documents are stored there, and not at other places, constructs a symbolic context for their understanding and interpretation. As Derrida has noted (as quoted by Dalbello, 2004) 'the "archive" [he uses the term broadly] is a context for transmission of texts', and so is the library.

Libraries as social institutions can be understood as functions, not places, in a networked information universe, where meaning is found in the information that documents contain, those selections which get read, and the paths taken through the body of represented knowledge which aggregates the results of all the perceptive and cognitive functions undertaken by individuals. Having seen this capacity for what is so often understood as a passive provision of a space in which information accumulates, to be transformed into a deliberative and culturally powerful selection – and so de-selection – of 'what counts', it surely becomes more possible to see every aspect of information practice as contributive to cultural meaning.

Shön (1983, 1987) has exposed the ineffectiveness of many professions, largely due to lack of interest in their social obligations, and librarianship is certainly one of these. Wiegand notes, 'Currently we lack a solid body of scholarship that critically analyses the multiple roles that libraries of all types have played and are playing in their host communities' (Wiegand, 1999), even though librarians are unavoidably involved in the cultural and scholarly activities that are related to knowledge creation, making meaning, learning and application processes, as noted.

There is much work to be done on evaluating the role of social institutions, such as libraries, in society. Evaluation of libraries has generally been undertaken from a managerialist, materialist and quantitative perspective, with little attention paid to wider outcomes. Numbers have been the significant means of expressing value, and these are associated with the scientific method, for a long time seen as the only way in which knowledge could be created. So, numbers are tallied by libraries: how many visitors they had, how much they spent on periodicals, how many books were issued, how many children's story hours were offered, and so forth. The focus has been clearly on the collections and how to manage them, not on the 'information flows' in society, as Castells (1996, 1997, 1998) put it.

None of these figures actually account for the difference that social institutions, such as libraries, make to the community and, indeed, this difference is recondite and longitudinal. There is a paucity of purpose-designed evaluation methodologies which can explore the performance of information work. Those drawn from otherwise-directed research paradigms have little efficacy in assessing information uptake or the programmes which support it. Fortunately, appropriate user-centred research objectives, measures and methods for the digital library are just beginning to emerge. There have been attempts recently in the UK to assess the economic value of libraries and museums, mostly through the Library, Archive and Museums initiative, and the British Library undertook its own study. Economic value is not directly related to finances, however, and so these evaluations cannot be subjected to accountancy regimes.

At the same time, there has been renewed interest in the notion of 'social capital', a phrase coined by Jane Jacobs in *The Death and Life of Great American Cities* (1961) in order to indicate those social conditions which unite a community to act against antipathetic business and government, although the term is used with different meanings by different people at different times. Essentially, 'social capital' refers to the networks, norms, trust and mutual understanding that bind together the members of human networks and communities, and enable participants to act together more effectively to pursue shared objects. Bourdieu (1983) identified social capital as part of cultural capital. It refers to the social powers accumulated by individuals and groups acting in concert, used to gain power over other individuals and groups, which is in turn used to negotiate, or contest, cultural or economic capital. The Organisation for Economic Cooperation and Development (OECD) definition of 'social capital' is 'networks, together with shared norms, values and understandings which facilitate co-operation within or among groups'. Measuring social capital remains difficult. Some consider the drop of 'bad' social phenomena, such as truancy and crime, and a rise of 'good' phenomena, such as lack of litter and higher rates of employment. However, as Widen-Wulff and Ginman note, 'A tool for measuring social capital must provide a common conceptual framework that helps unify [its] different dimensions' (Widen-Wulff and Ginman, 2004).

Libraries as political sites

Measuring the economic value or the social capital of libraries represents only one aspect of this issue, however. A primary goal of information work is thought to be to provide access to ideas so that people can constantly create knowledge, and this indicates that providing access to the records which contain information would be the chief function to achieve this. Information workers are, in this way, able to control the flows of information in society and influence the development of attitudes and opinions by facilitating or blocking access, whether this be physical access (to documents or to machines that store documents) or intellectual access (where language, degree of complexity and so forth can all impede access).

The word 'political' is used here in the sense of being concerned with dealing with the affairs of a community or society, or affecting the ways in which people make group or collective decisions, which are not necessarily involved with government administration per se. According to the principles of a free society, libraries are regarded as gateways to knowledge; as supporters of independent decision-making, cultural development, research, life-long learning, democratic values, the plurality and diversity of society; as contributors to the development and maintenance of intellectual freedom; as protectors of users' privacy and confidentiality; as promoters of responsible access to quality network information for all users; as opposers of censorship and all violations of human rights; and as bridges across the information gaps between the regions of the world (see, for example, the Glasgow Declaration formulated by IFLA, 2002). Libraries are vital for the maintenance of democracy, not so much as to have the 'informed electorate' which would support particular political systems, but to ensure that any government is responsible, transparent and accountable. Libraries also provide the space and place (even if digital only) for the creation of the type of 'public sphere' which Habermas (1991) envisaged.

That libraries can create real transformation and vigorous public debate, and even subvert authority, is evidenced by those acts of 'libricide' and furtive or overt censorship committed over the centuries, most notoriously by repressive regimes such as Nazism in Germany and Apartheid in South Africa, but also the Library of Baghdad by the Mongols in 1258 (and again in 2003 by invading US forces) and the Judaica collection at the library of Birobidzhan by Stalin. Once again, it is important to remember that such antagonism was not directed at libraries as organisations, or even books as objects: it was directed at the ideas recorded in such documents.

Day has remarked that 'Critical studies of professions need to reach out to a broader social and cultural context in order to understand professions as products of social forces other than themselves' (Day, 2000). While librarians choose to adopt a professionally 'neutral' stance with regard to bias, prejudice or opinion when supplying their users with information resources, their practice has nonetheless been implicitly hegemonic.[6] Power distributions are expressed not only in the economy but also in public policies which affect, *inter alia*, the funding and role of libraries and the functions of information in society. It is then quite easy to read libraries (as institutions) to be hegemonic, in spite of what librarians profess to believe, as conformity to the powers that be is often necessary in order to continue to receive funding. In spite of announcing goals of upliftment, development and so on, libraries are still prone to enacting social control surreptitiously, through selection processes, access protocols, dress and behaviour codes, opening hours and even classification decisions. The bland neutrality that is characteristic of most contemporary public libraries is in line with their most common use – entertainment in a consumer culture – and because of the claims of the discipline/profession to be 'scientific' in their neutrality.

Technology and teleology

Technology (*techne*) is more or less synonymous with 'tool' – any object that is made by humans to extend human capabilities. However, tools or technologies themselves have attributes and effects that are socially constructed. Heidegger (1977) noted that 'The essence of technology is by no means anything technological', and a remark by Goodman is often repeated to engineers: 'Whether or not it draws on new scientific research, technology is a branch of moral philosophy, not of science' (Goodman, 1970). Foucault noted that technologies make manifest certain social practices and values (Foucault, 1972) and can play a role in shaping social identities, knowledge systems and the ways in which things are done.

Google[7] and social media such as Facebook,[8] as well as various online databases, have certainly changed the ways in which people search for information. One could almost say that for many information was 'invented' by the Internet, as the immensity of the amount of human knowledge stored has never been so obvious as when millions of hits are identified by Google. There is little doubt that Google (and the Internet in general) can be seen as a threat to libraries – from a certain perspective anyway. But it would appear that skills in traversing the digital information universe are, by and large, lacking in the general population.

In 2008, the Centre for Information Behaviour and the Evaluation of Research (CIBER) group of University College London was sponsored by the Joint Information Systems Committee (JISC) and the British Library to examine how the 'Google generation' used the Internet, with specific reference to their information-finding skills. The results were not expected. The group found that most youngsters exhibited poor searching skills and this likely extends to the population at large, as few people understand how search engines work and how they determine relevancy. Google obligingly offers millions of results (of course, quite unusable based on quantity alone) and most users will be satisfied with these results. For most queries, most of the time, this is probably sufficient.

Librarians must be able to complement and contribute to the new information behaviours which are emerging in a networked and mobile world, and to demonstrate that they are capable of supporting those who inhabit digital information regions. Besides the fact that retrieving all this information is useless if the seeker is unable to understand it, critical thinking skills must be employed so that the information is accurately evaluated and interpreted for use (Webber and Johnston, 2003; Limberg and Sundin, 2006; D'Angelo, 2006). Librarians are perfectly positioned to teach such skills, which are different from the rather bland 'information literacy' approach so predominant in librarianship, which comprises little more than bibliographic instruction or how to use the library. Librarians should be able to encourage learning and critical thinking, so that more successful decisions can be made.

This responsibility can only be assumed by those who understand this social role, and Howard Winter (as cited by Shaughnessy) usefully describes the discipline/profession of librarianship as 'a systematically acquitted understanding of the nature of knowledge, its sources, its records and the human uses made of its records' (Winter, cited by Shaughnessy, 1979). This provides a neat summary of what a digital librarian should know.

Teleology

The matters mentioned above are but some of the social responsibilities that librarians must undertake as information professionals. Others would include issues such as censorship, information policies and the like, as suggested. The social purpose of professionals is to use their knowledge to help others, and the arena in which librarians work is that of helping to solve society's information problems. Sullivan (2007) sees professionals as 'moral agents' and believes that librarians should understand the importance of social responsibility and intervention. Like Schön (1983), Sullivan holds the view that, in the face of public distrust of social institutions such as banks, police, journalism and business, *inter alia*, all professionals must 'embrace a new way of looking at their role to include civic responsibility for themselves and their profession, and a personal commitment to a deeper engagement with society' (Sullivan, 2007).

This has implications for the future education of librarians. Aristotle used the term *sophia* to refer to wisdom, understanding or examination of the world. He further distinguished between several intellectual virtues or modes of knowing: *empeiria* (or *episteme*), *tekhene* and *phronesis*, and considered that all three were required to know something, with *sophia* (or understanding) as the supreme mode of, or mental attitude towards, discovering truth, or *theoria*, which also came to mean the investigation itself. *Theoria* implied an intellectual view of the world known as *nous*; eventually, an intellectual approach to the world came to suggest a rational explanation of it, known as an *episteme* (*Stanford Dictionary of Philosophy*, online). So there are five ways, according to Aristotle, in which a person may obtain the truth:

- *techne* – knowledge of making
- *empeiria* or *episteme* – knowledge proper
- *phronesis* – prudence or practical knowledge
- *sophia* – theoretical wisdom
- *nous* – intellectual approach, or intelligence.

Aristotle came to the conclusion that every well-functioning society was dependent on the effective functioning of all three intellectual virtues – *episteme*, *techne* and *phronesis*. However, *phronesis* has been largely ignored in the information professions, even though it is fundamental to any profession. Flyvbjerg (2001) points out that it is indicative of the degree to which thinking in the social sciences is dominated by the natural and technical sciences that there is no modern synonym for the one intellectual virtue which Aristotle saw as the necessary basis for social and political inquiry, and as the most important of the intellectual virtues. Flyvbjerg points out that 'Whereas *episteme* concerns theoretical *know why* and *techne* denotes technical *know how*, *phronesis* emphasizes practical knowledge and practical ethics' (Flyvbjerg, 2001). The object of *techne*, Flyvberg believes, is the application of technical knowledge and skills which emphasises the instrumental rationality which governs contemporary society: *phronesis*, on the other hand, is associated with a person who has knowledge of how to behave in particular circumstances, which Flyvbjerg describes as 'a sense of the ethically practical' (Flyvbjerg, 2001).

Many LIS education programmes tend to emphasise *techne* only, a dimension of the profession which is now largely subsumed by computers and the discipline of computer science. The various ways in which knowledge may be created and the *phronesis* (the ethical application of professional knowledge) has been somewhat ignored. Why *phronesis* has a particular value for professionals – and information professionals in particular – is that it considers the values of the profession with regard to its praxis, as *phronesis* is expressed in praxis. Praxis, as noted, is practice informed by theory, and an important component of theory is *teleology* – purpose.

Librarians have a distinct and demanding role in contemporary society. As Parker has noted, the fundamental aims and objectives of the Learning Society (social inclusion, lifelong learning and access to information) comfortably coincide with those of the cultural institutions sector (Parker, 2003). Caidi has extended this role, suggesting that the social role of libraries is to build civilisational competence (Caidi, 2006). As Caidi points out, libraries are social and cultural institutions that should enable individuals to lead successful lives by the acquisition of necessary skills and competencies. Information is not a commodity, but availability and understanding of information is vital to social and economic development nonetheless, because of its transformative powers. Information is capable of contributing to the knowledge base of an individual that will assist in making decisions that will have positive outcomes, and guiding actions that are likewise successful. Intervention in communication processes, between recorded ideas and those who wish to understand things (to put it as broadly as possible), should strengthen social and cultural networks of meaning and identity, and connect with the issues in people's lives.

How ICTs benefit the information professionals

Librarians now have the opportunity to become active agents in creating their new disciplinary and professional territory and forging new roles in the current environment, rather than remaining passive recipients reacting to external change, as has happened in the past (for example,

Lankes, 2009). Librarians can perform as principal actors for extending the library role to new or renewed functionalities in society (facilitator, educator or community agent).

The information worker can become a much more active agent in the interpretation of ideas and cultural heritage; an information interventionist (Myburgh, 2007) in the cycle of knowledge creation, distribution, understanding and new knowledge creation; a creator of learning contexts to encourage lifelong learning; and an intermediary in the social processes of information communication and knowledge creation. Information professions, positioned as they are in the flows of information, can assist people make sense and meaning of their lives out of the barrage of disparate messages with which they are bombarded. One of their primary social responsibilities is to connect people with the ideas of others, and assist in the construction of the social fabric through the communication of ideas. In this way, information professionals can keep the 'library' concept alive.

New skills will be demanded of this new generation. They will need to know how knowledge is created in different cultures and disciplines. As Thellefsen observes, concepts correspond to ideas and are conditional and provisional rather than fixed: they are not neutral, as they correspond to and are motivated by paradigms and ideologies (Thellefsen, 2004). This will enable librarians to be skilled cultural decoders and interpreters, enabling a narrative of continuity and coherence between users and information resources, so there is seamless engagement as part of the inquiry and learning processes. They can be agents of innovation and learning facilitators, supported by providing access to digital resources. Information professionals should know about and be ready to contribute to the development of information policies at the community, organisation and national level.

Conclusion

Librarians should therefore be elated by the increasing technologisation of their practice, as it promises so much that has been, until now, impossible. The work of information professionals must be directed towards playing a key role in managing and controlling information flows in society, and dealing with society's information (not technological) problems. This will go a considerable way towards individual, community and social development, the preservation of cultural heritage and the protection of freely available information as a basic human right. The distinction must be made between technologies and the ambitions of those who would use them solely for the construction and maintenance of power regimes to clarify to information and cultural workers – and to the wider public – that it is the ideologies at play, and not the technologies per se, that can pose threats.

Notes

1. For example, on 23 January 2007, the *Wired Campus Blog* of *The Chronicle*, an editorial that appeared in the *Washington Post*, suggested that books had become irrelevant, and that today's librarians were more concerned with teaching information literacy skills that comprised mastering computer skills.

2. In 1998, the UK Library and Information Commission released a statement entitled *New Library: The People's Network*, in which details of the ways in which public libraries were to function in the Information Society are given. At an international meeting held to discuss the recommendations of this report, the most typical roles of public libraries are described as little more than access nodes on the Internet, with librarians being charged with teaching the public how to use it (*International View: New Library: The People's Network*, 1998, online at: *http://www.ukoln.ac.uk/services/lic/newlibrary/intro.html*), giving a clear message that ICTs can replace, at the very least, the public library system.

3. In the United Kingdom, between 1993 and 2000, 203 libraries and 29 mobile libraries were closed, with a lack of local authority funding most frequently cited as the reason. But this is not the final tally: reports such as the following have been increasingly frequent of late:

107 libraries face closure

A total of 107 libraries across Britain are threatened with closure, the culture minister, David Lammy, confirmed. But Mr Lammy said that this was only a small percentage of the 3,500 libraries in the country, and that counties including Northamptonshire and Surrey had recently reversed plans to shut libraries. Mr Lammy wrote to councils in January to urge them to keep libraries open. Britain's libraries receive around 288 million visits each year. (*Independent*, 14 June 2006)

Libraries get £80m, but none of it to go on books

Libraries are to benefit from a new fund of £80 million of lottery money, but not a penny will be spent on books. Instead it will pay for buildings to be adapted for 'services', including Citizens Advice Bureaux, crèches, mother and toddler groups, t'ai chi and fitness classes.

The move comes as 50 libraries are believed to be earmarked for closure in 2006. Library campaigners are outraged, saying that libraries are about books and bookshelves, not about facilities for politically correct services. Christopher Hawtree, an author who ran a campaign to save a library in Brighton from closure, said: 'They should not become one-stop shops for council services. This is preposterous, they're turning librarians into *de facto* social workers.'

The plans were defended by The Big Lottery, which hands out money from the Lotto. The Big Lottery is preparing to distribute its £80 million 'community libraries' fund in June 2006. Stephen Dunmore, its chief executive, said: 'The whole idea is that libraries provide a focus for community activity, converting the space so that it can be used in a more imaginative way. Libraries are about books, but there are ways of learning which don't have to be book-based.' (*The Times*, 21 January 2006)

4. The dearth of theory and an underlying philosophy for the field has long been lamented in the professional literature. By 1931, Waples felt that librarianship was ready for a 'critical, academic approach' (Waples, 1931: 36). In 1992, Pierce pointed out that LIS does not have 'a common body of theory shaping the intellectual traditions of the field' (she stated that the field lacked 'dead Germans') (Pierce, 1992: 641). LIS presents what Foucault (1980: 108) calls a 'low epistemological profile'; the field has also been referred to as an 'academic impostor' (Manley, 1991: 70). Shön describes librarianship as a 'minor profession' which is 'hopelessly non-rigorous', one of the professions which suffers from 'shifting, ambiguous endings' and 'unstable institutional contexts of practice' (Shön, 1983: 23).

5. The DIK hierarchy has interesting origins, according to Sharma (2005), as it is first suggested in a poem by T.S. Eliot, published in 1934, called *The Chorus of the Rock*:

> Where is the Life we have lost in living?
> Where is the wisdom we have lost in knowledge?
> Where is the knowledge we have lost in information?

It is astonishing that information work should seek to have itself considered as a science based on a definition of the basic object of its knowledge domain that is given in a poem, but it is an equally surprising claim given that the DIK hierarchy does not add much to establishing the nature of these concepts.

6. According to Antonio Gramsci, a powerful group achieves hegemony when it gains control over a range of values and norms, to the extent that these become so embedded in society that they receive unquestioned acceptance.

7. *http://www.google.co.uk*

8. *http://www.facebook.com*

References

Abbott, A. (1988) *The System of Professions*. New York: Random.
Bourdieu, P. (1983) 'Forms of capital', in J. Richards (ed.) (1986) *Handbook of Theory and Research for the Sociology of Education*. New York: Greenwood Press.

Caidi, N. (2006) 'Building "civilisational competence": a new role for libraries?', *Journal of Documentation*, 62(2): 194–212.

Castells, M. (1996) *The Information Age: Economy, Society and Culture*, Vol. 1: *The Rise of the Network Society*. Oxford: Blackwell.

Castells, M. (1997) *The Information Age: Economy, Society and Culture*, Vol. 2: *The Power of Identity*. Oxford: Blackwell.

Castells, M. (1998) *The Information Age: Economy, Society and Culture*, Vol. 3: *End of Millennium*. Oxford: Blackwell.

D'Angelo, E. (2006) *Barbarians at the Gates of the Public Library: How Postmodern Consumer Capitalism Threatens Democracy, Civil Education and the Public Good*. New York: Library Juice Press.

Dalbello, M. (2004) 'Institutional shaping of cultural memory: digital library as environment for textual transmission', *Library Quarterly*, 74(3): 265–98.

Day, R.E. (2000) 'The "conduit metaphor" and the nature and politics of information studies', *Journal of the American Society for Information Science*, 51(9): 805–11.

Flyvbjerg, B. (2001) *Making Social Science Matter: Why Social Inquiry Fails and How It Can Succeed Again*. Cambridge: Cambridge University Press.

Foucault, M. (1972) *The Archaeology of Knowledge and the Discourse on Language*. New York: Harper & Row.

Foucault, M. (1980) *Power/Knowledge*. New York: Pantheon.

Goodman, P. (1970) *New Reformation: Notes of a Neolithic Conservative*. New York: Random House.

Habermas, J. (1991) *The Structural Transformation of the Public Sphere: An Inquiry into a Category of Bourgeois Society*. Cambridge, MA: MIT Press.

Heidegger, M. (1977) *Being and Time*. New York: Basic Books.

Hjørland, B. (1998) 'Theory and metatheory of information science: a new interpretation', *Journal of Documentation*, 54(5): 606–21.

International Federation of Library Associations (IFLA) (2002) *The Glasgow Declaration on Libraries, Information Services and Intellectual Freedom*. Online at: *http://www.ifla.org/publications/the-glasgow-declaration-on-libraries-information-services-and-intellectual-freedom*.

Jacobs, J. (1961) *The Death and Life of Great American Cities*. New York: Houghton Mifflin.

Kajberg, L. and Lørring, L. (eds) (2005) *European Curriculum Reflections on Library and Information Science Education*. Online at: *http://dspace-unipr.cilea.it/bitstream/1889/1704/1/EUCLID%20European%20LIS%20curriculum.pdf*.

Klein, J.T. (1996) *Crossing Boundaries: Knowledge, Disciplinarities and Interdisciplinarities*. Charlottesville, VA: University Press of Virginia.

Lankes, R.D. (2009) *New Concepts in Digital Reference*. San Rafael, CA: Morgan-Claypool.

Limberg, L. and Sundin, O. (2006) 'Teaching information seeking: relating information literacy education to theories of information behaviour', *Information Research*, 12(1). Online at: *http://InformationR.net/ir/12-1/paper280.html*.

Manley, W. (1991) 'Professional survival: it's academic', *Wilson Library Bulletin*, 65(6): 79–81.

Myburgh, S. (2007) *Defining Information: The Site of Struggle*. Adelaide: University of South Australia.

Ostler, L.J., Dahlin, T.C. and Willardson, J.D. (1995) *The Closing of American Library Schools: Problems and Opportunities*. Westport, CT: Greenwood Press.

Paris, M. (1988) *Library School Closings: Four Case Studies*. Metuchen, NJ: Scarecrow Press.

Parker, I. (2003) 'Psychoanalytic narratives: writing the self into contemporary cultural phenomena', *Narrative Inquiry*, 13(2): 301–15.

Pierce, S.J. (1992) 'Dead Germans and the theory of librarianship', *American Libraries*, 23(8): 641.

Schön, D. (1983) *The Reflective Practitioner*. New York: Basic Books.

Schön, D. (1987) *Educating the Reflective Practitioner*. San Francisco: Jossey-Bass.

Shannon, C. (1948) 'The mathematical theory of communication', *Bell System Technical Journal*, July and October, pp. 379–423 and 623–56.

Sharma, N. (2005) 'The origin of the "Data information knowledge wisdom" hierarchy'. Online at: *http://go.webassistant.com/wa/upload/users/u1000057/webpage_10248.html*.

Shaughnessy, T.W. (1979) 'Library research in the 70s: problems and prospects', *Californian Librarian*, 37: 44–52.

Sullivan, W.M. (2007) 'The Civic Life of Information: Teaching Professionalism for the Knowledge Age'. Online at: *http://www.alise.org/conferences/2007_conference/keynote.html*.

Talja, S., Keso, H. and Pietiläinen, T. (1999) 'The production of context in information seeking research: a metatheoretical view', *Information Processing and Management*, 35(6): 751–63. Online at: *http://www.uta.fi/~lisaka/taljakeso.pdf*.

Thellefsen, T. (2004) 'Knowledge profiling: the basis for knowledge organization', *Library Trends*, 52(3): 507–14.

Waples, D. (1931) 'The Graduate Library School at Chicago', *Library Quarterly*, 1(1): 26–36.

Weaver, W. and Shannon, C. (1949/1963) *The Mathematical Theory of Communication*. Urbana, IL: University of Illinois Press.

Webber, S. and Johnston, B. (2003) 'Information literacy in the United Kingdom: a critical review', in C. Basili (ed.), *Information Literacy in Europe*. Rome: Italian National Research Council, pp. 258–83.

Widen-Wulff, G. and Ginman, M. (2004) 'Explaining knowledge sharing in organizations through the dimensions of social capital', *Journal of Information Science*, 30(5): 448–58.

Wiegand, W.A. (1999) 'Tunnel vision and blind spots: what the past tells us about the present: reflections on the twentieth century history of American librarianship', *Library Quarterly*, 69(1): 1–32.

15

Flexible and agile university library and information services: skills and management methodologies

Caroline Williams

Abstract. In today's complex information ecology libraries and information services are cognisant of both maintaining and developing highly skilled and motivated staff who are agile and flexible so as to be responsive and relevant to the communities they serve. They are metamorphosing from hierarchical management of people grounded in the transactional model of content provision to collaboration and relationship building which enable the flows of information within our institutions. To achieve this transformation staff are looking through a number of lenses to generate the insights which will provide them with the next generation of practice for the profession.

These lenses include the re-examination of our skills in relationship management, e.g. from subject librarians to CRM, recognition of the value of social research methods in understanding user behaviour, and innovative approaches to information management from the curation of research data to cutting-edge UI and UX design. Another view is presented through changes in management and leadership thinking and practice: project-focused teams now work across existing organisational structures, and teams learn and vision and strategise together. Methodologies like OGC's Managing Successful Programmes (MSP) and PRINCE2 are becoming more and more established as tools to support the management of these new ways of working, as are self-conscious explorations of individual work preferences (e.g. Belbin) within teams to maximise the effectiveness of group working. For leaders the skills which are becoming vital are those which support working collaboratively, e.g. negotiation and influencing, and creating environments for change, e.g. action enquiry.

This chapter brings together these different lenses to provide reflections on latest practice to start to illuminate the routes from command and control to the collaborative and consensual direction of agile and flexible teams.

Keywords: agile, expertise, methodologies for managing, role, skills, subject librarians, teamwork

Introduction

In today's information overloaded world, library directors and managers are cognisant of the value of maintaining and developing highly skilled and well-motivated staff who are agile and flexible so as to be responsive and relevant to the communities they serve. The 2011 Horizon report highlights the trend away from traditional roles to 'models in which teams work actively together to address issues too far-reaching or complex for a single worker to resolve alone' (Johnson et al., 2011), and at number six in the EDUCAUSE review of the top ten issues for 2011 is 'Agility/Adaptability/Responsiveness' (Ingerman and Yang, 2011). This review spells out in no uncertain terms that 'technological change demands flexibility and nimbleness'. In our management of people we are attempting to metamorphose the functional groupings grounded in the transactional model of content provision into matrix and project-based structures to enable new flows of information within our institutions. The recent Research Libraries (RLUK) work (Brewerton, 2011) exploring new roles for subject librarians prompts reflection on transferable skills and extending the terms of engagement of the university information professional. At the heart of all this is delivering business value to our institutions and satisfaction to our clientele.

In job descriptions we ask for people who are flexible and agile. We have new recruits who are schooled in creative problem-solving and project management methodology, who have high levels of digital literacy and are full of ideas germinated in their experience of social network and mobile technologies. Yet harnessing this to create forward-looking and adaptable teams can be difficult to achieve in practice. In order to remain relevant, we need teams that can respond rapidly to changing priorities and new agendas. In these times of financial stringency, when battening down the hatches around our realms is all too tempting, it is even more challenging to create a working environment where silo-spanning activity flourishes. So how then do we build library and information services which respond quickly to the stimuli of strategic threat or opportunity? In this paper I will explore this question and these challenges, drawing on my experience in UK higher education (HE) libraries and information services. The themes I will cover are: teamwork – the good, the bad and the ugly; skills and expertise; and methodologies for managing – Managing Successful Programmes (MSP), Customer Relationship Management (CRM) and Agile.

Teamwork: the good, the bad and the ugly

Morrell and Capparell (2003) recount the Antarctic expedition of Sir Ernest Shackleton from 1914 to 1916 through a leadership lens. Shackleton recruited a team made up of the experienced to the novice, from the former Royal Navy and merchant serviceman as his deputy to the creative – a photographer. His advertisement for the team promised danger and grim conditions with only the possibility of safe return which would bring fame but not fortune. As we face an undefined future in HE libraries what are the skills, capabilities and attitudes/mindsets we need, and what is the new unwritten psychological contract (Rousseau, 1995)? Are we now asking our staff to be courageous and intrepid in the exploration of new territory, to take risks, to fail (the Shackleton expedition did not reach its ultimate destination) and to succeed (as Shackleton did by surviving)? If this is the reality of our library and information services now, then it is all the more vital to build high-performing teams.

'Teamwork remains the one sustainable competitive advantage that has been largely untapped' (Lencioni, 2005). Rather like Maslow's hierarchy of needs,[1] Lencioni presents a pyramid; his is of the dysfunctions of a team. As Maslow describes food and water as the physiological foundation without which we will not fulfil our higher-level psychological potential, Lencioni has as fundamental to effective teamworking the need for trust. He describes approaches to building trust which ultimately enable space for individual vulnerability to be revealed, where permission is granted for team members to 'say things like "I was wrong" and "I made a mistake" and "I need help" and "I'm not sure" and "you're better than I am at that" and yes, even "I'm sorry"'[2] – particularly difficult to do when the pressure is on to deliver more for less. Rising up the hierarchy of dysfunctions are fear of conflict, lack of commitment, avoidance of accountability and inattention to results. Lencioni describes tools to help overcome these: behavioural profiling such as the Myers-Briggs Type Indicator (MBTI), scoreboards or dashboards such as visual tools assessing success at any given point in time, and so on. He leaves us in no doubt that building successful teams 'requires levels of courage and discipline – and emotional energy – that even the most driven executives don't always possess'.

Building teams is not only a draw on emotional energy but also requires emotional intelligence. It is the relationships within teams that enable tasks and projects to move forward. Daniel Goleman (2007) writes of emotional intelligence and of the threat of the 'dark side' which can hijack teamworking. He describes 'The Dark Triad' of narcissists, Machiavellians and psychopaths:

> All three types share to varying degrees an unappealing, though sometimes well-concealed, core: social malevolence and duplicity, self-centeredness and aggression, and emotional coldness.

Extreme perhaps but this does resonate with some of the popular teamworking thinking that has crossed over to management from sports psychology. For example, sports psychologist Damien Hughes[3] talks of success in team sports where the individual puts the needs of the collective above those of their own. Returning to Shackleton, he did this by breaking down 'traditional hierarchies and cliques by training workers to do a number of jobs' (Morrell and Capparell, 2003) and he brought employees together to work on certain tasks simply to build trust and respect and even friendship. In so doing, he released his team from the tyranny of the power of the 'indispensable' specialist which can dominate decision-making and focus activity upon their own self-interest.

Building trust, understanding and friendship takes time. The time dimension and sense of evolution of the team is also evident in the familiar team development model of Tuckman (1965). His research into group dynamics gave us the stages of group development: forming, storming, norming, performing and adjourning. In my experience the two most challenging of these stages have been storming and adjourning, the former because giving time to (and not smoothing over) conflict is uncomfortable and finding ways to facilitate it so that the clashes are explicit, constructive and creative commands negotiation techniques, emotional intelligence and objectivity, the latter because stopping the work of a high-performing team may be about the diminishing relevance or value of the work (rather than quality standards) and because of the sense of loss that comes with disbanding a team where there is high level of trust. On the other hand, adjourning in line with project management methodology does encourage us to celebrate project successes and learn lessons.

Skills and expertise

At the time of writing I have recently established a project team to deliver a research data management infrastructure for my university. We have some of the necessary expertise already – particularly in developing the technical infrastructure – and an understanding of who can be retrained and redeployed, and have recruited two new staff, one who brings data management expertise from the commercial domain and another who has redeveloped her librarianship skills to be finely tuned to the needs of the research community. In this and other situations, as there are a number of variables, getting the right roles, skills and expertise and allocating the right level of effort can feel more like an art than a science.

Over recent years, I have found myself drawing together the threads of expertise around the centrality of the user experience and using that as the fulcrum of the development activity. I will illustrate this with a case study – a mobile development project. This was a 12-month project to develop mobile applications and search interfaces for two digital library databases to enable academics and students researching 'on the road' not only to store information, but also easily to find the location, access and contact details at a touch of a button. The mobile interfaces were developed in collaboration with the UK researcher community, firstly by working with them to prioritise and better understand requirements and secondly through user testing.

To deliver this project a team was established with wide-ranging skills sets and the project team roles emerged accordingly. The project manager was not PRINCE2 (Projects in Controlled Environments)[4] qualified but offered more by having plenty of practical experience of project management. She possessed the ability to keep the team focused on the end goal and had a good grasp of resourcing and scheduling. She planned and managed the project, ensuring that reporting requirements were met, the budget was effectively managed and the project was delivered on time to quality standards. Because of her expertise in social research methods, the project manager doubled up as market researcher to work with the service team to design and analyse the survey and focus groups of users. She also supported dissemination activity which was incorporated into the established service communication channels. Most importantly, across the sense of ownership and priorities inherent in the organisational structures she had to navigate between the service team and the mobile project team, the technical infrastructure team and the project team, and the service users and the project and service team.

In terms of technical development we initially thought one person could do the job. However, in early discussion it became clear that we needed the skill sets of two individuals because of the importance we had placed on a user-centric approach. One was experienced in user experience (UX) and user interface (UI) design and another delivered the backend technical development, translating service functionality to mobile devices. This team worked well together, some of the reasons for which included the following:

- There was a clear focus on output and the outcomes for users.
- Team members had respect for each other's skills sets.
- All team members had the ability to juggle the priorities of this project alongside their other commitments.
- They embraced working on a project that was, at the time, innovative.
- All members of the project team had the communication skills and emotional intelligence to build and manage relationships across the whole organisation.

This small team took the project from an idea to delivery. In doing so, they demonstrated a whole host of skills and aptitudes, which, as well as those already mentioned, included:

- horizon scanning;
- strategic thinking;
- identifying funding opportunities and writing bids;
- requirements gathering and user testing;
- high levels of digital literacy;
- risk management;
- stakeholder relationship management;
- benefits management.

To find all this embodied in a small team may be the exception rather than the rule so we are more often considering investment in skills development and team-building. Many HE library and information services can support individual and group training and development. At the group level, training tends to be aimed at groups undertaking similar jobs or at similar levels in the organisational hierarchy. Other than team-building in one-off events, it is more unusual for teams across staff levels/ grades and functional roles to come together to learn collectively. I was part of a team which did just that and in so doing built capability and capacity to respond flexibly to changing priorities and demands. The annual team-training programme was intentionally tailor-made to meet emerging requirements. This programme covered, among other things (including the ubiquitous Belbin (1981) analysis of team roles), chairing and facilitating meetings, creative problem-solving, negotiation skills, and presence and impact. We could share out the load of managing the communication with others, support each other and change roles as the situation demanded. In addition, Lencioni's (2005) environment for vulnerability and trust was enabled through the collective learning together. With such a level of trust, the norm (outside of the development programme) was to say things like 'will you write that – you're better than me' or 'show me how to ...' or 'take a look at this ...'.

However, building expertise and capacity internally is not necessarily sustainable or desirable especially as our thinking in relation to shared services and outsourcing extends and matures. In his weblog, Lorcan Dempsey discusses issues of scaling in the context of services and collections. His points have implications for staffing and indeed can be reapplied to thinking about the deployment of skills:

> Questions about sourcing and scaling are becoming much more common ... What does it make sense to do at institutional level? What does it make sense to source elsewhere (repository services in the cloud, for example, or institutional email services from Google)? And what should be left entirely to other providers? At what level, or scale, is it best to do things? Locally, or within a consortium, or ...?'[5]

Shared services and outsourcing allow us to do things more efficiently and potentially respond more quickly and flexibly to peaks and troughs in demand and changing stakeholder requirements. We do already have examples of shared services in helpdesks, cataloguing and collection management, so what next is appropriate and feasible to deliver as a wider collective or to outsource and what activity is best retained in-house?

Methodologies for managing – Managing Successful Programmes, Customer Relationship Management and Agile

> The world around us is messy. Inevitably, then, when we set up ourselves and our systems to be neat and orderly, we're creating a sort of barrier, with high randomness on the outside and low randomness on the inside. But while the barrier may succeed in keeping out mess, it can also cut us off from the very aspects of the outside world that are critical to our success. (Abrahamson and Freedman, 2006)

There are methodologies which give structure and allow us to work outside of formal hierarchies and functional groupings. Project management is commonplace. It concentrates our minds on delivering outputs and it gives us lines of accountability, stakeholder management, the disciplines of resource allocation, scheduling and progress reporting, planning, risk management and the management of project closure. Projects in library and information services often apply PRINCE2 with a 'light touch' and organisations create their own methodologies based on it. Yet it is not always appropriate for delivering change and service development; there are other methodologies which can help us to manage for flexibility and agility in response to changing user needs and behaviour, three of which I mentioned earlier and will discuss further now – Managing Successful Programmes (MSP), Customer Relationship Management (CRM) and Agile.

The Office of Government Commerce's (OGC) Managing Successful Programmes methodology is a framework which challenges us to think deeper than project management to focus on delivering stakeholder benefit and organisational change. Programme management also provides a mechanism to split up what could initially appear to be a sprawling range of work into phased (tranches) segments (projects) of activity with clear interdependencies and unified outcomes. One of the most significant documents of the MSP methodology is the Blueprint, the role of which is to outline the characteristics of the current and the desired 'future state'. This does two significant things:

- It ensures that the challenges, strengths and weaknesses of the present service are clearly articulated (as opposed to being a mass of problems or solutions described in different documents and raised at numerous meetings, which often do not come together to highlight underlying systemic deficiencies).

- It articulates the vision of the future in sufficient detail to enable staff to unite behind it without necessarily understanding all the specifics.

This document also initiates the briefs for the projects that make up the programme. Management of the projects and project teams can then be allocated across staffing structures, creating a temporary matrix organisational grouping. Another part of MSP is the stakeholder relationship management and benefits realisation, both of which help to keep the focus on what is of value to the business and the target audiences. In summary, MSP is a useful methodology for managing complexity, change, working across organisational boundaries and structure, and work at scale.

Both CRM and Agile are associated with the IT industry. They can be applied as they stand to library and information services and also offer something to our thinking in broader terms through the concepts upon which they are based and the problems they address, quoting once more Lorcan Dempsey who comments on 'a general move towards "customer relationship" (or engagement, or research and learning support, or ...) and away from infrastructure management as the primary locus of library activity'.[6]

In 'Introducing CRM into an academic library', Mei-Yu Wang (2007) tells us 'Relationship marketing aims to identify, maintain, and build up a network with individual customers and to continuously strengthen the network for the mutual benefit of both sides through interactive, individualised and value-added contacts over a long period of time.' There are many interactions between academic and library and information staff and services. Harnessing, collecting and sharing information about these interactions potentially provide not only management information to inform service development but also a more holistic response to users. However, it is not widely deployed in university libraries, yet the associated process and focus of staff on customers is potentially of great value and has been masked by attention to the technology that accompanies CRM implementation which has been problematic: 'Approximately 70 percent of CRM implementations fail to meet basic company goals.'[7]

A methodology which has been developed in response to the delivery of software solutions which do not meet business needs is Agile development.

> Agile is a collective term for methodologies (and practices) that have emerged over the past two decades to increase the relevance, flexibility and business value of software solutions. (Cooke, 2011)

Its fundamental objective is to focus on delivering outputs which create the highest 'business value for the organisation' and 'encourage ongoing communication between the business areas and technical team members to increase the relevance, usability and quality of delivered software' (Cooke, 2011). Applying these objectives to digital library development is difficult – to some extent we are hostage to the interfaces of library management system suppliers and e-publishers. It is a concern that the pace of development of software solutions for the searching of our digital collections and our prioritisation of stability are barriers to agile development in response to user expectations and behaviour.

Conclusion

As a flock of birds moves as one in response to stimuli then we should assume the behaviour of complex adaptive systems to ensure long-term survival through agility and flexibility as individuals, teams and services. In summary, the features which will facilitate this kind of behaviour include: a working environment which is trusting and challenging; multi-skilled staff who are open to learning; an ability to cut across functional structures; high-performing multidisciplinary teams; knowledge sharing systems and information banks about customers; and more external partnerships and commissions – all with the business needs of the host organisation and customers absolutely central.

Notes

1. *http://www.abraham-maslow.com/m_motivation/Hierarchy_of_Needs.asp*
2. Ibid.
3. Damian Hughes, LiquidThinker, online at: *http://www.liquidthinker.com/ sports-psychology.aspx*.
4. A process-based method for effective project management; see *http://www. prince2.com/what-is-prince2.asp*.
5. L. Dempsey (2011) *Sourcing and Scaling: The University of California.* Online at: *http://orweblog.oclc.org/archives/002175.html*.
6. L. Dempsey (2011) *The Service Turn* ... Online at: *http://orweblog.oclc. org/archives/002152.html*.
7. Ibid.

References

Abrahamson, E. and Freedman, D.H. (2006) *A Perfect Mess: The Hidden Benefits of Disorder.* London: Weidenfeld & Nicolson.

Belbin, R.M. (1981) *Management Teams: Why They Succeed or Fail.* London: Heinemann.

Brewerton, A. (RLUK Work Force Think Tank) (2011) *Research Project: Investigation into the 'Subject Librarian' Skills Sets Required to Effectively Support the Information Needs of Researchers in the Current and Future Research Environment.* Online at *http://www.rluk.ac.uk/node/657.*

Cooke, J.L. (2011) *Agile: An Executive Guide.* Ely: IT Governance Publishing.

Goleman, D. (2007) *New Science of Human Relationships.* London: Arrow.

Ingerman, B.L. and Yang, C. (2011) 'Top-ten IT issues 2011', *EDUCAUSE Review*, May/June.

Johnson, L., Smith, R., Willis, J., Levine, A. and Haywood, K. (2011) *The 2011 Horizon Report.* Austin, TX: New Media Consortium.

Lencioni, P. (2005) *Overcoming the Five Dysfunctions of a Team: A Field Guide for Leaders, Managers and Facilitators.* San Francisco: Jossey-Bass.

Morrell, M. and Capparell, S. (2003) *Shackleton's Way: Leadership Lessons from the Great Antarctic Explorer.* London: Nicholas Brealey.

Rousseau, D.M. (1995) *Psychological Contracts in Organisations: Understanding Written and Unwritten Agreements.* London: Sage.

Tuckman, B. (1965) 'Developmental sequence in small groups', *Psychological Bulletin,* 63(6): 384–99.

Wang, M.-Y. (2007) 'Introducing CRM into an academic library', *Library Management,* 28(6/7): 281–91.

16

The future of academic libraries in the digital age

LiLi Li

Abstract. Impacted by the evolving web search engines and innovative information media, academic libraries are facing more unexpected competition in today's networked information society. Published by the *Chronicle of Higher Education* in January 2011, Brian T. Sullivan's 'Academic Library Autopsy Report, 2050'[1] triggered another round of debate about the demise of academic libraries. In this chapter, the author analyses six key factors Sullivan used to declare the death of the academic library. After examining current academic libraries from four different aspects, the author highlights six driving forces that will impact the infrastructure and operations of academic libraries in the future. Utilising the web-based library information technology architecture, he outlines a number of features that future academic libraries may have in future.

Keywords: academic libraries, Cloud, digital age, digitisation, emerging technologies, Semantic Web, twenty-first century

Introduction

In the digital age, the Internet has become a primary technology platform for academic libraries to deliver and disseminate information for faculty and students. Challenged by powerful web search engines such as Ask,[2] Bing,[3] Google[4] and Yahoo,[5] a number of academic administrators, executives, faculty, librarians and other professionals are debating whether or not it is still wise to invest in academic libraries. Since web search engines are so popular today, do we still need academic libraries to search academic and scholarly information for teaching and learning?

Do undergraduates and graduates still need information literacy instructions regarding library resources and searches? Since the arrival of the Internet, it is not uncommon to hear talk of the demise of the library from time to time.

Impacted by the evolving web search engines and innovative information media, academic libraries are facing more unexpected competition in today's networked information society. On 2 January 2011, the *Chronicle of Higher Education* published Brian T. Sullivan's paper titled 'Academic Library Autopsy Report, 2050' which again shook the library world and attracted a lot of debate about whether or not academic libraries will survive in the digital age. In his paper, Sullivan concluded that 'The academic library has died.' His major perspective came from the following observations:

- Book collections have become obsolete.
- Library instructions are not necessary.
- Information literacy instruction is fully integrated into the curriculum.
- Libraries and librarians have been subsumed by information technology departments.
- Reference services disappeared.
- Economics has trumped quality.

Because of these six reasons, he thinks that 'we'll never know now what kind of treatments might have worked. Librarians planted the seeds of their own destruction and are responsible for their own downfall' (Sullivan, 2011).

After a careful review, the author believes that these six factors are still not sufficient to predict the demise of academic libraries. The rise of e-books indeed has had a great impact on current library printed book collections. However, it is still a little too early to claim that e-books will completely replace traditional printed books. Even so, academic libraries still will be able to offer access to e-books and other academic e-databases for students and faculty. Without a network or a power supply, e-books are not accessible at all. In service-oriented and student-centred academic library settings, essential library guidance is still indispensable to undergraduates. It is not practical to rely on web search engines or e-database vendors to replace customised library instructions in dynamic and interactive academic learning environments. A general user-friendly interface cannot solve all kinds of local access problems for students on and off campus. As for information literacy, this is an eternal topic. To foster and promote skills in creative thinking, decision-making and problem-solving, academic faculty and librarians need to work together to integrate information literacy into the curriculum. The persistence of librarians has resulted in more and more colleges and universities having launched campus-wide information literacy programmes. It is not reasonable to assert that librarians have 'lost faith in their ability to impart useful knowledge to students' (Sullivan, 2011). Information literacy is not library literacy. Information literacy refers to general experience, knowledge and skills of obtaining information and knowledge in many different subject categories. Library literacy is the essential capability for accessing and searching information in a library setting. Librarians cannot replace other teaching faculty to impart specific career experience, subject knowledge and industrial skills in many different academic programmes. In view of the fact that academic libraries are contributing different teaching functions and social responsibilities to the infrastructure of institutes of higher education, it is impossible for IT departments to take over academic libraries completely, even though the library's 'collection development became a mere matter of maintaining database subscriptions recommended by faculty' (Sullivan, 2011) and 'cataloguing became the exclusive purview of the vendors of digital-book-and-journal collections' (Sullivan, 2011). In the digital age, academic libraries have more functions and roles than computer labs can handle. Just because academic libraries are using information technologies does not mean that academic libraries and librarians will be 'subsumed by information-technology departments' (Sullivan, 2011). Utilising innovative information technologies, reference services in academic libraries have not disappeared. On the contrary, reference services, which have been enhanced and integrated to information services with IT departments, have expanded their service ranges to reach more faculty and students. In addition to the popular Wikipedia[6] and Google Scholar,[7] there are so many powerful academic databases and network consortiums available. Moreover, the quality of information resources and the scale of library collections in academic libraries have been recognised as one of the critical criteria for academic institutions and programmes to retain their academic accreditations. Up to now, a lot of teaching faculty have not accepted Wikipedia as a creditable scholarly resource. Google Scholar cannot replace many other important academic and scholarly databases and network consortiums.

Without a thorough examination of current functions, infrastructures, operations and services of academic libraries in ever-changing academic learning environments, it is impossible to foresee correctly in which direction academic libraries will move in the digital age. As an experienced e-information services librarian, the author believes that the developing trends in cutting-edge and emerging technologies will have direct implications for current and future academic library information resources and services. Before we make any predictions, we need to examine how and where innovative information technologies will impact academic libraries via the Internet and the World Wide Web. In addition, any predictions without a timeframe do not make any sense. Utilising the web-based academic library information technology architecture, the author predicts where the future of academic libraries will move by the end of the twenty-first century.

Current academic libraries in the digital age

In the long journey of history, libraries appeared to be repository spaces to preserve the essentials of human civilisations. Defined by the *New Oxford American Dictionary*, the library is described as 'a building or room containing collections of books, periodicals, and sometimes films and recorded music for people to read, borrow, or refer to' (Mckean, 2005). Since the ancient Roman Empire, libraries have been used as places to store all kinds of information, including artistic, historical, literary, military, musical, reference materials and so on. Having gone through so many changes and innovations over the past 2,000 years, what functions and roles have academic libraries displayed in the modern society? What new inventions, innovations and products are changing ways of information delivery and dissemination in academic libraries? How will the digital revolution impact on academic library information resources and services in the future? Once we find out all of these answers, it will be much easier for us to predict correctly which way the future of academic libraries will evolve in the digital age.

Current functions and roles of academic libraries

In the digital age, academic library buildings are not only utilised as repository places to support teaching and learning activities. In dynamic and interactive academic learning environments, an academic library has become a centre for information access and distribution, learning and teaching activities, presentations and exhibitions, and social network connections. In an effort to attract and retain more undergraduates and graduates, academic libraries are also used as the incarnation of learning manners and styles in academic learning environments. In campus tours, academic libraries are introduced as support centres for excellence in teaching and life-long learning. To support all kinds of researches and studies, academic libraries are making their best efforts to provide students and faculty with the qualified information resources at affordable cost. At the same time, academic libraries are taking primary responsibility for promoting cultural, economic, educational and social associations between institutions and local communities.

Web-based information technology architecture in an academic library

Since the late 1990s, the Internet and the World Wide Web have become the primary technology platform for libraries worldwide to deliver web-based information resources and services. From Figure 16.1 based on the web-based three-tier client/server information technology architecture, we can see that different library computers, including desktops, laptops, netbooks, smart phones and tablets, are located at Tier 1 (also called web clients at the frontend). Middleware, which contains web server and many other business rules, is located at Tier 2. Various data repository objects, including HTML/XML-based documents, catalogues, data warehouses, digital libraries, e-databases, knowledgebases, web forms and other digital assets, are located at Tier 3 (also called the backend).

Over the Internet platform, academic libraries are able to set up web-oriented information resources and services, such as Ask-A-Librarian, Bibliographic Instructions, Computerised Library Catalogues, Distance Learning Services, e-Government Information Resources, Information Literacy Programmes, Instant Messaging (IM) Reference Services, Interlibrary Loan (ILL) and Document Delivery Services, Library Online Workshops, Virtual Classrooms, Virtual Library Tours, Virtual Reference Shelves and so on. All of these library information resources and services are, in most cases, accessible from HTML (Hypertext Markup Language) and XML (Extensible Markup Language) documents located at the frontend. As for other scripting languages, such as CSS

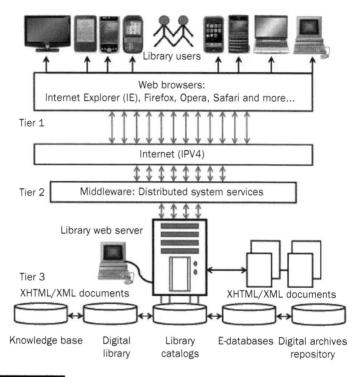

Figure 16.1 Three-tier library information technology architecture

(Cascading Style Sheets) and Java Scripts, they can be located either at the frontend or the backend. At the backend, server-side scripting languages, such as ASP (Active Server Pages), ColdFusion, JSP (Java Server Pages), .Net Framework, PHP (Hypertext Preprocessor) and so on, are providing controls and responses to web users' access rights, inquiries, inputs and other related web activities. Invisible to web browsers, the primary role of server-side scripting programming languages is to generate dynamic and interactive web pages.

Web-based library information resources and services

Associated with the Internet and the World Wide Web, academic library information resources and services in the digital age have the following features:

- *Web-based* – academic libraries in the digital age are using the Internet platform to offer their primary information resources and services.

- *24x7* – web-based information resources and services in academic libraries are accessible 24x7, no matter whether users are on campus or not.

- *Open-access* – specific fee-based academic library databases are accessible to students, faculty and staff, while other general databases and information resources are free to the general public.

- *Multi-formats* – current information resources and services collected by academic libraries have multi-format support, including paper format and e-format.

- *Multi-language support* – utilising web language translation tools, such as Applied Language Solutions' Free Translation Tools,[8] Google Language Translation,[9] Yahoo Babel Fish[10] and so on, many web-based information resources and services offered by academic libraries have multi-language support.

In addition, many academic libraries in the world are offering a new innovative library information service model called Information Commons or Learning Commons. An Information Commons/Learning Commons is a type of collaborative service model provided by academic information services librarians and IT specialists in networked learning environments.

Library expansion and innovation projects

Christopher Stewart has said, 'At many colleges and universities, the library building is located at the heart of the campus. It serves as a powerful symbol of academic life and is often one of the largest facilities on campus' (Stewart, 2010). Based on his statistical data, 99 new academic library buildings were built across the United States between 2003 and 2009. At least 14 new library buildings were built each year over a seven-year period following the terrorist attack on the United States on 11 September 2001. According to the studies made by Harold B. Shill and Shawn Tonner in 2003, more than 350 academic library projects, including constructions, renovations and additions, were completed in America between 1995 and 2002. Obviously, academic libraries in the digital age are still expanding their spaces to satisfy the dynamic need for learning space and storage capacity. Sullivan's speculation that academic libraries

Figure 16.2 The new Zach S. Henderson Library, Georgia Southern University in the USA

will be dead by 2050 is not borne out by the growing functions and roles of academic library buildings on campus. Inspired by the 'information explosion' and the digital revolution, many academic libraries need to generate more inventions and innovations to meet dynamic needs to support teaching and learning activities on and off campus. More and more library expansion and innovation projects will only strengthen the status of academic libraries as information gateways in the digital age. At the cost of US$22.75 million, the new innovative Zach S. Henderson Library at Georgia Southern University occupies 233,000 square feet (see Figure 16.2). Completed in the fall of 2009, the library contains one Learning Commons, one exhibition hall, one presentation room, three classrooms, three demonstration booths, plus one Zach's Brews (a coffee shop). The library currently offers 1,900 seats, expandable to 3,400, whenever needed. Four hundred computer (PC and Mac) workstations are connected with a wired/wireless cable network. In addition, the first automated retrieval system installed in the southeastern part of the United States provides more than seventy years of collection growth capacity as the institutional repository (Zach S. Henderson Library, 2008).[11]

Driving forces to change the future

As the greatest achievement of science and technology in the twentieth century, the prosperity of the Internet and the World Wide Web provides academic libraries with more challenges and opportunities in the digital age. However, which cutting-edge and emerging technologies will decide whether or not academic libraries will survive? From the perspective of an e-information services librarian, the author thinks that the following evolving information technologies will become decisive forces in shaping the future of academic libraries in the digital age.

Artificial Intelligence and Machine Translation

Artificial Intelligence (AI) is a new science and technology which studies theories, mechanisms, developments and applications on how to simulate human intelligence via computerised robots, voice recognition, image recognition, natural language processes, expert systems and so on. With the assistance of Artificial Intelligence and related computer technologies, Machine Translation (MT) refers to the conversion of and translation from one natural language to another natural language. For academic libraries and librarians, new achievements in AI will be brought in to change information services in future academic libraries. When the author happened to watch America's favourite quiz show *Jeopardy!* in early 2011, it was astonishing to see how easily IBM Robot Watson (IBM Watson, 2010) beat two human competitors and won the Jeopardy Championship. From IBM Watson's victory, we can foresee how information services will look in future academic libraries. Since English is not the only language used for information delivery, the development of MT will speed up the exchange and sharing of information across the different countries and regions. Also, it will be helpful to promote collaborative reference, which is an innovative library information services model performed by different academic and/or public libraries in different geographical locations, among librarians speaking in different languages.

Cloud computing

Cloud computing is the revolutionary development of running computer applications and data savings over the Internet platform. Cloud computing combines distributed computing, parallel computing and grid computing together. In terms of the architecture of cloud computing, the concept of the 'cloud' means groups of computers. Each group of computers includes thousands and thousands of computers connected by the network. Each 'cloud' is a computing centre designed to provide cloud users with cloud applications and cloud data storage. Cloud users can run cloud application interfaces, such as word processing and web searches, via web browsers. Data can be accessible from and storable in databases in the 'cloud'. Importantly, cloud computing has laid down a solid technological foundation for academic libraries to design and develop web-based course-reserved materials, digital libraries, dissertations and theses databases, tutorials, and other archived information repositories in the cloud computing environments.

Library digitisation and digital library

Library digitisation refers to the process of digitising library collection materials. Utilising computer software and other computer devices, library digitisation is a process of collecting, copying, scanning and transforming library materials from a printed format to a digitised format. A digital library is a virtual software application running over the Internet platform. Via web browsers, a digital library provides a software interface for library users to access and search digitised library materials, including images, graphs, pictures, texts, videos and other media. For the first time, the development of library digitisation and the digital library has provided academic libraries with the power to impact the process of knowledge production. Relying on the library digitisation and digital library applications, academic libraries will be able to survive in the competition with web search engines. Unfortunately, Sullivan did not realise this in his work.

Mobile and wireless access

Building ultra-high-speed computer networks over the Internet platform is the technological precondition for academic libraries to expand their information service ranges in service-oriented and user-centred academic library settings. Utilising the new generation of wireless technologies, for example, academic libraries will be able to reach more library users at a much faster speed across a greater distance range. Academic faculty and students will have access to academic library information resources and services not only in classrooms and offices, but also in any other places they prefer. To improve teaching and learning effectiveness, academic libraries will need to launch new mobile websites for faculty and students who need to access and search academic databases and course-reserved materials in mobile and wireless computing environments.

Multi-formats and multimedia

In simple terms, a format is a way of delivering and disseminating information, while a medium is a tool to access, display, receive, transfer and transmit information. In the digital age, the evolving cutting-edge and emerging technologies will keep creating new information formats and media for information delivery and dissemination across many different applications, databases, networks, platforms and systems. The development of innovative information formats and media will eventually change ways of accessing, collecting and storing information resources in academic libraries. Any changes in multi-formats and multimedia will impact the categories in and ranges of library collections. Policies and standards for academic library collection development will also need to be adjusted to reflect the evolution and revolution of multi-formats and multimedia. In today's information world, as long as the most essential medium, paper, is still in use, printed format and e-format will remain the two primary information formats available for academic library collections. For a long time into the future, printed books and e-books will be collected by global academic libraries at the same time.

Semantic web

The current Web is the collection of web pages. Each web page on the World Wide Web is identified by its unique URL (Universal Resource Locator) address. A general web search method uses keywords and Boolean operators as one of the primary methods to scan related web pages before a list of search records is generated. As a result, this list of search results contains a lot of unrelated information, since computers cannot understand the complex relationships between the multi-format information coded by the machine readable language and the multiple semantic meanings implied by the syntax of natural language sentences. The semantic web is the next generation of the Web. Proposed by Tim Berners-Lee in the late 1990s, the Semantic Web is designed to explore the hidden and implied relationships between data and information. Via databases and web technologies, the semantic web provides a common framework – the Resource Description Framework (RDF) – to define metadata for web information. The promise of the semantic web is the hope for the next generation of web searching. New advances in the semantic web will be the key not only to improve the effectiveness of the future web search, but will also shape the infrastructures of future academic libraries in the digital age (Li, 2009).

The future of academic libraries

After we understand how these driving forces are going to change ways of information delivery and dissemination in the future, the future vision for academic libraries will become much clearer in the coming years of the twenty-first century. Ahead of strong competition from web search engines, an academic library will still exist as a physical space, contributing those multiple functions and roles that web search engines cannot replace in academic learning environments. Based on the evolving three-tier client/server information technology architecture in academic library settings, the author believes that future academic libraries are expected to have the features described in the sections which follow.

Future functions and roles of future academic libraries

Because of the Internet and information technologies, academic libraries have given up their primary role as storage places for information and knowledge. At the same time, cutting-edge and emerging technologies have created more opportunities for academic libraries to expand their range of services. For example, innovative media such as e-book readers, smartphones, social media networks and tablets have enabled academic libraries to deliver and disseminate multi-format information to library users in mobile and wireless computing environments. The further development of science and technology will create new implications for the function and role of academic libraries in the networked information society. Future academic libraries will integrate and enhance their infrastructures and operations to follow current developing trends in information technologies. As one of the valuable components in institutions of higher education, future academic libraries will keep functioning as information centres, learning centres, teaching centres, presentation centres and social network centres for students, faculty, staff and other local community users. No matter how they will change their infrastructures in the future, academic libraries will always be used as a support for academic learning and as an institutional repository.

Future academic library information resources and services

Via the Internet and the World Wide Web, future academic libraries will continue to offer reputable web-based information services and resources for students, faculty and staff. Future information services in academic libraries will be both staffed and unstaffed. One of the new achievements for academic information services will be unstaffed information services provided by advanced human intelligent robots, which could be designed and developed from the IBM Watson prototype. New advances in human intelligence and machine translation will give robots the capability of providing multi-language translation services too. In addition to common information services, academic information services librarians, who are both subject experts and information technology specialists, will take responsibility for maintaining and updating computer programs for these robots. With the advances in the Semantic Web and voice recognition technology, web translation software such as Google Language Tools and Yahoo Babel Fish will automatically generate lists of correct search results while web users are asking and/or typing their questions.

Future academic library collection development

Based on the emerging trends in information technology and its implications for academic learning environments, more and more digitised information materials, including animations, e-books, e-databases, e-papers, graphs, MP3 music, videos and other digitised information resources, will become primary information resources for future academic libraries in the digital age. Digital Asset Management (DAM) will become one of the critical processes in the future of academic library collection development. Academic cataloguing librarians and other library staff will use specific computer software, technical mechanisms and tools to annotate, catalogue, retrieve and store digitised library materials. As long as paper is still in use, both the paper format and the e-format will become information formats collected by future academic libraries in the digital age. There is still a long way to go before the e-format can entirely replace the paper format in academic learning environments.

Future library digitisation and digital libraries

To support a variety of academic missions, library digitisation will keep expanding the subject scope of the digital library collections. Future digital libraries will become open-access digital archives for the national and international scholarly communities. Google and Google Scholar are unable to cover all the peer-reviewed academic and scholarly information resources in multi-languages, since they are only accessible from academic databases designed and developed by other competitive information vendors. Therefore library digitisation and digital libraries have enabled academic libraries to become information and knowledge producers in the chain of knowledge production. The development of library digitisation and digital libraries is laying down solid cornerstones for future academic libraries to compete against web search engines over the Internet platform.

Future academic librarians

Librarian positions in future academic libraries will reflect innovations driven by cutting-edge and emerging technologies applicable to academic learning environments. To follow the current developing trends in information technologies, for example, academic libraries in the digital age will need more digital services librarians, emerging technologies librarians, information services librarians, system/metadata librarians, web services librarians and so on to meet the dynamic needs of academic library users. The developing trend is that academic librarians will become information technology specialists. With general reference librarians and subject librarian positions in decline, information services librarians who can transform themselves into information technology specialists will survive. In the face of the challenges and opportunities emerging from cloud computing and the Internet, future academic libraries will need to have more competitive and technical compound expertise.

Future library and information science (LIS) programmes and professionals

It is an old cliché to say that cutting-edge and emerging technologies have changed information delivery and dissemination in the digital age. LIS graduates need to know how academic library information resources and services over the Internet platform are changing. Rated as the best LIS Master's programmes in the United States, the LIS Master's programmes offered by the University of Illinois at Urbana-Champaign, the University of North Carolina at Chapel Hill and Syracuse University are expected to spark creativity and promote innovations in future automation and digitisation at academic library settings. In addition to highly recommended LIS courses in the fields of cataloguing and classification, all three of these top American LIS programmes focus on courses in the fields of data modelling, distributed computing, human–machine interaction, information systems analysis, information technology architecture, network security, relational database management, telecommunication and network management, web design and wireless networking. It will not be surprising if future LIS programmes merged into those of computer sciences, information sciences, and information systems. All of these top three American LIS programmes indicate that future LIS professionals will become information systems specialists in academic libraries in the future.

Summary

As Laurie A. MacWhinnie, Head of Reference Services at Mantor Library of the University of Maine at Farmington in the United States, has pointed out: 'The academic library is not doomed by technology' (MacWhinnie, 2003). In the digital age, academic libraries will not only be the best places for excellence in teaching and life-long learning, but also the evolving repository spaces for academic and scholarly information resources. The more information media cutting-edge and emerging technologies create, the more challenges and opportunities academic libraries will meet. No matter how different their functions, infrastructures, operations and organisations will be in the future, academic libraries will keep expanding the range and scope of information services via the Internet and the World Wide Web. Academic faculty and students will still need to use academic libraries for their teaching and learning activities, though they do not need physically to present themselves inside library buildings each time. In the coming years of the twenty-first century, academic libraries will still exist as indispensable information gateways in service-oriented and student-focused academic learning environments.

Notes

1. Sullivan (2011). Online at: *http://chronicle.com/article/Academic-Library-Autopsy/125767/*.
2. *http://www.ask.co.uk*
3. *http://www.bing.com*
4. *http://www.google.co.uk*
5. *http://www.yahoo.co.uk*
6. Wikipedia: the free encyclopaedia that anyone can edit. Online at: *http://www.wikipedia.org*.
7. Google Scholar. Online at: *http://scholar.google.com/*.

8. *http://www.appliedlanguage.com/free_translation.shtml*
9. *http://www.google.com/language_tools?hl=en*
10. *http://babelfish.yahoo.com/*
11. *http://library.georgiasouthern.edu/DDDC.htm*

References

IBM Watson (2010) *Final Jeopardy! and the Future of Watson.* Online at: *http://www-03.ibm.com/innovation/us/watson/what-is-watson/the-future-of-watson.html.*

Li, L.L. (2009) *Emerging Technologies for Academic Libraries in the Digital Age.* Oxford: Chandos.

Mckean, E. (2005) *The New Oxford American Dictionary.* New York: Oxford University Press.

MacWhinnie, L.A. (2003) 'The information commons: the academic library of the future', *Libraries and the Academy*, 3(2): 241–57.

Shill, H.B. and Tonner, S. (2003) 'Creating a better place: physical improvements in academic libraries, 1995–2002', *College & Research Libraries*, 64(6): 431–66.

Stewart, C. (2010) *The Academic Library Building in the Digital Age: A Study of Construction, Planning, and Design of New Library Space.* Chicago: Association of College and Research Libraries.

Sullivan, B.T. (2011) 'Academic Library Autopsy Report, 2050', *Chronicle of Higher Education.* Online at: *http://chronicle.com/article/Academic-Library-Autopsy/125767/.*

Syracuse University, Master of Science in Library and Information Science (MSLIS) (2011) Curriculum. Online at: *http://ischool.syr.edu/academics/graduate/mls/mls_curriculum.aspx.*

University of Illinois at Urbana-Champaign, Graduate of Library and Information Science, *Master of Science Curriculum.* Online at: *http://www.lis.illinois.edu/academics/programs/ms/curriculum.*

University of North Carolina (UNC), School of Information and Library Science (2011) *SILS Course Information.* Online at: *http://sils.unc.edu/courses#40.*

17

Roadblocks, potholes and obstructions on the path to new library futures

Steve O'Connor

Abstract. There are many forces in the current environment tugging at why libraries exist, how they are perceived and what the future holds for them. Their roles and operations are being seriously questioned. Their technologies and those in the digital and publishing industries are changing rapidly, greatly affecting futures. This survey provides an overview of the major forces at play in our education systems and at the academic level especially. The technological environment both present and future is scoped while the rapidly changing publishing environment is surveyed.

The chapter is written for those engaged in strategic thinking and who require an overview of the major driving forces which will affect them. It is written from a global internationalist perspective but with local insights.

Keywords: collaboration, expertise, future, information professionals, open access, role, skills, technology

Introduction

There are many forces in the current environment asking why libraries exist, how they are perceived and what the future holds for them. Their roles and operations are being seriously questioned. Their technologies and those in the digital and publishing industries are changing rapidly, greatly affecting their futures. This survey attempts to overview the major forces at play in our education systems and at the academic level especially. The technological environment both present and future has been scoped while the rapidly changing publishing environment has been surveyed.

The paper has been written for those engaged in strategic thinking and who require an overview of the major driving forces that will affect them. It has been written from a global internationalist perspective but with local insights.

It is clearly a very difficult time to be managing libraries. There are many pressures in terms of the traditional relationship which they have to publishers and content, their relationship to their traditional users and even their traditional role in their communities. Perhaps none of this is surprising, but for those who are charged with planning these services for the future, it is very difficult to reconceptualise a traditional service into something quite different and even new. The pressure to create something new which is vital and workable is difficult when the environment is so thoroughly infected with change. Marshall McLuhan, the communications guru, used to call his work 'difficult stuff' – even in this area, it is an understatement.

Preparing the mind

This chapter is intended to survey the future field for obstacles and pitfalls that may confront the planner and the librarian engaged in positioning the library or information service. It is not intended to deal with methodologies but to assist the various views of the future field that can be adopted. Like many scenic positions in a national park, the view can be different from different positions. So it is with our views of the future of our library. One angle or perspective will deliver differing insights from another perspective. Often our conventional or long-held perspective is the most difficult from which to escape. But unless other perspectives are included, a more complete and balanced view will never be gained. This future field will vary across the globe but most of the trends discussed in this paper will be valid in some fashion.

Rick Anderson, writing on 'The Crisis in Research Librarianship' (2011), highlights three issues that could apply to any library in any sector anywhere on the globe. He says that the problem is not that libraries fail to offer value to their constituents. The crisis stems, instead, from the following three facts:

- Perception matters more than reality.
- Patrons genuinely do not need librarians as much as they once did.
- Value that is not valued is not valuable.

Implicit in these three statements is a different way of looking at the present. In many ways it is an unpleasant set of statements in that it implies that no matter what we are doing we are challenged; no matter how well we think we are doing we are challenged; no matter what perception we have of what we are doing we must stop and think again. The author of this chapter strongly believes in the three statements and all the self-examination that must seriously happen with each of our organisations and us. The reader will be reminded of these perspectives throughout the course of this paper and any resulting actions that the reader undertakes beyond the scope of this chapter.

Managing libraries for the future is complex and so time and space needs to be applied to the exercise to remove the mind and prejudices from the realms of the present and past. So what are the broad issues?

Reconceptualising

'The future is not what it used to be.' This was the smart assessment of a comedian to the task of predicting the future. Of course, it is also true. The future is always different from what we had or even expected, but for the most part we do not recognise this in that the future creeps up on us. This is especially the case if we let the future happen to us, rather than setting out to make something happen. If we just let the future happen, then the only way to see what has changed is by looking to the past. Looking back we can see the many, many changes that have happened in the way in which we do business or the way in which we operate. If we were honest, we would also recognise that our users have also changed, as Rick Anderson has highlighted. Our users have changed the ways in which they access and assess information. So we must be alive to those changes and not just hold on to our existent practices. We need to assess our services in the light of what our users are practising. What is the perspective of our users toward libraries and librarians? Do they regard the services offered by libraries and librarians as valuable any longer? Or are our users doing fine without our expertise and services? In an honest self-examination we would have to conclude that our users have a huge variety of alternative approaches at their disposal now. They can 'google' it! They can 'google it' even if they do not understand or perhaps care what they are getting access to. Their perception of what is 'adequate' is the reality and we have to respond accordingly. Their perception is our reality. Our reality is irrelevant to their perception. We may still believe that our realities are true and important but unless we are able to present them in a manner which the user believes to be true, then they are irrelevant. It is also clear in such a situation that they do not regard our services as valuable and therefore they are valueless.

A few areas for reconceptualisation are *search*, *content* and *organisation*. These are but a few areas demanding a different view but they are good areas in which to commence.

The reconceptualisation of *search* is the 'Google doctrine'. As librarians we have sought to create MARC (Machine Readable Cataloguing) records as the basis for keyword searching but have always assumed that our users want and need all that power at all times. In many ways the MARC record was ahead of its time but our approach to *search* has not adjusted to the times. We still believe that our users require the full exposure to our indexed content when they conduct a search. What if they only wanted brief information or a simple search rather than the full exposure? What if they do not know the difference between a book, a symposium or a journal article? Do they have to learn the difference or do they just get to the information that they seek? Do they have enough metadata in our records to retrieve the item they want using *their* language? The Library of Congress Subject Headings are very narrowly framed and set in a past time. They cannot respond to contemporary searching need.

There is a strong software movement across the library software world now towards 'discovery', which is empowering the user to search much of the library's content regardless of the form in which it is held, regardless of whether it is in print, digital or audio-visual form. Our concept of *search* needs to be based not on our present data structures and technological capabilities but about what we research our future user needs and preferences to be.

Reconceptualising content is another major issue. It is very simple and true to state that much of the world's content is being locked behind digital firewalls. It is also the case that print content is being beautifully scanned by companies such as Google who will then effectively 'own' the world's intellectual output, again behind digital firewalls with cash registers at the entrance. It is true that some of this content will be free but most of it will not. How many digital 'buys' would justify the retention of a print copy? The notion of the free library service is quickly being made redundant and free access to information as the backbone of any free and democratic society is becoming a phenomenon of the past. So from a future library perspective, what is the notion of content?

Do we continue to own any content? Do we only license content? Do we allow access arrangements only for the life of a licence agreement or 'in perpetuity'? Do we buy print content only for the present and not 'in perpetuity' or for long-term storage and access? The very concept that a user can access the content that they want from a free library service is a huge strategic issue. What is the impact of this?

Our concepts of *content* are in transition. We have concepts here that are amalgams of the past and the present while we are becoming victims of the future. What shape to this concept of *content* do we want to achieve?

In many senses libraries have paid publishers for content over the years. They have, in effect, been paying for the publication of books and journal content. Publishers now reap significant profits from their enterprise or their exposure to the risk of business. Libraries are now strongly moving into the creation of institutional repositories into which they are placing the pre-published versions of the work of their community's authors. They are making this content available to the world through the Internet. So are libraries publishers of content? Is this a new and vital role for libraries? Regardless of whether it is or not, we have to choose the concept of *content* which we wish to use into the future. Is it one that is chosen for us by publishers or is it a different concept of *content* that libraries will create? Or is it a combination of both approaches. What do our users want?

Risk

Risk is a very difficult concept. Risk is not failure. Change without risk is not possible. Risk also does not happen in a culture of blame. Blame limits risk and therefore success. Thomas Watson,[1] a former head of IBM, said famously that if one wanted to succeed, one had to double the failure rate. The creation of a culture in which risk and failure are acceptable is a strong priority. Risk and innovation obviously go hand in hand; innovation in an environment of rapid change and disruption is crucial in order to forge new and exciting futures. These concepts are highlighted here to remind us that the work culture we create has to deal positively with each of these issues. Action is not possible unless the culture is one which allows our people to suggest, to avoid blame and to take risk, to think differently, to turn old concepts on their head and to realise new solutions which may fail. The engagement with risk and the management of change are vital for any scenario of change.

Staff

Our staff are our greatest resource. Our people will help the library achieve its purpose, but they can also be the force resisting change with potential fragmentation of clear directions. So it is important to engage our staff in why change is important, to embed the staff inside the process of change, to openly and transparently infuse the process with their own ideas. Staff are invariably responsive to this kind of inclusion.

In times of significant and constant change, it is very desirable to create work cultures which are open to new and different ideas. The very nature of work is changing so much of what we do. It is always interesting to draw out the different ways which staff can think about issues. Each of our experiences will be interpreted in differing ways depending on a wide variety of factors. The educational psychologist Howard Gardner[2] articulated seven different types of intelligence rather than the limiting arithmetic and linguistic. In his research outcome lies the secret to the broad capability of a whole staff. So many perspectives can be released to motivate a whole operation. Many of the perspectives for the future will be gained from good library literature but many of the most acute insights will be from the allied literatures of business and the social sciences.

The library organisation for the future requires not only professional librarian expertise but professional expertise from other disciplines. These disciplines include: database managers, web designers, graphic artists and marketing professionals. It is no longer appropriate to employ a librarian-marketer but rather a marketing professional, not a web designer-librarian but a web designer professional. The new team of professionals should complement each others' skills but be driven by common strategic and professional goals.

The identification of new skills for the professional librarian is an issue of ongoing concern and development. The skill set has as much to do with the issues involving our people as professionals as the state of the content communication. The debate and practice surrounding the development of and access to content in e-form will impact on the appropriate skill development. The two issues are intertwined.

The delineation of the roles of the professional and the paraprofessional librarian will come more and more into sharper relief as the roles of the physical and digital libraries evolve. Too often the professional roles have slipped into the operational realm when this should be resisted, creating sharper and defined roles complementing each other for the benefit of the future library. There are clearly managerial roles for the professional but the professional and paraprofessional should both gain satisfaction from clear and satisfying roles.

Key to the success of any library staff is their ability to be able to collaborate, to be able to establish viable and tangible partnerships to work with others. Working with others will include different units in one's own library, as well as allied institutional departments such as Educational Development and Marketing Information Technology. Most important will be the partnerships or working relationships beyond the borders of one's own institution, even one's own country. To collaborate is the new way of working; it is the new way to achieve outcomes. Living within one's own silo severely limits what can be achieved and also one's perspective of what the strategic game really is.

Technology

Technology for libraries has become synonymous with efficiencies in the first instance and now with outreach. However, with advances in technology occurring so quickly it is difficult for libraries to always stay in touch. Therefore there are a few issues to be considered strategically.

Firstly, the constraints of proprietary systems need to be addressed in periods of rapid technological and service changes. These systems are very good providing stable platforms for operations but lack the flexibility to respond to local service need. The advent of Application Programming Interfaces (APIs) enables the creation of plug-ins to basic systems providing the freedom to customise for local service need and innovation. Innovation is clearly linked strategically to the achievement of flexibility in technological capability.

This is not to say that proprietary systems are inappropriate but it is to indicate that the system architecture should be viewed as comprising a database of library data including the MARC records and user information, with separate service components which shape the service mix. There is no reason why a library's technological mix cannot be sourced from a variety of vendors and local producers. The sharing of locally produced API's among libraries should also be considered as being desirable. This can be loosely considered to be part of the Open Source movement which allows much more sharing of local initiatives rather than being captive to the power of the major software players in the market.

Secondly, consideration of Open Access is so important as a vital component of any future technological mix. In a publishing environment which is both increasingly business focused and fluid in the future sense, Open Access is a vital force for change and flexibility. Open Access enables libraries to deliver content in pre-published versions via their institutional repositories. It also enables them to create content using standards such an EPUB (electronic publication) for free and open e-book publication. This is especially powerful as libraries create content for their own communities.

Thirdly, the apparently strong motivation for devices such as Radio Frequency Identification (RFID) should attract a lot of close consideration before any action is undertaken. It is important to understand exactly why tags such as RFID are being considered. Is it to save staff time? Is it to be able to locate certain physical items? This is an important issue especially when the amount of print material being purchased by libraries is less and less. Many libraries already spend around three-quarters of their budgets on electronic resources. It is also the case that projects, such as to RFID entire collections, are very intensive exercises requiring a lot of staff time and, most especially, will distract the entire library organisation from other more important strategic directions.

Organisational issues

Most of us continue to live with traditional organisational structures but the nature of work and collaboration is increasingly offering, even requiring, different approaches to the way we are organised. Our workplaces are increasingly organised in team structures but while the library as a physical edifice is increasingly remote from the clientele, other staff structures should be considered. If many of our primary clientele, especially academics in an educational institution, rarely if ever attend the library, then close and active consideration ought to be given to embedding professional staff within the faculty. This is a highly desirable outcome with strong benefits and a number of risks.

Another governance issue arises in collaborative ventures. If these collaborative ventures are significant in size and complexity, it may be that a different legal governance structure is required for future sustainability. There are a number of enterprises now around the globe which deliver benefits to groups of libraries which have formed themselves into legal company structures. These include large organisations such as OCLC,[3] large consortia such as Lyrasis[4] and

Caval,[5] and even large collaborative storage facilities such as the Joint Universities Research Archive (JURA).[6] The company structure offers many advantages to operating such ventures within existing educational institutions. It offers permanence, independence, transparency and a vehicle for the development of future collaboration.

User engagement

This is the most crucial area and one in which we, as librarians, cannot delude ourselves. I have mentioned earlier in this paper the three excellent reminders from Rick Anderson. These are that *perception* matters more than reality, that patrons genuinely do not need librarians and finally that a service is only valuable if it is valued. If we ignore these three edicts then we will most certainly fail and condemn libraries to oblivion. These three edicts should guide our thinking every time we plan or need to respond to an issue. Even more now than in the past we need to be firmly engaged with our user communities, to understand their pressures, their driving purpose, their projects and their desired outcomes. Collections for collections' sake can never be our driver. We must adapt and adopt new strategies and services, all the time being relevant to our community. This does not mean that we abandon our profession or its ethics or standards. It does mean, however, that our business model, or the way in which we do business, needs to be entirely focused on what our clients need, on how they perceive the library service and on how patrons can genuinely need and find value in what we do.

Conclusion

The precise determination of the impacts on our environment by the variety of forces affecting our future is very difficult. Sometimes it seems that we are immersed in a fog with glimpses of our future being revealed as the fog swirls this way and then that. But in this fog, the entire picture or field of opportunities is never clear. What has been written in this chapter provides a strategic overview of the library world from the perspective of this author. It is an overview laced with questions which will hopefully challenge the reader to ask 'Why?' and to then re-examine their own environment in a different light.

Notes

1. *http://thinkexist.com/quotes/tom_watson/*
2. Howard Gardner (1985) *Frames of Mind: The Theory of Multiple Intelligences.* New York: Basic Books.
3. *http://www.oclc.org/*
4. *http://www.lyrasis.org/*
5. *http://www.caval.edu.au/*
6. *http://www.julac.org/?page_id=258*

Reference

Anderson, R. (2011) 'The crisis in research librarianship', *Journal of Academic Librarianship*, 37(4): 289–90.

Index